£1

SWEDEN

SWEDEN

A traveller's history

Eric Elstob

BOYDELL PRESS

© Eric Carl Elstob 1979

Published by Boydell Press Ltd
PO Box 9, Woodbridge, Suffolk IP12 3DF
and Rowman & Littlefield Inc
81 Adams Drive, Totowa, New Jersey
07512, United States of America

First published 1979

British Library Cataloguing in Publication Data

Elstob, Eric Carl
  Sweden.
  1. Sweden – History
  I. Title
  948.5   DL648

  ISBN 0-85115-111-6

Photoset by Rowland Phototypesetting Limited
Bury St. Edmunds, Suffolk
Printed in Great Britain by St. Edmundsbury Press Limited
Haverhill, Suffolk

For my mother, who never lived to read it

Contents

List of Illustrations

Drawings and Maps

Illustrations 1, 4, 6, 8, 9, 13, 14, 16, 18, 20, 22, 27, 29, 34 by Kurt Bengtsson; 19 by Gösta Sörensen; 15, 17, 21, 24, 25, 26, 28, 30, 31, 32, 33 National Museum, Stockholm; 2, 3, 5, 7, 10, 11, 12 author.
Maps by Liz Cazalet. Drawings by Ricardo Cinalli.

ACKNOWLEDGEMENTS

This book owes its completion to the constant encouragement and a bit of pressure by various generous friends. First and foremost is Richard Barber, who has brought a professional writer's encouragement and a professional publisher's discipline to a rank amateur; but I must also mention Ruth Marris and Kevin Crossley-Holland. The quality of the writing and the errors of the text remain mine.

I also owe warm thanks to my cousin-in-law Kurt Bengtsson for all his photographs and to Ricardo Cinalli for his drawings. I am grateful to the National Museum in Stockholm for permission to use their photographs of portraits in their collection.

1. The Prehistoric Age

The year is 6839 B.C. The Swedes have, with their customary efficiency, worked out an exact date for the beginning of their history; so let us imagine a tourist travelling northwards near the end of the last European Ice Age. It has been an early spring, and already in April the ice has begun to melt, dribbling from the foot of the great glaciers that fill the Scandinavian valleys. Soon in Egypt and Mesopotamia, men will plough the fields, while priests and kings will build palaces and pyramids; but in the North there is only the barren tundra across which roam the wolf-packs, as the ancestors of the modern Swedes cower in their damp caves.

The tourist we are following would have been able to make his way dry shod up from Denmark across the Sound into Sweden, for the Baltic has only recently forced an outlet into the North Sea. When the first prehistoric tribes entered Sweden, the Baltic was still a fresh-water lake, and even today its water has a very low salt content. The whole country was still in the grip of the Ice Age, which lasted far longer here than in the rest of Europe. At the very heart of Sweden, where Stockholm, Uppsala and the farmlands of Uppland now lie, there was nothing but a vast lake.

Now, if our tourist has chosen his date right, he will reach the shores of this lake on the day when the spring thaw raises its level to record height; suddenly the water breaks over its eastern lip and empties itself into the Baltic. All that remains is the water in the deep furrows of its bed: and there it still is, in the peculiar fretted outline of lake Mälaren with its countless peninsulas and fiords.

How on earth is it possible, one may well ask, to date a geological event to within a couple of months in a particular year? It is a fascinating story. At the beginning of the present century, a Swedish geologist, Gerhard de Geer, was taking samples of the sediment at the foot of a cliff and observed that the soil was composed of hundreds of layers of differing thicknesses, one above the other. He soon realized that each layer was the deposit of one year's dirt and grit that had been carried downstream by the flow of water from the melting glacier. It was then easy to chart the thickness of the various layers, which showed whether the year's thaw had been slight or strong, and the chart thus drawn up corresponded exactly with charts produced in other places. As he worked northwards, so the charts overlapped, following the shrinking ice-cap, until de Geer reached the foot of one of the surviving glaciers in Lapland, where the summer thaw was laying the most recent layer on the bed of a stream. All that remained was to count down to the exceptionally thick layer which

1

marked the sludge carried by the bursting lake in the year that first properly defined the country of Sweden.

The land was inhabited even then; though little trace is left of these prehistoric peoples. Life must have been very hard, and the struggle for food and warmth must have occupied almost all their energies – yet not all.

The Stone Age inhabitants of Sweden found time and strength to build megalithic tombs as fine as those of their cousins in kinder, southern lands; and, of course, a country where every field is full of granite boulders lends itself to megalithic architecture. Neolithic man chose to live in the most tolerable parts of the land, the fertile plains of Skåne and Gothland, and there their beautifully shaped stone axes are often turned up by the plough; at Nörrköping, a harpoon of bone has been found lodged in the skeleton of a seal at the bottom of a dried-out lake.

These people belonged to that mysterious race who built the stone monuments found throughout Europe from Malta, through Brittany and the British Isles to Scandinavia. Sweden cannot boast a Stonehenge or a Carnac, but many long barrows survive. Especially on the plain between the lakes Vänern and Vättern, these massive dolmens, stripped of their mounds of earth, rise above the cornfields.

The largest megalithic tomb in the whole of northern Europe is at Barsebäck in Skåne. Here the earth mound of the great wedge-shaped barrow has survived intact. From the broad end a long passage with walls and roof boulders leads to the chamber itself, which is so large that a man can stand upright there in a room eighteen feet wide. The stones which form the roof weigh up to eighteen tons each, and those of the walls are of equal proportions.

At Haväng, on the eastern coast of Skåne, there is another of these barrows, but here the winds straight from the Russian steppes have blown away the whole mound of sand and earth to leave just the dolmen. It stands on a dune a hundred yards from the Baltic by a wide, sandy beach. The path to it leads from an old farm, which is now a youth hostel, through a botanist's paradise, where the short turf is thick with such flowers of the heath as wild thyme, thrift or the rare scented *Anthericum liliage,* past a copse of beeches whose roots have failed to bind the sand and now twist naked from the hillside. The Stone Age chieftain chose his grave well. Still today it looks out over the sea, within earshot of nothing except the waves. The tomb itself is built with granite boulders silvered by moss and lichen. Archaeologically it is a remarkable tomb, for the dolmen is surrounded by a wall of small upright stones in a square, giving it a very rare shape for a barrow. The whole heath is scattered with menhirs: stone circles rise from the long grass and stone ships sail through the gorse. In contrast to Stonehenge, with its new car park, nature has if anything grown wilder here, and it is still possible to feel something of the vast loneliness in which ancient man lived amid the hostile world.

However, these Stone Age builders were eventually displaced as they were everywhere else by stronger tribes armed with strange and fearful

2

new weapons of metal. Scandinavia must have been one of their last refuges. It is only at the beginning of the second millennium B.C. that firm evidence of the invaders appears. They were Aryans, like the ancient Greeks; but they are known throughout the North, after the form of their weapons, as the Boat-Axe people. Sweden has some of the richest copper mines of Europe, so once the techniques of smelting the metal had evolved, her inhabitants had no lack of bronze. They used it for weapons, of course, and jewellery and even drinking horns. Several small bronze images of gods have been found, including the fat fertility goddess now in the State Historical Museum at Stockholm, a descendant of the famous Venus of Willensdorf.

The Bronze Age megalith builders left their finest monument in the astonishing grave at Kivik, which is, in its way, as remarkable as Stonehenge. Kivik is a small fishing village on the eastern coast of Skåne. Its only other claim to fame is the great gipsy market which is held every summer on the sandy hills near by. Suddenly, for one week, the streets of this sleepy village are crowded: dark-haired, sallow-skinned Romanies mix with the blue-eyed, fair-haired locals, and the drunks reel down to the beach to sober up in the sea wind. The Kivik tomb itself is a mile to the south of the village. As it stands today, it is an enormous round cairn, almost seventy-five yards across and rising to ten feet at the centre. Since it has been used as a quarry for the past five hundred years, there is no telling what the original height may have been. It is built out of the small boulders that litter the fields around, and its size alone is enough to make it archaeologically significant, but it hides a treasure far more dramatic.

When two farmers were taking stones from the cairn during the eighteenth century, they broke through to a chamber at its centre. This they promptly ransacked to find the trolls' gold which, as everybody knows, is buried in such chambers. They found no gold; what they did find was one of Europe's outstanding prehistoric remains. The chamber comprised a large coffin, the sides of which are formed by eight great stones, about four feet high, whose inside surfaces are all carved with complex pictures. The original discoverers were not interested in such works of art. After the stones had been drawn by a local worthy who was interested in archaeology, they were dragged off and used as building material. One is still missing, and another was lost until a few years ago when a house in the village fell down and pieces of the carved stone were found broken up in the wall.

The carvings on these stones show two distinct styles. Six of them are decorated with symbolic shapes that are comparatively common at other sites. There are the heavy double-headed axes like the ones at Stonehenge, there are the sun wheels with four spokes, and there are ships with their crews. These motifs and others yet more strange are to be seen on many Swedish rock-carvings. What is unique is the carving on the two remaining stones.

These are pictures in the modern sense, each showing a complete scene, and they can fully qualify as figurative art. Both pictures are

3

composed in rows, like a strip cartoon. At the top of the first stone, two men with swords lead away two others, and behind them a man drives a chariot drawn by two horses, the reins being carved straight up like bits of wire to avoid cutting across their bodies. Underneath are a fish and two more four-legged animals; then, in the bottom row, walks a man, with his hands up in the air, followed by eight robed figures – at least, one may assume they are human beings, though they look more like seals. The other pictorial stone is even more fascinating. Unfortunately, this is the stone that was found broken up in the house wall and only a few pieces were recovered. We must thank that eighteenth-century archaeologist for our best knowledge of how it looked. At the top, two men inside a circle may either be hanging a sacrifice in a tree, or else beating on two suspended gongs. That the interpretation can be so different shows how enigmatic this art is. Four other men approach them, two blowing on great curved horns. Underneath are the eight robed figures of the other stone, on either side of a font-like object. The bottom row is even more mysterious; four figures are walking towards the mouth of a reversed C, and this group is repeated twice. It seems reasonable to guess that the robed figures are priests; this kind of Ku-Klux-Klan uniform is common to primitive societies and magic ritual all over the world; and one may assume that the scene portrayed is a religious ceremony, probably a sacrifice.

The Kivik tomb has recently been scientifically excavated, but such had been its maltreatment that the results were meagre. However, a few

Kivik tomb

4

fragments of bronze were found, which allow it to be dated to the Boat-Axe period, but no other contents have survived.

The geological necessity that obliged the ancient Swedes to commit their art to the granite has been our good fortune. Today, Sweden possesses a wealth of prehistoric rock-carvings, regrettably little known in the outside world. There are literally thousands of these *Hällristningar* throughout the country. Of course, if you happen to live in a country where the original rock breaks through on every hillside, and it is impossible to walk any distance without meeting a big bolder, the obvious thing to do is to carve on it. Indeed, the motifs of some of these graffiti have survived unchanged for thousands of years. They must have existed throughout prehistoric Europe, but further south they would have been painted, and only a happy accident has preserved a few in the caves at Lascaux and elsewhere in the Dordogne. There are even a few prehistoric paintings left on protected rock-surfaces in the far north of Sweden. Once carved on granite, however, their only enemy is the concealing moss, and it is certain that there are thousands more waiting to be discovered in Scandinavia.

One cannot know the exact reasons for these works, but it seems fairly certain that they were magical. In any primitive community, men believe that to possess an image of something gives power over the original; so when the tribe was preparing for a hunt, their tribal priests or witch-doctors would carve or paint a portrait of their quarry to make it submit to their magic. Much is to be learnt of our ancestors' diets from these wishful menus in stone, and they explain some of their most usual subjects. The act of carving seems to have been far more important than the finished work, for one often finds later pictures on top of older ones.

Up in the far north there is a long and violent rapid called Namforsen, and long ago this was a favourite hunting place. The ancient huntsmen would start their prey in the forests and then, like a pack of hounds, would drive it into the rapids, where it would be pounded to death on the rocks, so that all that remained was to retrieve the victim, even if it was *pâté*, from the calm waters lower down. All around on the rocks and cliff-faces are carvings. Animals of all kinds are to be found here, though mainly, of course, elk and deer, but there are several lively looking salmon, and even a fisherman in his boat. These carvings in remote Ångermanland were discovered by engineers planning a new hydro-electric power station. Now, thanks to the electricity board, they are among the most accessible of Sweden's northern rock carvings, and there are paths and gangways along the rapids. Even so, Namforsen retains its atmosphere. The thundering, surging mass of water is as wild today as it was then, and beyond the power station lies the open fell, purple towards the horizon. As the spray spatters the visitor's face, it is easy to imagine the pack of men hunting with their stone axes. Their village has been fully excavated and the Historical Museum at Stockholm has their stone querns and bone needles.

By no means all Swedish rock-carvings are hunting magic. Certainly in

5

the south they often express a far more sophisticated concept of life and are the work of settled farmers rather than of migratory tribes. As glimpses into what our remote ancestors believed about life and death, these carvings are fascinating. Their religion was obviously concerned with fertility, of men and of crops and of herds, and its traditions are not dead yet. At the beginning of the present century, it was still common in Norrland for the farmer's wife to bake the round sun bread in the spring, which was then shared between the ploughman and his horse while the crumbs were mixed in with the seed-corn. I have seen a pair of scissors underneath the mattress of a baby's cot, in a farmhouse with a television set and a deep-freeze, a memory of the days when cold metal would protect the child against the Stone Age men whom the Bronze Age farmers had driven out.

This religion has left traces in written history as well. In the Viking pantheon, as it is described in the old poems, there are certain gods, Freyr, Freya and Njord, who are called the 'Vanir' or the old gods. They have survived as the pre-Olympians, Chronos and Pan, have in Greek mythology. Freyr, we know, was a fertility god, his distinctive attribute being an exaggerated phallus; his wife Freya was the guardian of the crops. They seem out of place among the warrior companions of Odin; and, indeed, they belong to a more ancient culture. The archetypal fertility symbol, the maypole, is even found carved on a rock at Lilla Gerum near Tanum. At its top there is a horned figure, and three men

Rock carving at Lilla Gerum near Tanum

dance round it holding the traditional ribbons. Midsummer Eve, when the sun sets throughout the North for at the most a couple of hours, is still celebrated in the country with a party round the maypole. It is one of the best times to be in Sweden, when the landscape swims in the heat of high summer and, in every village the boys and girls dress up in their gaudy folk costumes and dance their complicated reels and square-dances. The great bonfire has been baptized with the name of St John, but its origins are pagan enough.

One of the most popular single motifs in rock-carvings is the ship, often highly decorated and manned with rowers. It has two possible interpretations. Many anthropologists think that this is the ship which carries the sun across the sky. On the other hand, our knowledge of later beliefs suggests a funeral cult. The idea that death is a voyage on to which each man must be launched is far older than the Vikings, who sent their chieftains to rest at sea in a blazing longship. It may be that each man of importance needed his picture of a ship to ferry him to the next world.

There are many themes and symbols that constantly recur. The sun was obviously an important god, for circles empty or with a cross inside are to be found everywhere. The tradition appears to have been that the sun wheel was carried on a cart at festivals. Some years ago, a model of such a cart was found in a bog in Skåne, and two more have been found in Denmark; the Swedish one is now in the Stockholm museum. Unfortunately, only the four wheels and the base, a thin frame about a foot square with rests at the corners, survive. The sun cart is found carved in many places.

One of the most amusing subjects in the carvings is the many pairs of feet. Probably they were intended as a sign of ownership, and a footprint was taken as a sign of possession.

In all of Sweden, it is the province on the coast north of Gothenburg, called Bohuslän, that is the richest in prehistoric rock-carvings. For those who prefer comfort in their archaeology, Gothenburg museum has an excellent collection of casts, but the countryside of pine woods and granite repays the exercise needed to see the originals.

Not far outside the town at the village of Kirkeby Nedergård, there is a fleet of ships on a stone near the church. There are also such mysterious figures as bird-men with clearly carved wings, and a fisherman in a boat who has caught a fish twice as big as himself at the end of his line.

At Ylleneis, there is an entire decorated cliff-face. This displays no less than twenty-five boats and a complete hunting scene of two bowmen, their dogs and the deer they are chasing. Strangest of all is a depiction of two men holding on to the rump of a stag; only when looking closely at the hind legs does the viewer realize that this is a man dressed in a pelt and holding antlers on his head. The analogy that leaps to mind is the animal dances painted in certain Etruscan tombs.

Thorsbo boasts a gigantic boat fully five yards long and manned by 125 oarsmen. It is carved at the foot of a cliff on whose head stand three Bronze Age round barrows, plundered now and desecrated; perhaps one of them held the chieftain for whose last voyage the boat was shaped.

At Vitlycke, the old road runs beneath a cliff which is decorated with one of the largest surfaces of rock-carvings in the whole of Scandinavia. Across it sail whole fleets of ships, and scattered among them are other fascinating scenes. Two warriors fight across a dotted line. There is a procession carrying some kind of an idol that can no longer be identified. Away to one side, an enormous snake coils towards a man with his arms in the air; is he sacrifice or priest?

Near Litsleby, carved on top of older boats, is a man, larger than life, with an erect phallus and brandishing a spear, whose pose recalls the Long Man of Wilmington in Sussex, England. A hundred yards to the east of him there is an entire battle scene in which soldiers on horseback charge at each other, waving their spears and their square shields.

The ideal centre from which to study these rock-carvings is the village of Tanum in Bohuslän. There are outstanding examples in all the surrounding countryside, and most of them have been signposted clearly by the Swedish Tourist Society with the word *Hällristningar* on the notice boards.

On the other side of Sweden, at Nörrköping on the bank of Motala river, there is a remarkable group of carvings; these are on the main road near Himmelstalund, and have been freshly painted up. There are many pictures of animals and men, but the glory of the rock is a whole fleet of ships sailing bravely on the west wind.

In due course, however, the Swedes begin to appear on the fringes of European history. In his *Germania,* Tacitus describes how, beyond various odd tribes on the edge of the known world, dwelt the Gotones and Suiones, in other words the Goths and Swedes. The Swedes, or *Svear,* lived in the area round modern Stockholm and in Uppland, the Goths in central Sweden in what is now East Gothland and West Gothland. They were already a seafaring people, and Tacitus mentions admiringly their ships with a prow at both the bow and stern. Indeed, there was considerable trade between the Swedes and the Romans. Roman coins and Roman glass are often found in graves, and the Swedes had a virtual monopoly of two luxury items of the empire: fur and amber. They soon realized, too, that the export of slaves was a remarkably easy and profitable industry. In Ptolemy's map of the world, drawn in about A.D. 150, there is an island to the north of Europe near Ultima Thule called Scandia, and this is the first historical record of Sweden as a country.

Small tribes must have been constantly fighting throughout the country, and even across the Baltic, if for no other reason than to obtain slaves. On the island of Öland, there survive no less than sixteen great fortresses built during the Iron Age, which in Sweden lasted until the advent of Christianity and written history. They are an imposing testimony to the dangers and disorders of the Folk-Wandering period, even among the barbarians themselves, and in the whole of Sweden there are scores of such fortresses. However, the largest and best preserved are those on Oland, which lies like a thin reef off the coast of Småland.

Maypole and reconstructed Iron Age house at Löjsta

They are really towns surrounded by stone walls which still stand higher than a man, and interrupted by gateways leading on to what is now only a great meadow. The houses were of wood, so their only trace is the stone foundations; the ruined walls enclose oaks and junipers growing in the poor soil, and the turf between the stones is thick with wild flowers. The three most impressive of these towns are Ismanstorp, Gråborg and Eketorp.

To get to Ismanstorp means a long drive down narrow lanes into the forest, then a mile's walk through hazel woods, till suddenly the country-side opens and there, in a broad field, stands the grey wall enclosing a site of several acres. Inside are the foundations of the rectangular houses, built along the radii of the circle. The stones of the wall are piled one on top of the other without any mortar, like the drystone walls of the West of England, and there are no less than nine gates. I have visited Ismanstorp on a sweltering summer's day when the broken walls stood out like a Greek ruin against the blue sky, the junipers dark as cypresses and the air throbbing with the singing of the grasshoppers. It was as if Mycenae had been removed by magic to the far north.

Gråborg is very similar; but here the site was taken back into occupa-tion in the Middle Ages, and used as a place of refuge from the Danes. One complete medieval gate still survives, and outside the walls are the remains of a little twelfth-century chapel dedicated to St Knut. Gråborg is the largest of these fortresses, over two hundred yards in diameter; at their base its walls are a good thirty feet thick, and still stand to almost twenty feet high.

Eketorp is the only one to have been excavated so far, and it has answered a number of questions. Like Gråborg, it lacks Ismanstorp's romantic position in the depths of the forest, but lies surrounded by rich fields. The excavators found the same fan of houses along the inside of the walls and the traces of many layers of occupation. The deepest dates were from the period of the Folk-Wandering, but above this are clear signs of use during the Viking era and the early Middle Ages. A reconstruction of a house is being built.

The ruins of Öland are fascinating for their sheer natural beauty. The island is famous for its wild flowers, its lilies and bulbs; when spring comes, the whole countryside, and above all the heaths (*alvaret*), burst into a carpet of bright colours, so the walker wades through the tall grass to find rare orchids that seem as common as harebells. The old stone walls are like grey ribbons tied round bunches of vivid flowers.

Most of the prehistoric monuments of Sweden have a particular charm, which they owe to the emptiness of the country. In Britain, such remains are more often like Avebury, where the village has taken over from the temple and cosy cottages have covered the awesome origins of the place. In Sweden, none of this has happened. The landscape is still as wild and as lovely as when men first made a clearing in the forest for their daub and wattle huts. Wolves are not yet extinct and elks are common. To look at the work of ancient man in such a country, after a rough drive down a cart track, or better still, after a long walk across the heath, is to be carried back to the world of ever-present danger and harsh survival in which they lived. Both exhilarating and frightening, the experience is the most effective way to feel what such a past must have been like.

2. The Viking Era

The Iron Age in Sweden was a poorer time than the Bronze Age; the weather grew colder and the collapse of the Roman Empire meant a virtual end to trade in Europe. Many of the Northern peoples went south; the Angles and Saxons decided on England, and some islanders from Bornholm in the Baltic moved to the Rhine, where they founded Borgundarholmr, or Burgundy. So what we usually call the Viking expansion is only the last and most famous stage in a southward migration that had already begun in the second and third centuries.

Our earliest written source of Swedish history is the Old English epic, *Beowulf*. Beowulf himself seems to have taken a lively interest in Scandinavian politics, lending Adil the Swede an army to throw out his uncle Onela and become king. Nor are Adil and his grandfather Angantyr mere figures of legend, perhaps howed in the great barrows at Uppsala, for they are mentioned independently in the *Ynglingatal,* a Viking genealogy of the kings of Norway. The Sweden of those days consisted only of the province of Uppland and the area around lake Mälaren, the original home of the Swedes. To their south lived the Goths in the provinces of East and West Gothland, while other Vikings had sailed across to Finland and the Baltic States, where they conquered the local Wends. These three tribes form the nucleus of modern Sweden, and even today the full title of Karl Gustav is 'King of the Swedes, the Goths and the Wends'. This, too, is the origin of the Swedish royal arms – the three crowns set on a blue field – which is still to be seen on every piece of government property, from tanks to writing-paper. The whole southern end of the peninsula, the provinces of Skåne, Halland and Blekinge, belonged to Denmark, and towards the end of the Viking period, Olof Skötkonung's attempt to seize them ended in his utter defeat by Canute the Great.

In Britain, the Vikings always tend to be thought of as pirates who plundered the coasts of these islands, and who eventually conquered and settled the Danelaw in the north-east; but what is seldom realized is that they voyaged out to the East as much as to the West. Their exploits in Byzantium and Persia are as dramatic as the discovery of America. Each of the three Scandinavian nations sailed out from their own coasts: the Norwegians to Scotland and Iceland, the Danes to England and the Swedes to Finland and Russia. Northern trade was centred on the Baltic, in the middle of which lies the strategically placed island of Gotland. Its

11

merchants were exporting furs from the Arctic, amber from their own shores, and, as slaves, anyone who had the misfortune to be weaker than they were. In return came silver from the Moslem empires, silks from Byzantium, for silk has been found in a grave in Birka. In the whole of Sweden over 85,000 Arabic coins have been found. Not that the Swedes failed to venture westwards. One of the discoverers of Iceland, Gartharr, was a Swede, and they seem to have had their fair share of any English money that was going, to judge from the runestones at Grinda and Orkesta which were raised to men 'who had fetched their Danegeld in England' and from finds of many English pennies.

One has only to see the high mountains and fells flanked by lonely forests that separate Sweden from Norway and the west to understand why their main expansion should have been eastwards, where a swift longship could cross the Baltic in a couple of days. The earliest explorers

The Viking trade routes to the east

settled on the west coast of Finland, but Norse colonies were soon dotted all along the Baltic's eastern shore, as at Grobin in Latvia, where a whole town and its cemetery have been excavated to yield typical Viking weapons from the graves. They penetrated into Russia, first as traders, then as settlers. The very word 'Russia' derives from their presence; it means the land of the Rus, which was the Slav name for the Vikings and which was used by the Greek historians of the Byzantine empire. The Finnish name for Sweden, Ruotsi, has the same root, which perhaps is simply the verb *rodr*, 'to row'. Other Russian names seem so typical that no one would imagine they were Norse; who would look for Waldemar in Vladimir or Olof in Oleg, or, for that matter for Nygård, 'the new farm', in Novgorod? The country in which they settled was in a state of primitive turmoil, and the *Nestorian Chronicle* of the twelfth century proudly records how the Rus first brought law and order to Russia. They did so under three brothers, two of whom soon disappeared to leave Rurik to become prince of Kiev in 882, and to found a ruling house that survived for several centuries. There were, however, never enough settlers to provide more than a thin ruling class, which was absorbed into the native population during the chaos of the Tartar invasion that cut the trade routes to the Black Sea.

Two routes led southwards from the city of Novgorod; both followed the rivers, leaving only relatively short stretches of country to be crossed on foot, when the Vikings calmly took their ships with them. In one poem there is a description of how they cut down trees and, using them as rollers, heaved a whole ship laden with goods down to the Dneiper. This river, each of whose rapids had both a Norse and a Slav name, flows down to the Black Sea, where a few days' sailing took them to what was then the largest and richest city in the world, Constantinople, which they called Miklagård, quite simply 'the great city'. Not that this inspired the Vikings with any considerable awe; they made two attempts to sack it. Meanwhile, further east, the voyage led down the Volga to the Caspian Sea, and thence on to the cities of Baghdad or Bokhara. It seems a long way from the battles of King Alfred on the downs of Wessex to the capital of Harun al-Rashid and the *Thousand and One Nights,* yet the same man could easily have experienced both. What is more, the trade balance seems to have been in favour of the Vikings, to judge by all those Arab and Byzantine coinhoards found in Sweden wherever some thrifty merchant failed to withdraw his deposit account of the precious metal of the age.

The only traces of the Vikings in Russia today are their graves. At Gnezdeve, there are perhaps 4,000 barrows, and those few that have been opened have yielded superb swords and rich bracelets, all typically Scandinavian. Ibn Rustah, an Arab merchant, wrote a description of a Viking funeral which he witnessed and which obviously rather shook him. The dead chief was placed fully-clothed in a grave built like a hall, with his weapons, coins, food and drink. Finally, to make sure that every need was catered for, a drugged slave-girl was first violated by all the guests at the funeral and then strangled by an old hag and laid out beside him before he was ritually cremated. Another merchant, Ibn Fadhlan, stayed at a Viking camp on the banks of the Volga. He found the men tall as palm trees, with red hair, and always armed with at least an axe and a sword. For every 10,000 dirhems a man possessed, he had a necklace of silver made for his wife, a precise measure of wealth, and the women also wore capsules of metal over their breasts. Ibn Fadhlan also complained that the Rus were exceptionally dirty.

Trade with the Greeks was even more active. For over two centuries longships anchored off the Golden Horn were no uncommon sight. In southern Russia, the Vikings received a steady source of income in protection money from the local tribes, and in 860 they had the insolence to try the same technique at Constantinople, culminating in an unsuccessful attack on the city. Later the Rus signed a formal treaty with the joint emperors Leon and Alexander, but they did not observe it for long. In 941, a Viking fleet again attacked Constantinople, and was only driven back from the walls by the deadly secret weapon of the age, Greek fire. It is a reflection on the confidence which the Greek emperors had in their fellow countrymen that, in the tenth century, they should have formed the Varangian bodyguard of Viking mercenaries to protect themselves.

The most famous of the Varangians was Harald Hardrathi, the Norwegian prince who led the first invasion of England in 1066 and was killed by Harold at Stamford Bridge. After the defeat of Hastings, many Saxon nobles who would not stay as serfs in England went to Constantinople to end their days in the guard. One homesick Viking carved a rune, now sadly illegible, on a lion at the Acropolis of Athens. The lion stands today at the gate of the Arsenal in Venice, where it was taken by a later Swedish mercenary who commanded the Venetians at the tragic sixteenth-century siege of Athens when the Parthenon was blown up. On the marble screen in the south gallery of Hagia Sofia, one Halvdan has scratched his name as a good tenth-century tourist. Nor were these men forgotten at home; at Kyrkstigen in Uppland is a runic inscription to Röngvald, who served as a captain in the Varangian guard.

By the end of the eleventh century, the hordes from the steppes had put a stop to Scandinavian trade southwards, and at home the clearing of the forests began to satisfy the land-hunger of the earlier Vikings. On the south coast of the Baltic, the expansionist role was taken over by the Teutonic Knights, while in Finland there were crusades all through the early Middle Ages until the whole country became a Christian Swedish province. The last important Viking link with Russia was the marriage of Olof Skötkonung's daughter to Prince Jaroslav of Kiev, and Olof Skötkonung is the first Swedish king about whom enough is known to lift him from legend into history.

It is easy to forget that the Vikings led other lives apart from being pirates and merchants, but at home they slowly drove back the untamed forest and opened up their country. They lived on subsistence farms that were almost small villages, where the *bonde* or farmer ruled his family and perhaps as many as twenty thralls and their dependants. It was a tough life, where starvation was an ever-present threat. One hard winter could wipe out a little community completely, and every spring was touch and go, when, as an old proverb says, the cow dies while the grass is growing. A useless mouth to feed was an impossible burden, and it was generally accepted that the old killed themselves when they could work no more – there are several cliffs whose names today show they were used for this grim duty and there was thus never any moral stigma attached to suicide.

It was, in fact, the simple need for food which lay behind the Viking raids. Many of those who went to England or to Russia were genuine settlers, looking for a land where life was not so harsh; others, the real pirates, set off from home when the harvest was in, leaving its fruits to be consumed by their women and children. To most men, a Mediterranean winter of trade, or plunder if the other side were not strong enough to enforce payment, was vastly preferable to sitting snowed up in a Scandinavian log-cabin. Their diet was plain: bread, fish, meat when lucky, and honey for sweetening, with beer and mead to drink. Salted herrings and rosehips are still traditional foods in Sweden, and modern science has proved that rosehips are the purest form of Vitamin C in nature. Mead, too, is still to be drunk: in the Odinsborg inn at the foot of the royal howes in Old Uppsala it is served in silver-bound horns. One of the joys of Valhalla, the Viking heaven, was that the struggle for food was solved, for there the mead-horns never ran dry, and the boar Saehrimnir, after being roasted and devoured every night, was found whole again each morning. In Viking society, pain and cruelty were accepted as normal. A favourite punishment was the 'blood eagle', when the victim's chest was slit vertically where the ribs meet and, once the muscle holding them together was cut, they flew open like eagle's wings to expose the heart and lungs. The rest of Europe not unreasonably regarded the Vikings as wild animals. Adam of Bremen, in his history of the northern missionaries, gives a fairer description, with credit for their honesty among themselves and mentioning one trait that has not been bred out by civilization. 'The Swedes,' he writes, 'are moderate in all things save in women.'

Unfortunately, the simplicity of Viking life means that there are very few remains for us to look at today. Their great halls were all built in wood, and so none has survived. Historically, these structures were the predecessors of the great halls in Norman castles, used for living, eating, sleeping. The actual construction was like a Canadian log-cabin, whole tree-trunks piled one on top of the other and the cracks filled with moss; but there is one difference of which we can be certain, judging by a few ancient churches that have survived in Norway, and that is that every log was carved with patterns and gaudily painted. The open hearth was in the centre of the hall and the smoke escaped through a hole in the roof; along the walls were the locker benches still to be seen in old farms. The walls, so the old *Edda* songs tell us, were hung with tapestries to help preserve the warmth. The most famous medieval tapestry is, of course, that of Bayeux, which tells the story of the Norman conquest of England;

and the women who wove it were the grandchildren of Rolf's Vikings. Only a few fragments of Swedish tapestries have been saved in the Historical Museum in Stockholm.

In Sweden, only one Viking town has been properly excavated, and this is Birka on the island of birches about eighteen miles west of Stockholm. Today there are only a few earthworks to be seen, but we know a good deal about Birka from various sources. It was an important market, well known as far south as Hamburg, and Rimbert, who worked there as a missionary, praises its size and wealth in his life of his predecessor Ansgar. The rediscovery of Birka is romantic. An archaeologist collecting amber on the beach was advised by the local farmer to dig in an area called the Black Earth, where he would find much more. The Black Earth was Birka; it covers about thirty acres within a six-foot rampart, and at the southern end is a hill fort on a cliff. In its two natural harbours were the remains of heavy oak jetties, and an enormous mound of ashes marked the site of the town's beacon, which would have been visible as far as the entrance to the Baltic. A wealth of domestic objects have been found as well, including a pair of skates made of bone, pottery jugs and drinking glasses from the Rhineland, weights and scales, the inevitable coins of course from distant lands, and, furthest travelled of all, a bronze statuette of Buddha from northern India. Birka seems to have been abandoned towards the end of the Viking period, probably when the land level rose and the harbour silted up.

The Swedish Iron Age lasted effectively into the Viking era. It would be a mistake to see the Vikings as entirely separate from a prehistoric context. Iron ore is, even today, one of the most valuable natural resources of Sweden, but the first smiths dredged it in oxidized lumps from the shallow lakes of Småland and Darlecarlia, where the water has a dirty red colour and the stones on the bottom are covered with a film of rust that can be wiped off with a finger. The Viking smith was a man of great skill; on a dried-up lake on Gotland a farmer recently ploughed up a whole tool-chest, which must have gone to the bottom, either in a summer wreck or else through the ice in winter. The tools are quite sophisticated: several pairs of pliers, hammers, ladles, a little cauldron for melting the iron, and even a hand balance.

The quality of Viking sword blades and axes could be warranted for by many a monk; but far more admirable is the skill and workmanship lavished upon the hilts. Often the whole pommel is carved with an endless, twisting pattern which has then been inlaid with gold; at the centre may be the head of an animal, a god or a lucky charm such as Thor's hammer. The same art is used on anything metal, so that a bridle, a belt buckle, a shield-boss, the bands of a drinking-horn are all treated as pieces of jewellery. Little use is made of precious stones; the beauty lies in the craftsmanship. This art is essentially non-representational; it seems to grow like the wild vegetation of the untamed forest, with all the lavish, meaningless wealth of nature that the Vikings were so close to. There seems little purpose in something as weak as man to those who live with

16

something as strong as the sea. They saw beauty in form and pattern, in light and shadow on worked surface without the need of a subject or a story to justify itself. When an animal like a horse or a snake is actually represented, it is treated as a pattern, the gripping beast whose body has become one complicated knot, so that it is hard to recognize the original. These artists had a horror of empty spaces, which made them cover every inch of the surface on which they were working.

The outstanding survival of Scandinavian art from just before the Viking period is the Sutton Hoo treasure in the British Museum; but the Historical Museum in Stockholm has a large collection of similar objects. The boat-grave at Vet. lel, where the ship had completely rotted away, yielded in compensation a superb helmet and sword. The helmet has a long low crest, perhaps copied from the Romans, but the face-guard is unique with two eyeholes underneath beetling eyebrows, and a bearded head at the bridge of the nose. Stranger still are the gilt bronze pennants that presumably flew from a warship's mast-top or prow. Only six have been found in Sweden, but they are all remarkably beautiful, each being shaped like a bird's wing and with a fantastic twisting dragon set inside the border. As is usual, the finest objects have been found as grave-goods: amazingly intricate work in gold and silver, inlaying even sword-hilts and axe-heads with precious metals.

Sadly, no grave has been found in Sweden to compare with Oseberg or Gökstad in Norway, where the whole wooden longships that were to carry the dead on their voyage to the next world have been preserved in the clay. Not that every Viking grave had a real ship buried in it; that would have been very extravagent. Instead, stones were raised to form the outline of a ship, the tallest at the prow and the stern, and such

Ale's stones, near Kåseberga

skeppssättningar are to be found the length and breadth of Sweden. At Badelunda in Västmanland, a wide clearing in the dark pine forest holds a whole fleet of these stone ships, the blocks of granite throwing their long shadows on the turf that swells like the sea and the wind in the trees at the forest's edge sounding like an echo of the waves for those long-dead sailors. The biggest such ship stands on top of the sandcliffs which plunge into the Baltic at the south-easternmost corner of Sweden above the little fishing village of Kåseberga. The stones stand in a meadow thick with wild thyme, ready to sail out on to the sea a hundred feet below. Nor is the man who chose to sleep so dramatically to the music of the sea forgotten, for these are known as Ale's Stones.

Thanks to the Oseberg and Roskilde finds, it is possible to reconstruct Viking ships with some precision, and they were remarkable examples of scientific seamanship. The exploits of sailing to America were convincingly put to proof in 1893 when Captain Magnus Anderson and his Norwegian crew sailed an exact replica of the Gökstad ship across the North Atlantic in under a month, and he was full of praise for her seaworthiness. The keel was always made of a single tree-trunk, which could bend several inches under the pressure of the waves, and the hull was clinker-built with the thickest strakes at the waterline. She was steered by a rudder fixed to the right or 'steerboard' of the stern-post. The great square sail hung from a single yard-arm, with no boom but only spars that could be fastened at any angle. In the Visby museum there are a couple of runestones showing longships under full sail, and the Lärbro stone shows the crew holding the ropes. The longship, with its low, elegant lines, was exclusively military; for trade, shorter, deeper ships with a hold beneath the deck were used, like those found in the Roskilde fiord.

A longship was the proudest of a great man's possessions, and the battles of the age were all fought at sea, as when Canute the Great defeated Olof Skötkonung's son on the Holy River in Skåne. Loyalty to those kings was more a matter of personal liking than of geography, and the king was more a war-leader than a ruler. Local government was handled by the Ting, a meeting held in the open country which every freeman could attend. The most famous Tingsplace is at Old Uppsala, where every February all the Swedes would gather by the great flat-topped mound to make their laws. Human life was cheap and the usual penalty for murder was a practical cash payment to the bereaved. If revenge was insisted on, the form was for a duel to be fought on an island from which only the winner returned. Society was divided into three classes: at the bottom the thralls, often the unhappy victims of distant raids; then, with his own farm, the freeman or *karl,* which is the original form of the name Charles; and lastly the *jarl* or warrior, which oddly enough only survives as a title in the English and Scottish 'earl' and has been lost in Scandinavia.

What Viking literature has survived comes exclusively from Iceland, where the old sagas were written down in the twelfth and thirteenth

The Larbrö stone

centuries. History owes an incalculable debt to Snorri Sturluson, an
Icelandic scholar and statesman, who deliberately set out at the beginning
of the Christian era to collect all he could of the old Norse myths before
they were forgotten. His work covers several historical sagas as well as
the *Prose Edda*, which is the story of the Norse gods.

Only one saga has come down to us with a Swedish hero, that of
Yngvar the Far-Travelled, who led an expedition to the court of Jaroslav of
Russia and then on to Constantinople. Many of the episodes belong to the
fantastic world of the folktale, but the basic story of a voyage to
Constantinople is quite plausible. In reality, Yngvar's expedition seems to
have been something of a disaster. No less than twenty-five runestones in
different parts of Sweden commemorate Vikings who fell with Yngvar;
one outside Gripsholm Castle is to his brother Harald. 'They journeyed
boldly, far afield after gold; in the east they gave food to the eagles. They
died in the South in Serkland.' Serkland was the Viking name for the
Byzantine Empire.

19

The *skald* or poet was an important and admired man, richly rewarded by his patrons, for in a heroic society where fame is the supreme goal it is important to have the journalists on your side. Scaldic verse had two main uses: either to tell an epic saga or to fix points of law as in the *Havamal,* or *Wisdom of Odin.* The verse is alliterative not rhymed with the same consonant recurring again and again at the beginning of the words in each line.

> Nothing I know lives nor lasts longer;
> Deathless is doom over dead men.

Plenty of Viking texts survive in Sweden, but they are carved on runestones which do not lend themselves to recording whole epics. There are over 2,500 runestones known in Sweden, more than in any other country, and over 1,000 in Uppland alone. The oldest, in fact, have no runes. They are just free-standing stones whose surfaces are covered with pictures, a more advanced form of rock-carvings. The finest are from the island of Gotland, like the Tjängvide stone, now in Stockholm or the Lärbro stone, on which Odin rides his eight-legged horse Sleipnir above a longship under full sail; with its battle scenes and hangéd men. The style of these stones is simple: no sense of perspective or proportion, but a superb sense of composition, where a horse's tail curves to link two groups, or a raven fills a blank space. It was always guessed that the runestones were painted, but proof was lacking until 1956 when an old church on Öland was pulled down and from the rubble fell pieces of carved stone painted red, black and white.

As the runes begin to appear on the stones, so the pictures begin to disappear; words replace images until at last even the dragons are reduced to long curling bands on which the runes are written. The runes themselves were secret and holy, and the carver of runes had something of the status of a magician. Each letter had a magic value, so we often find T, the letter of Thor, on a sword-blade or an axe-head. The runes themselves are derived from the Latin and Greek alphabets, modified into straight lines as they had to be carved on wood or stone instead of being written with a pen. Some letters, like R or B, are the same as today, while others like ᚦ for O, or ᚼ for H are unique. Originally the runic alphabet had twenty-four letters, beginning FUTHARK, but these were soon reduced to sixteen in the new futhark-line. According to the Havamal, it was Odin, the God of Wisdom, who discovered the runes; but he bought his knowledge dearly, for he had to hang for nine days from Yggdrasil, the ash tree at the centre of the world, pierced by a spear, until he understood them. All through the Middle Ages, the runes survived alongside the universal Latin script, which, of course, was used by all the clerks; for if there was an inscription to be made by someone other than the priest, he would use the old letters which his ancestors had invented before the Church came. As a popular script, their last use was on the runestick, a calendar which was formerly used in every farmhouse. It is a

The Rök stone

flat piece of wood like a ruler, on which the calendar is carved, using a different rune for each day of the month, and examples can be seen in museums dated from as late as the early eighteenth century.

Sometimes the magic of the runes is so complicated that it is impossible to interpret them. The biggest runestone in Sweden stands at Rök in East Gothland, but it has puzzled every scholar who has tried to read it; it seems to be either a curse or else a spell to protect the honour of the family. This stone has no pattern at all; the whole surface is covered by vertical rows of runes. Some stones were raised for more mundane reasons, to commemorate the building of a bridge or a causeway. The most usual purpose is as a monument to a dead man whose grave lies far away; some even record voyages to Jerusalem.

Quite often the artist who carved the stone has signed it, so that we know of Asmund Kåreson, Balle, Fot and Opir. Balle has left us the big stone at Litslena in Uppland, where two dragons facing each other are woven into a pattern so complex that it strains the eye to follow it. Not so many runestones remain standing on their original sites, and while moving the old stones from their home robs them of romance, it is certainly more convenient to wander round the collections in the Historical Museum in Stockholm, the Cultural Museum in Lund, or the 'Stone Hall' in Visby.

Few people appreciate how many runestones date from the Christian era. Often the inscription asks for Christ's mercy on the dead man's soul; but sometimes it is the other way round, and pagan legends are used on a Christian object. The wooden font from Lockne in Jämtland, which is as late as the thirteenth century, shows Gunnar in the snake pit.

The success of Christianity is traditionally taken to mark the end of the Viking age. Its acceptance brought the practical advantages of a superior civilization; though there were many, like the Norwegian Kjartan, who stuck to Thor on the high seas. In Iceland, the whole question was very sensibly put to a vote at the *Ting,* and when Christianity won a majority, it was accepted as the official religion, with the proviso that those who wished to hold fast to the old gods might do so in private. The 'barbarian' Vikings were remarkably civilized on the often thorny problem of religions. Only the Swedes proved to be really obstinate pagans, and Christianity there was not generally accepted until the twelfth century.

It was appropriate that Sweden should have remained so loyal to the old gods the longest; for it was the most remote of the Scandinavian countries, and the centre of resistance to the new religion was the holy place of Uppsala. There, beside the three enormous Kings' Howes, is a hollow in the plain where the grass is a richer green, marking the site of the two sacred springs, Urdal and Mimir. Here the wind still shivers in the coppice of aspens that must be at least ten generations from the trees in the sacred grove, though the Christians have long since felled the ancient yew dedicated to Odin. Every ninth year came Fröblod, the greatest festival of the gods of Valhalla, and on that yew tree were hanged nine males of each species and left there to rot. One of the names of Odin

22

is the God of the Hanged, and when we hang our presents on a Christmas tree we are making an unwitting sacrifice to him. Adam of Bremen recorded a vivid description of Fröblod from an old man in the monastery who had witnessed the ceremony and seen nine men die there on the tree.

Even today the old church that was once a cathedral is dwarfed by the gigantic mounds, and the mood of Old Uppsala is far more pagan than Christian. Recent excavations in the actual choir of the twelfth century church have revealed the foundations of that heathen temple which was famous throughout the North. It was a square building of wood with an aisle running all round the outside, presumably built of upright staves and carved and painted like the earliest churches. According to Adam of Bremen, at the centre of the shrine there stood three statues, larger than life and covered with beaten gold; in the middle was Thor with his raised hammer, on one side Odin and on the other Frey, distinguished by an enormous phallus. It is strange not to see Odin given the most important place. The temple is, in fact, a last gesture by the doomed religion, seeking pathetically to imitate and rival the Christian Trinity, when it displaced the profound and mysterious Odin by the simple Thor.

By the middle of the eleventh century, Christians had broken into the temple and destroyed the idols, but many traces of heathendom survive in Swedish life today. Christmas is still called by the old name of Yule, the festival of midwinter.

Such surviving traditions of the old religion give far too kind an impression. The Viking gods were hard and cruel, like the lives of those who worshipped them. The gift of good or ill fortune was completely arbitrary, and like the gods of Olympus, the gods of Valhalla had no moral purposes in their interferences in the world of men. The Vikings shared with the Homeric Greeks the cult of heroism, but added to it their own kind of fatalism. Again and again in myths that are sheer adventure stories come flashes of profound insight into the eternal problems of humanity. The three norns, for instance, who tended Yggdrasil, were called Urd, Verdandi and Skuld, respectively fate or past, being or present, necessity or future; it would be hard to make a terser or more lucid summing up of the human situation. Odin was the greatest of the gods and he had a dual personality: on the one hand, the God of Wisdom and Thought, the writer of runes and teacher of poets; on the other, the God of Frenzy and War, under whose protection berserk warriors fought armourless, and whose daughters, the Valkyries, brought them to Valhalla when they were killed. To die in one's bed was the most shameful of ends. Thor, on the other hand, was a much simpler character, travelling the world in search of adventure, a great trencherman who was once tricked into trying to drain a horn, the other end of which was set in the sea, and who almost dried up the ocean. Thor's taking the place of Odin shows the spiritual decline of the old religion.

The poem called the *Havamal* is an interesting summing up of the Viking attitude to life. A kind of versified Book of Proverbs, its advice is

23

tough and eminently practical: 'Be especially careful with beer and another man's wife.' The author had no time to sentimentalize life. There are a few qualities which are absolutely fundamental: courage, moderation and absolute honesty among equals. To the Vikings, a man was nothing but his reputation; and to believe that is to impose a very high standard upon oneself.

What is unique about the religion of the Aesir is its tragic pessimism. It is the only religion in the world where the gods will all be killed never to rise again. Unlike the Greek Titans, the northern giants are not securely bound. At the end of the world they will break their chains, and Loki will lead them to storm Valhalla. This is Ragnarök, and it is to fight in this battle that the bravest of men had been taken to Valhalla when they fell. In this conflict there will be no survivors. Thor will kill the great serpent which is coiled round the edge of the world, but die of its poison; Odin will be devoured by the grey wolf Fenrir; when all have fallen, the blazing earth will sink into the boiling sea. This myth expresses something very deep in the mind of every Scandinavian, which is still detectable in writers like Strindberg: the sense that it is hopeless to try to control life, and that the end, even for the best of men, is only death.

Among these stories of blood and violence, the myth of Balder appears like a burst of sunshine on a stormy day. Balder was Odin's son, handsome and gentle, so loved by the gods that all things alive and dead took an oath never to hurt him. Loki, however, managed to get him killed by the mistletoe that had been forgotten, hidden in the oak. There are two versions of the story, one being just another triumph of darkness over light. In the other, however, Balder returns after Ragnarök to rule over a world of peace and love. No one knows whether this was an ancient myth or whether it grew out of Christian influences, but the early missionaries proclaimed Christ as the White Balder, and in his name the new religion conquered the North.

3. The Early Middle Ages

By the ninth century the Vikings were seriously disrupting life in the more civilized parts of Europe, until Louis the Pious concluded that the only hope of controlling the menace was to convert it. So, in 829, a monk called Ansgar set off for the far north from the court at Aachen. By the time he got to Birka, he had already been captured by pirates, who stole all Louis's gifts for the Swedish king. However, he was allowed to build a church, though his parishioners consisted mainly of Christian slaves.

Ansgar is always called the Apostle of the North, but his mission was really only a flash in the pan. After two years he returned south to become the first bishop of Hamburg, and his Frankish successor at Birka was soon driven out. Ansgar's biographer, Rimbert, who also took part in the Swedish mission, describes him as an energetic and saintly man with the vital strength of personality necessary to launch Christianity in the heathen North, which came under his diocese. Even in Hamburg he was on the frontier; for, in 845, the city was attacked and stormed by a Viking fleet, and Ansgar had to remove his see to the greater safety of Bremen. Christianity was not to gain a permanent footing in Scandinavia for at least another century, and although Ansgar regretted on his deathbed that he had not become a martyr, it was hardly for want of trying.

By the year 1000, both Denmark and Norway had been converted, and Sweden's first Christian king, Olof Skötkonung, was baptized in 1006. He made several attempts to destroy the pagan temple at Uppsala, but his people were having none of it, electing his pagan son Anund Jacob to be king instead. At a *Ting* they obliged Olof to choose the best province of his kingdom and build his church there, so he chose West Gothland, and built his first cathedral at Skara on the site of a temple to Freya.

Olof needed priests to teach his people, and he turned to Ethelred of England, who sent him Sigfrid of York and Eskil. Eskil interrupted a heathen sacrifice and promptly got martyred at a place still called Eskilstuna. The missionaries came from two directions, the south and the west, and throughout the early Middle Ages in Scandinavia there was a struggle for influence between Canterbury and Hamburg; indeed, it was only after William the Conqueror reorientated the politics and trade of his new kingdom towards France that the English lost interest.

Olof fetched more than his religion from across the North Sea. He was the first Swedish king to strike a coinage; and his mint-master, Godwin, was an Englishman whose crude silver pennies carry his own and the king's name around a distant imitation of the emperor's head on a Roman coin with a cross on the obverse. Within the church itself, both liturgy and architecture show English influences. Nothing remains of the first church at Skara; but after he was murdered by pagans, Olof was buried in the lovely Husaby, which must be typical of the first dour Romanesque churches of Sweden. He was succeeded by another of his sons, Stenkil Olofsson.

Now is the moment to point out a very troublesome aspect of Swedish history. For a long time, no family had a surname. Instead, they just put son after the father's Christian name and used that – Stenkil Olof's son. This makes Swedish history quite as confusing to write as it is to read; and the habit continues today, to the bane of the Swedish Post Office, for in spite of annual appeals by the postmaster-general to get people to change their names, Anderssons still occupy some twenty pages of the Stockholm telephone directory. Even today, when the father has an unusual Christian name, the children take it and create a new surname. The easiest thing for the reader to do is to remember that the name moves backwards one place each generation. The oldest Swedish noble families have very simple surnames, like Bonde, meaning 'farmer', or Nattochdag, meaning 'day and night' because their shield was half white and half black; but always using the name in ——son as well.

Stenkil Olofsson was an ardent Christian who established Adalvard as the first bishop of Sigtuna, only a few miles from the pagan centre of Uppsala, whence he was promptly expelled. Indeed, for the next century the bishops are in and out of Sigtuna like jacks-in-a-box. Although the nobles might become Christian out of snobbery, their thralls at the best added Christ to the pantheon of Valhalla. In war or famine, there was almost an automatic return to the old gods, for catastrophes were blamed on the neglect by a Christian king of his most important duty, that of priest.

The only part of Sweden about which we know much in the eleventh century is Skåne, then a province of Denmark, which was altogether a far more advanced kingdom. The first cathedral in Skåne was founded at Dalby, where its remains form part of the present parish church. Its patron was the Danish king, Sven Estridsen, and its first bishop the pugnacious Egino. However, within six years the see was transferred to Lund a few miles away, and work soon began on the magnificent Romanesque cathedral which still stands there. In 1103, the vast missionary diocese of Hamburg was split up, and Ascer became the new archbishop for the whole of Scandinavia with his seat at Lund.

By tradition, the kings were elected at the *Ting*; but fortunately the hereditary principle soon triumphed and Sweden was spared the bloody and tragic history of Poland. The oldest code governing these elections is the West Gothic Laws, dating from the early thirteenth century. There, it is written, the Swedes have the right to elect their kings and to throw them out. The laws also cover the other duties of the king. Immediately after his election, he is to ride through the country on his Eriksgata so that his people will know him in battle; he also had to be supreme judge at the

Ting. Each province had its own code of laws, that of Uppland being completed in the 1290s under the chairmanship of Birger Persson, the father of St Bridget. They include many far older traditions, and oaths are often 'by the gods'.

At first society was organized as it had been in the Viking age, but with time Sweden fell into the mould of feudalism, copied from the rest of Europe, with the three Estates of the Lords, the Church and the Commons, except that the Commons were divided into burgers and yeomen, who managed to retain more rights and freedoms than their class enjoyed in most other countries.

The kings of Sweden in the early Middle Ages are shadowy figures, belonging partly to legend and partly to history. There is Inge the Elder, who was poisoned at the royal manor of Vreta, and the first church there was probably built over his grave. Near him lies his daughter Margareta Fredkulla, who was married to a Danish prince who ruled over parts of Sweden. Often a man would be accepted as king by only one province, and there might be several kings in permanent civil war.

The most noteworthy ruler of the century was Sverker, who became king in 1139. He was an East Goth, whose family estate lay at the foot of Omberg on the shore of lake Vättern, and the founder of a line that was to provide Sweden with kings for over a century. His reign saw a remarkable flourishing of the Church. The temple at Uppsala was gone and the missionary bishopric of Sigtuna was transferred on to its very site. Sweden's first monastery was founded at Alvastra, and several others followed in quick succession. The whole Christian civilization of the medieval world burst into flower in a few short years.

Alvastra, too, lies near Omberg, that strange mountain that rises so dramatically between the lake and the plain; and it was in 1143 that Sverker's queen, Ulfhild, wrote to Bernard of Clairvaux to send her monks for her monastery. We do not know the name of the first abbot, but the second was a certain Bernard of Utrecht. He returned to Clairvaux, as St Bernard had promised him, leaving behind a noble life's work in a wild and distant land. Also founded direct from Clairvaux was Nydala, whence the monks went out to Roma in Gotland in 1164. The Church in Sweden was obviously ready to be absorbed into the Church Universal of Rome, and in 1153 the papal legate, Nicolas of Albano, convened a meeting at Linköping, whose bishop, Gisle, was King Sverker's chancellor. There, in the presence of all the great men of the realm, the Swedish Church was officially recognized, and all lax practices, such as failing to pay tithes to Rome or allowing the clergy to marry, were ceremoniously abolished.

Sverker died in 1156 and a certain Erik was elected to succeed him. But the principle of the elective monarchy was not established and we shall see that, for almost a hundred years, there was constant civil war between the descendants of Sverker and the descendants of Erik as each family tried to assert itself as the house of the hereditary kings. Erik was destined to become a saint, indeed, the patron saint of his country. There is little historical evidence of his sanctity, but his relics soon began to work miracles and the monks of Uppsala naturally cultivated so lucrative a legend. During his reign, the church of St Laurence at Old Uppsala was completed and richly furnished by the king himself.

St Erik is best remembered for his crusade in Finland. The story is told in the fourteenth-century frescoes of the de Geer family chapel in Uppsala cathedral. There are twelve scenes (reading from the top downwards), beginning with his coronation. Then there is the preaching of the crusade, and the ships full of soldiers sail across the gulf of Bothnia to force a landing. After various battles, the Finns are baptized. The last fight, however, is against the Danes, and there St Erik is defeated; we see him kneeling to be executed, and finally his body his carried to Uppsala. The facts of his death are vague; but he certainly came to a tragic end which was warmly remembered in the fireside tales of his people.

The Danish army was probably helping Sverker's son Karl to gain the throne. This was the usual course of events, with the losing side appealing to the Danes and the Danes supporting them in the hope of becoming overlords of Sweden. Only one act of importance happened in Karl Sverkersson's reign, and that was in France. In 1164, Stephen, a monk from Alvastra and perhaps an Englishman, was consecrated the first archbishop of Uppsala in a ceremony at the brand-new cathedral of Sens, where the builders were experimenting with the earliest Gothic. When he returned to the rough North, Stephen must have carried with him the memory of all that light and youthful energy to spread among his flock so recently emerged from the darkness of paganism. Stephen's seal has been preserved and shows him standing with his pastoral staff in his right hand and an open book in his left. Under him, Stephen had six more dioceses: Linköping, Skara, Strängnäs, Västerås, Växjö and Åbo in Finland. The real reason for raising the status of Uppsala, although it was still subordinate to Lund, was to punish the Danes, who had joined the Germans in supporting the antipope; but it was an apt expression of the rising sense of Swedish nationalism.

Karl Sverkersson did not enjoy his kingdom for long; in 1167 he was murdered by St Erik's son Knut. Knut Eriksson had obviously not inherited any of his father's alleged sanctity. A ruthless and efficient ruler, he set about consolidating his kingdom by such practical but utilitarian works as reforming the coinage, suppressing pirates and building strongholds in the countryside. He probably built the first castle at Stockholm. Knut allied himself to the Church, whose monks welcomed a strong central government instead of the anarchy which they usually saw around them. The pope himself was interested, and the monument to the reign of Adrian IV is the ecclesiastical organization of Scandinavia. Perhaps, when he was still the English monk Nicolas Breakspear, he had heard stories from his countrymen about their work among the wild Norsemen.

When Knut Eriksson died in 1196, he had arranged to be succeeded by his son Erik, but it was the turn of Sverker's family to provide the king; and Erik Knutsson was driven out almost immediately by Johan Sverkersson. He took refuge in Denmark, where he received the support of the king, but it was not enough to win back his throne, and the history of the years which follow is one of confused civil war. Johan Sverkersson received significant support from a group of noblemen called the Folkungs. Unfortunately, this name is also used for a later royal family, but originally it seems to have been a political party which opposed the hereditary crown and tried to restore the ancient Swedish right to elect their kings. Its policy was essentially democratic and divisive against the centralized feudal state that Knut Eriksson had tried to found.

This chaos did not halt the development of Sweden in other ways. One class which almost always benefits from wars is that of the merchants, and the struggle between the Sverkerssons and the Erikssons showed no exception to the rule. The only trouble was that, in thirteenth-century Sweden, the merchants were usually Germans.

These years saw the beginning of a strong German influence. The economy was still very primitive, though forward-looking kings like Knut Eriksson tried hard to encourage a more active commercial life, for Sweden had plenty to export, such as the iron and copper which provide much of her wealth today. Her one essential import was salt, followed by cloth. Much of the cloth came from England, and Henry III issued a special letter of privileges to Odelrik, chief of the German merchants of Visby.

The trade of Northern Europe at this time was controlled by the Hanseatic League, to which most of the cities of northern Germany belonged. They were free within the empire, like the Italian merchant republics, and were as independent as any state, while many non-German cities also belonged. The Hansa controlled almost all the trade of the Baltic, and served as bankers to many kings, some, indeed, being so deeply in debt that Sweden was often almost a client kingdom. The capital of the league was Lübeck, then, as now, a frontier town of Christendom; but it included both Hamburg and Bremen.

However, probably the greatest monument to the Hanseatic League is the city of Visby on the island of Gotland. Visby is a northern Carcassonne. Its wall, bastioned by more than thirty towers, is still complete, and within the gates little has changed since the Middle Ages, save that of its twelve proud churches eleven are ruins and only the cathedral stands in its original grandeur. Visby was founded about the middle of the twelfth century as a depot half-way on the route between Lübeck and Novgorod. In its many-storeyed warehouses, some of which are still inhabited, were kept furs from Russia, swords from Bergslagen, wine from the Rhine, cloth from Norwich, gold from Byzantium. Gotland had been an island of merchants since the Viking days, but the Gotlanders themselves lived on their farms, and it was only the German immigrants who gathered together in a city. Commercial rivalry and national tension were inevitable; and in 1288 these broke out into open war, which ended in

Town walls at Visby

favour of Visby and the Hansa, no doubt partly thanks to the security of the great walls.

The merchants' club in every northern town is the Guild of St Knut. Visby's died with the decline of the city; but in Ystad the guild survives today to claim descent from the Hansa. Ystad is another town that has changed little since the days when kings and armies made the crossing from its harbour to Stralsund in Germany.

Nor did civil war interrupt the business of crusading in Finland. In 1220, the chronicles report, the king and the bishop of Linköping both died miserably on a crusade in Estonia; but usually these crusades were a success. They were a continuation of the Viking expeditions eastwards, and, on a wider stage, part of the *Drang nach Osten* of the Germanic nations. These Swedish crusades along the north-eastern shores of the Baltic were matched on the southern ones by the conquests of the Teutonic Knights. Of the German advance, nothing now remains; Königsberg, Marienburg, East Prussia – all were returned to the Slavs at the end of the Second World War after a thousand years of western-ization. Finland is all that is left of this expansion, for there a Swedish aristocracy has grown together with the Finnish people to become one nation, which is still officially bilingual. Eventually the German victories spelt the commercial ruin of Gotland, because they opened up a safe route to the East along the coast which had before been the dangerous haunt of heathen pirates.

Every king turned his attention eastwards as soon as he had an oppor-tunity. A Russian chronicle records an invasion by Sverker of sixty ships. Few Scandinavians took part in the crusades to Palestine; instead, they put their religious fervour to a more practical use nearer home. Progress was not fast. One papal Bull complains that the Finns begged ardently for priests whenever a crusading army appeared, but threw them out the moment the army had left.

Erik Knutsson had managed to get himself crowned in 1210, the first recorded Swedish coronation, and he found himself sole king in Sweden after Johan Sverkersson was killed crusading. He did not enjoy this state for long; he died in 1222, leaving a posthumously born heir, Erik Eriksson. Folke Jarl, the leader of the Folkungs, immediately dispossessed the baby and had his own candidate, Knut the Tall, elected king.

Unfortunately for Folke, Erik's sister had been married to one of the most able men in Swedish history, Birger Jarl, who naturally set about winning back his brother-in-law's kingdom. The Folkungs were decis-ively defeated at the battle of Herrevads Bro, and when Knut the Tall died there were no more rival claimants and the long civil war was over. For all practical purposes, Sweden was ruled by Birger Jarl, at first because the king was a child, but later because the wretched Erik was totally in-adequate; indeed, he was nicknamed 'Erik the Halt and Lisping'.

Birger saw that what his ravaged country needed was peace and stability, and his natural ally in this was the Church, where his brother Bengt was bishop of Linköping. His ecclesiastical policy was rewarded with the Council at Skänninge in 1248 under the papal legate William of Sabina. He led one successful campaign in Finland and conquered Tavastland. In trade, Birger made an alliance with the Hansa, and extended their privileges. At home, he is famous for founding the town of Stockholm, and he built the first keep at Örebro. Finally, there is his reputation as a lawyer.

The church in Sweden needed its council. In 1244, the convent at Vreta, today a beautiful ruin, was raided by the noble Lars, and the nun Benedicta, granddaughter of King Sverker himself, was carried off. The pair fled to Norway, where Lars soon died, at which Benedicta promptly returned to Sweden and married someone else. Chastity was clearly not her calling. The whole story is preserved in the contemporary folksong, 'Junker Lars' Theft from the Cloister'.

A happier tale is that of Petrus de Dacia. He was born on the island of Gotland, and became a priest after taking refuge from pirates in a church. A good scholar, it was as a student in Cologne that he met Christina of Stommeln, a nun famous for her visions and prophesies. Between them sprang up one of those strange sublimated love affairs of the Middle Ages. Back in Gotland, he kept up a long correspondence with her that was intended to become her biography, but it became his own as well, and grew into a moving story of medieval faith and love. Petrus is known as Sweden's first author; he became prior of the monastery of St Nicholas in Visby, and died there in 1289. His church is now a majestic ruin, and every summer his life is acted as a mystery play, set to music by Friedrich Mehler, in the roofless choir where he lies buried.

The miserable King Erik died in 1250, and the next king was his nephew, Birger Jarl's son Valdemar, who was crowned in the new cathedral at Linköping. In 1266, the old Jarl died. He had effectively ruled Sweden for over forty years, and during that time he had led his country out of the miseries of anarchy and civil war to a prosperity and a security it had never before known. His wise policies brought Sweden into the medieval world as an accepted state rather than as a barbarous territory on the fringe of Europe. The Council of Skänninge was symbolic, for there the Church recognized and confirmed his achievement. To later history, Birger is known as the first of the Folkungs, and it is under that incorrect name that his descendants ruled Sweden. He himself was the last of the Jarls.

Valdemar did not make much of a king, in spite of the influence of his father. Most of his energies were devoted to an affair with his sister-in-law, Jutta of Denmark, whom a chronicle describes as 'fair as an angel in heaven'. However, there were no enemies to disturb the peace. Work had begun on a new cathedral at Uppsala in 1258 on a different site, for the town had moved some five miles to be on a navigable river. There, on the hill, was raised a greater church than any yet seen in the North, in pure French Gothic style. Under Archbishop Laurence, the work went swiftly ahead, and in 1273 the relics of St Erik were translated with due pomp from Old Uppsala, and the new cathedral was dedicated.

Valdemar's careless rule bore hard on his younger brother Magnus, who was the real heir to their father's energy and ability. In 1275, Valdemar made the tactical error of going to Rome on a pilgrimage, and no sooner had he left than Magnus seized power. The unfortunate Valdemar returned home to find he had no throne, and lacking all support from the nobility, he soon quietly withdrew to obscurity.

Many hoped that the revolt of Magnus meant a return to the good old days of free-booting chaos before Birger Jarl's time. They were so swiftly disillusioned that the great lords rose in rebellion the very next year, only to be defeated in battle and most of them executed. Yet Magnus had seen the strength of the opposition to the new order among the great families, and in 1279 he came to terms with them at Alsnö. The Ordinances of Alsnö represent the final codified triumph of feudalism in Sweden, defining the various privileges and rights of the different estates. The Church which had supported Magnus was rewarded well. The old nobility were bought generously with the grant of freedom from taxation, but in return they were bound, as elsewhere in Europe, to maintain the standing of knighthood and to lead their vassals to the king's armies; their ranks, too, were diluted by the admission of many men of lesser birth who had proved themselves worthy royal servants. Magnus also reorganized the whole civil service. The old title of *jarl*, which had carried so much power, was abolished; the next man to the king was the *kanzler* or chancellor, with two new officials to help him, the *marsk* or marshal and the *drots* or steward of the realm.

Magnus continued the domestic policies of his father, increasing the prosperity of the nation. The earliest reference to the great copper mine at Falun is dated 1288, and it is interesting to see on what a democratic basis it was organized, for the greatest share in the mine was owned by the free miners who worked it. Indeed, the wealthy miners of Falun were an important force in politics throughout the Middle Ages. Magnus was one of the most popular of all Swedish kings. His reign was marked by prosperity and peace; he fined the citizens of Visby for fortifying their town without his permission. He particularly protected the common people, and forbade the custom whereby a lord could oblige a farmer to feed him and his retinue as long as the stores lasted; for this Magnus was nicknamed Ladulås or 'barnlock'. Such was the love he had inspired, that when he died the loyal farmers carried his coffin on their shoulders all the way from Visingsö to Stockholm.

His religious foundations are numerous, and the most famous of them is the monastery of the Franciscan Friars on the Riddarholm in Stockholm. Their church is now the burial place of the kings of Sweden, and on a wall survives an almost contemporary portrait of Magnus Ladulås himself.

When King Magnus died in 1290, his eldest son, Birger, was still a minor. The council of regency was dominated by Torgil Knutsson, the marshal. He was a good soldier who had led several Finnish crusades in person, and he built the splendid lowering fortress of Viborg to guard the natural frontier on the isthmus between the gulf of Finland and lake Ladoga. Viborg only fell with the collapse of the Swedish empire in the eighteenth century; it fell a second time at the Russian invasion of Finland in 1940 and is still occupied today.

The reign of Birger Magnusson was confused and bloody, with at least four different parties struggling for power. No sooner had Birger reached his majority and been crowned than his younger brothers, the Dukes Erik and Valdemar, made their claims and were driven into exile in Norway, where – to keep the pot boiling – the king gave them the fief of Bohuslän on the Swedish frontier. Duke Erik then managed to get the grant of the fief of Halland from the Danish king, so that he controlled a stretch of territory centred on the great fortress of Varberg, just where the three Scandinavian kingdoms met: an admirable base for a troublemaker.

The brothers were reconciled in time to join the bishops in ousting Torgil Knutsson. The marshal himself was captured, tried and executed as a heretic, one who had opposed the interests of the Church. Duke Erik was intent on keeping Swedish politics exciting. That same autumn of 1306, he invited his brother the king to Håtuna, and promptly locked him up, playfully naming the incident 'The Game of Håtuna'. He then forced Birger to grant him special privileges. One cannot tell quite what Duke Erik's objectives were, whether he wanted to create a separate kingdom out of his territories or whether he merely wanted to become king of Sweden, for he changed sides so often and his whole career was so treacherous and unscrupulous that the truth is entirely lost. However, that is the view of later ages. At least one of his contemporaries saw him as a peerless knight, and that was the author of the *Chronicle of Erik*. This is Sweden's oldest surviving verse chronicle, and it is a superb epic. The action leads up through the brothers' struggle for the kingdom to the hero's horrible death, and the tragedy closes with the retribution on his murderer.

For the next few years, Sweden was divided more or less peacefully between the three brothers and seemed doomed to disintegration. This, however, was not to be, thanks to King Birger's long memory. It was nearing Christmas in 1317, and Birger had invited both his brothers to celebrate Yule, the festival of the family, with him at Nyköping. He did not fail in his duties as a medieval host, and by the time dinner was over both the dukes were so drunk that they were lost to the world, in which state they were carried away by Birger's servants to sober up in one of the dungeons. There their host came to see them and asked if they remembered 'The Game of Håtuna'. 'And,' he continued, 'you will find this game just as entertaining.' After which Birger threw the keys of the dungeon into the river at Nyköping, and Erik and Valdemar duly starved to death. The Guest-night at Nyköping was a bit too much even for the fourteenth-century Swedes; the whole country rose against Birger, his son was killed and he was driven out to die an exile in Denmark.

The steward, Mats Kettilmundsson, took control of the kingdom in the name of the baby son of Duke Erik and his wife Ingeborg, princess of

Norway. The previous years had left a lot of work for the council of regency. Most important was peace with Russia, which was signed at Nöteborg in 1323, confirming the conquests of Torgil Knutsson, and making the steward himself lord of the castle of Viborg.

The Duchess Ingeborg seems to have had much in common with her late husband. Effectively ignoring her son, she married a Danish nobleman called Knut Porse, and set about creating another independent state for herself based on Duke Erik's possessions around Varberg. She married her daughter Eufemia to Duke Albrecht of Mecklenburg in an attempt to encircle Denmark, and her policy was amply rewarded when the country simply fell apart under Christopher II, 'The King without Lands', to end in ten years when there was no Danish king at all. Knut Porse used the opportunity to seize Halland, and even parts of Zealand itself. In Skåne, he was forestalled by Count John of Holstein to whom king Christopher had pawned the province.

Meanwhile fate dealt kindly with young Magnus Eriksson. Even before he was declared king of Sweden in 1319, his Norwegian grandfather had died leaving the three-year-old boy his heir, so that Magnus was the king of the whole of the northern part of the Scandinavian peninsula. By 1332, the rule of John of Holstein had become so incompetent that the archbishop of Lund formally asked Magnus to take possession of Skåne too; and the count of Holstein was glad to sell his title for a large ransom which Magnus paid, nearly bankrupting his own kingdoms.

The prosperity Sweden had enjoyed in the previous century was completely lost, and in 1349 Sweden was struck by natural disaster, the Black Death. That summer an English ship arrived at Bergen with a cargo of cloth and the plague bacillus. By the following year the plague's ravages had carried off perhaps a third of the population of Sweden. In his film *The Seventh Seal*, Ingmar Bergman produced a frighteningly vivid picture of the stricken country where the terror of death lurches between religious fervour and carnal indulgence. As elsewhere, the plague brought economic chaos; serfdom was already dying when Magnus Eriksson abolished it on his *eriksgata* in 1335. Unhappily Sweden had no native class of entrepreneurs, and trade was almost a German monopoly. Desperately short of money, king Magnus had to pawn castles and counties to the German merchants, and his brother-in-law, Albrecht of Mecklenburg, was the foremost of these money-lenders. Large areas of the country were passing into German control as security for overdue loans.

However, the reign of Magnus Eriksson was made notable by a woman, perhaps the first Swede whose life was of international importance. St Bridget is one of the most striking of medieval saints. She was born the seventh child of Birger Persson, who was descended from King Sverker, while her mother was a Folkung. Her father was one of the great lords in the party of Mats Kettilmundsson, and had helped to revise the Uppland Law. Bridget was every inch an aristocrat, and her politics were those of the nobility; she was a remarkably forceful personality, ready to

St Bridget: a fifteenth century statue by Johannes Junge at Vadstena

impose her will in any field, the true heir to those Viking matrons who had ruled kingdoms while their husbands were at war. Had she been a man, she would have become the *jarl* of Sweden, but since a political career was closed to her, she became a saint instead.

In 1316, she married Ulf Gudmarsson, governor of Närke, to whom she bore eight children, and the ruins of their home at Ulfåsa still exist. There she learnt the homely metaphors of field and hall that light up her grim and severe prophesies. As a lady-in-waiting to the young queen Blanche of Namur, she exercised considerable influence over the young couple to make them support the great lords. Already one can trace her ideas of a theocracy administered by the nobles. The king was ordered by the saint to sleep with his wife; but Magnus reacted against this domineering woman, and started to sleep with the stableboys instead. One of his favourites was the young Bengt Algotsson, whom he even made a duke when Bridget was out of the country. After that, her most powerful sermons were directed at the three devils in Sweden: drunkenness, lust and sodomy.

In 1341 Bridget, and her husband, who was completely under her thumb, made the classic pilgrimage to Compostela; on the way, she found time to tell the kings of France and England to stop the Hundred Years War. Ulf Gudmarsson died on his return, and, freed from earthly duties, Bridget cast away her wedding ring to follow her religious vocation. The next years she passed near Alvastra with her old friend, disciple and biographer, Petrus Olavi. In a vision she saw the Virgin ask Christ to give her Vadstena as a convent to be ruled by an abbess with its own chaplains, and Bridget soon bullied Magnus into giving her the royal manor there for her new foundation.

The pope refused to sanction the new Order; and in 1349 Bridget set off for Rome, accompanied by Petrus Olavi, where she was joined by her daughter Katherine. The rest of her life was spent trying to obtain papal approval for her new Order. They were long and humiliating years. Bridget was wholly out of sympathy with Rome, where the Renaissance was already stirring. Shocked by its worldliness and laxity, she said so, until there were riots against the Scandinavian witch. Back at home, Magnus trying to make himself independent from the lords, banished her son, Karl of Ulfåsa; at which Bridget had a vision of all the Folkungs from Birger Jarl onwards burning in hell – a vivid expression of the hatred felt by the Swedish nobility for strong royal government. When Urban V returned to Rome after the long exile of Avignon, Bridget was waiting there with the rules of her Order. When Urban pointed out that the founding of new Orders had been forbidden, she promptly had a vision of him in hell too, along with all her other opponents. At last, in 1370, a Bull was granted for Vadstena under the authority of the Augustinians.

Bridget's work was over, but, before she returned home, the old lady – regardless of Saracens – made the pilgrimage to Jerusalem. On the way back her son Karl died at Naples, legend having it that this was in answer to her prayers that he should not be seduced by the beautiful queen Johanna. Back in Rome, Bridget died herself, but on her deathbed her last vision reassured her of the future of Vadstena. Her daughter Katherine duly set off across Europe with her remains, and in the spring of 1374 St Bridget came home along a triumphal *eriksgata* of flowers.

The Bridgittine Order of nuns still exists in the Roman Church and it is unique for the power and independence it grants to women. Its founder was a remarkable woman who possessed, to an exceptional degree, that medieval blend of worldliness and sanctity. In one light, she was an aggressive and unpleasant politician, but she was also one of the great mystics, and using her administrative talents to a higher end, she founded one of the most useful Orders of the Church.

To rule both Sweden and Norway had, in fact, proved to be beyond

Magnus, and he only kept his throne thanks to the support of Bengt Algotsson. In 1356, he appointed his son Håkon the heir to Norway, and his son Erik the heir to Sweden. Erik showed his gratitude by joining the nobles in a rebellion that forced his father to surrender to him Skåne, Småland and East Gothland. Erik turned out to be a hopeless ruler, and was soon no more than the client of Albrecht of Mecklenburg.

Magnus saw his whole kingdom falling apart before his eyes, and in a last attempt to reassert his authority he summoned the four Estates to meet him at Kalmar. There, in the great hall of the castle, the nobles, clergy, burghers and free yeomen of Sweden met for the first *Riksdag* in their history. The significance of this parliament lies in its summons, which laid down the precedent for that attendance of representatives from each class in community. Though it achieved no more than a truce, the Kalmar *Riksdag* had immense constitutional significance.

Unfortunately for Magnus, one of Denmark's greatest kings had just entered into his inheritance. Admittedly that inheritance scarcely existed at the outset, but King Valdemar had one purpose: to re-create Denmark. He is nicknamed Atterdag, 'Another Day', from his habit of saying, 'There will come another day.' Magnus offered Valdemar the town of Hälsingborg, the twin of Elsinore, in return for his help in driving his son Erik out of Skåne. However, when Erik died suddenly, Valdemar failed to suspend his campaign, and went on to conquer Skåne, Blekinge and Halland for himself.

Valdemar decided to strike next at Sweden's commercial wealth, and, landing his army in Gotland, marched on Visby. The only resistance came not from the Hansa but the Gotlanders themselves, and Valdemar defeated them in a battle fought beneath the very walls of the city. The cross set up by the survivors still stands with its brief and tragic inscription: 'In 1361 on the third day after St James the Goths fell into the hands of the Danes before the gates of Visby. Here they lie. Pray for them.' *Hic sepulti. Orate pro eis.* Those two laconic phrases are the end of the great age of Gotland. The mass graves of the Gotlanders were found by accident at the beginning of this century. The dead had been thrown into the pits as they fell, skulls white inside their chainmail, arrows jammed between ribs, the bones of severed limbs. The islanders had given all to resist the invader, and the real epic of the battle was told in the archaeologists' laboratories. The remains belonged to men of all ages and all stations, the rich in armour, the poor in leather, to boys and to cripples, even to women. The free yeomen of Gotland had fallen together in the last desperate fight against Valdemar's professional army. Visby's mighty walls were not besieged by Valdemar; let us hope because there were no men left to hold them. Instead, a breach was made to the south-east and Valdemar entered in triumph.

Then followed a scene famous in folklore: the ransom of Visby. Three great ale vats were set up in the market-place, and the citizens had to fill them with gold and silver or see their town sacked. Coffers and warehouses were emptied, and in front of the jeering Danish soldiers the gold and silver were stripped from the churches. Only when the women of Visby had cast their personal jewels on the pile was the brim reached. Valdemar was not destined to keep his plunder, for a Baltic storm sank his treasure ship on its voyage home.

In spite of this, Magnus was obliged to ask for Valdemar's support against his own nobles, and in return his only surviving son, Håkon of Norway, was married to Valdemar's daughter Margareta. This wedding in 1363 was to be of profound importance in later years. The Swedish nobles promptly met at the *Ting* at Mora, and deposed Magnus and his son to elect the younger Albrecht of Mecklenburg king instead.

The nobles hoped to have an easy puppet in this rich foreigner and welcomed him to Stockholm that autumn. Together they defeated and captured Magnus Eriksson at Gataskogen; but Håkon of Norway continued the struggle with the help of his father-in-law Valdemar, who was fighting his own war with Mecklenburg. Albrecht at last compromised by giving Magnus West Gothland and the provinces on the Norwegian border, and when the unhappy old man was drowned in a shipwreck, his son took them over.

Albrecht, almost in self-defence, gave the most important posts in the kingdom to his German followers; Vicke von Vitzen was steward of Kalmar and Raven von Barnekow steward of Nyköping, and these two made themselves particularly hated for their greed. In folklore, the memory of the German stewards has become a byword for oppression, and the nuns of Vadstena wrote that the birds of prey had settled on the mountain-tops. At last Albrecht was forced to hand over control of even the royal lands to the Council of the Realm, who then shared out the loot between themselves. One man who did spectacularly well was Bo Johansson Grip. As steward, the basis of his power was the province of Finland, where he defended the frontier, but he added to this vast estates in Sweden and fortresses like Kalmar. His court was virtually royal and his contacts international; the French *Roman d'Alexandre* was translated for him. He used his wealth well to redeem many of the Swedish castles that had been pawned to the Germans by Magnus Eriksson. When the steward died in 1386, Albrecht tried to seize Grip's legacy for himself, but this was the one thing that the late steward did not intend should happen. In his will he left all he possessed to the council to use as they thought fit, so when Albrecht tried to take what amounted to half his kingdom, the executors made over Grip's estate to Margareta of Denmark.

For Valdemar Atterdag had died, one of Denmark's greatest kings, and been succeeded by his five-year-old grandson, Olav, the heir to Denmark through his mother Margareta and to Norway and Sweden through his father Håkon. Within a few years, the whole of Scandinavia was peacefully united. Then, in 1387, the young king died, and it seemed that the whole North must be plunged back into anarchy.

Queen Margareta, however, was a child worthy of her father. No sooner was her son dead than she ordered the Estates of Denmark to proclaim her 'wife and steward and regent of Denmark', the Norwegians soon granting her similar titles. When the crisis in Sweden was precipitated by the death of the steward, there was only one claimant fit for the enormous power which Grip's heir would wield, and that was the wife and the mother of the last of the Folkungs. The Council of Sweden invited Margareta to become their ruler too.

So this middle-aged widow took over her dead son's empire, and ruled it with an energy and a statesmanship which those lands had seldom known. Albrecht maintained himself with his troops from Mecklenburg, but in 1389 he suffered a crushing defeat at Falen, where his heavy German cavalry rode straight into the marsh and he himself was captured. His supporters were reduced to the role of pirates, known as the Vitalien Brotherhood, who raided the Baltic from their base in Gotland. Stockholm at last surrendered to Margareta in 1395, and at the Peace of Lindholm, Albrecht finally renounced the Swedish crown and was allowed to ransom himself.

4. The Late Middle Ages

So the king without trousers, as Albrecht had unwisely named Margareta, had won. When Albrecht emerged from six years of captivity in Skåne, there was nothing left of his empire north of the Baltic; even the island of Gotland had been sold by that level-headed pirate Sven Sture to the grand master of the Teutonic Order, when Albrecht's cause was hopeless. It took the queen a few years to tidy up her new empire. She bought back Gotland from the grand master, and in 1399 Bo Johansson's son Knut Bosson Grip did homage for Finland which he had been ruling independently.

By 1395, however, Margareta was recognized as queen, from the German Empire to the White Sea and from the Orkneys to the frontiers of Russia. Never before or since has the whole of Scandinavia been happily united under one ruler, and with the collapse of Margareta's kingdom after a stormy span of just over a century, the whole idea of Scandinavianism was forgotten until quite recently. Yet it is a union which has every logical justification. Sweden, Denmark and Norway all speak dialects of the same language, which had spread widely into Finland with the colonists from across the Baltic. Even today, all Scandinavians can talk together and read one another's books; all, that is, except the Icelanders, who still speak Old Norse which requires a philologist to bridge a gap of a thousand years. In race, they are all far more closely related than, say, the English and the Scots, who have managed to stay united for much longer. The only real reason why this natural union had not come about much earlier was simply the vast areas occupied by the Nordic peoples. In days when it could take a courier months to get from one end of the empire to the other, having a single ruler presented considerable physical difficulties.

There was some truth in Albrecht's taunt; for it was impossible in the Middle Ages for a woman to be a monarch. Even her loyal Danes had recognized Margareta as only regent. The first problem of her reign was therefore to find an heir who could be recognized as titular head of the united kingdoms. The tragic death of her own son meant that there was no one in direct line of descent; instead Queen Margareta chose her sister's son, Erik of Pomerania, then still a boy but already elected to the throne of Norway, to be elected king of Sweden also at Mora in 1395.

Two years later, the representatives of the three kingdoms met at Kalmar, the great fortress that guards the road into Sweden from Denmark. There, on Trinity Sunday 1397, the twelve-year-old Erik was crowned with great pomp as king of Denmark, Sweden and Norway, and all the deputies swore homage to him, since when this great Scandinavian empire has been known as the Union of Kalmar.

After the ceremonies came the business of deciding upon the form and constitution of the union. By a remarkable stroke of fortune, two of the original documents have survived in the Danish royal archives. The first is the official proclamation of King Erik's coronation and of the oaths of the delegates, with a special blessing for Queen Margareta. It is written on parchment, and beneath it hang the magnificent seals of the seven Swedes, six Danes and four Norwegians who spoke for their countries. The second document is less grand but far more significant. It is a draft of the laws of the union, dated a week after the coronation, but it is written only on paper on to which the seals have been stamped directly. Nor did all the delegates sign it; none of the Norwegians did and only three of the Danes. Was it ever officially accepted? To that question time has destroyed the answer.

However, this document known as the Letter of Union is of enormous interest, for it is almost a constitution. By it, Erik was recognized as king of all three countries, and on his death that all should be ruled by one and the same king. The successor should be chosen from Erik's direct heirs if possible, and if there was no candidate, then the councillors of the three kingdoms should elect someone acceptable to all. In foreign policy, the enemy of one kingdom was to be the enemy of all, and embassies to other lands should represent all three. While each kingdom kept its own laws and customs, an outlaw in one could not seek sanctuary anywhere else in Scandinavia, and every ancient feud was to be forgotten between them. Six parchment copies of this letter should have been made, but if they ever were, then they have been lost. It may be that its purpose was to limit the power of the monarch in the two elective kingdoms of Sweden and Denmark, and this would explain why the Norwegians, whose king was the heir by divine right, failed to sign it.

Some historians have claimed that the whole reason for the Union of Kalmar was economic, to prevent Scandinavia becoming totally dominated by German merchants and adventurers, and that its collapse was inevitable once this external threat faded away. Certainly the reign of Albrecht of Mecklenburg had threatened to make Sweden a German colony. Queen Margareta herself had followed very closely the policies of Bo Johansson Grip in Sweden, and in Denmark she restored the old frontier against the German advances.

At home, Queen Margareta succeeded in doing what many men had failed to do. She reformed the primitive system whereby taxes were raised, and by efficient administration enormously increased the revenues of the crown. At the Meeting of Nyköping, she forced the surrender of all the royal estates which the nobles had appropriated during the confusion of Albrecht's reign, among them the wealthy mining district of Bergslagen. The technical name for this process is a reduction, and there have been reductions all through Swedish history –

the Swedish upper class seems to have been quite exceptionally skilful at adding to its lands at royal expense. Margareta even succeeded in reducing some of the wealth of the Church, which won her the double-edged epitaph from the nuns of Vadstena, 'She was very successful in matters of this world.' Although the queen had all the energy and personality of St Bridget, she also possessed the gift of personal charm, and was sincerely loved by her subjects.

To them her reign appeared as a golden age during later troubles, and when she died suddenly on board ship at Flensburg in the autumn of 1412, the loss was sincerely mourned. She lies buried in the lovely Danish cathedral of Roskilde, the effigy on her tomb showing a highly intelligent forehead and strong features. Her achievement was unique, and she is part, not just of Danish history, but of the whole of the North. The *Rhyme Chronicle* rightly ends with the words, 'Late will a woman her like be born.'

The empire which Erik of Pomerania now had to rule in person as well as in name was an impressive one; but by its very existence it could not avoid being at war with the other great power of Northern Europe, the Hanseatic League. There simply was not room for both of them. Queen Margareta had prepared the diplomatic ground very well. The obvious commercial rival to the Hansa was England, and the merchants of London were delighted at the prospect of stealing Lübeck's trade. The first suggestion was that Erik's sister should marry Henry V, but then Catherine was given to the king of Bavaria, thereby outflanking the Hansa to the south. Instead, Erik married Henry's sister, Philippa, to seal a good commercial bargain.

Every Swedish child knows from his first history book that Erik was an evil king, whose taxmen robbed the widow and the orphan so that he could live in luxury at Copenhagen; but, like King John of England, Erik deserves a certain amount of rehabilitation. In fact, he was an able but very unlucky man. His empire was bound to be an administrative problem for anyone, and things were not made easier by there being two very different schools of political thought. The king wanted to rule as an absolute monarch, like his colleagues in Germany, with obedient lieutenants to carry out his orders in each county. However, the Swedish peasants were free men, not serfs as in Germany, and they only carried out orders if it suited them. At the other end of the scale, the Swedish nobles had an old tradition of jobs for the boys under which they were invested with a county for life, and they did not relish the prospects of having to become conscientious civil servants. The result was that Erik had to employ his own servants as *fogdar* or stewards, and the people became even more reluctant to pay taxes to foreigners.

For most of his reign, Erik was actually at war with the Hansa, both in Slesvig and on the Baltic. It was a struggle for survival on each side, and a very expensive one, so it required a lot of taxes. This weighed particularly heavily on the Swedish economy, being far from the front line for the money was never spent in Sweden, where the king had in any case debased the coinage with his notorious black pennies. The royal tax collectors were, in the main, very conscientious men. The steward of Darlecarlia, a Dane called Josse Eriksson, was known to smoke recalcitrant peasants over the fire in the great hall of Västerås castle as a way of encouraging payment. Västerås is the capital of Bergslagen, the industrial province of medieval Sweden. There, in the middle of the forest, were the great open-cast mines for iron and copper which was exported all over Europe. They were worked by free miners (many of them German immigrants) who actually owned the mines themselves. The charter of the Falun mine dates from 1347, which makes it one of the oldest industrial corporations still in existence. Bergslagen was more hurt by the war than anywhere else. The Hanseatic fleet was blockading the harbours of Sweden, and even after King Erik's naval victories, the markets of Lübeck and the other German towns remained closed to Swedish merchants. The whole country was suffering from a lack of salt, and in those days this was a serious matter, for salt was the only known way of preserving food for the winter, but at least there was in general enough food. This was not the case in Bergslagen, for there the copper and iron lay unsold and nobody had any money to buy the necessities of life.

The king seldom came to Sweden, for he had to stay at the centre of the war in Denmark, and although queen Philippa spent much of her time there, the Swedes began to feel themselves as second-class citizens in a union whose wars were no concern of theirs. Unrest was near the surface when the archbishop of Uppsala died in 1432. The chapter elected their dean his successor before King Erik could make his will known, for they knew that the royal candidate would be someone who would divert the cathedral revenues into the Exchequer. Erik promptly threw the new archbishop out and installed his own man, to the great scandal of the general public.

Matters came to a head in the summer of 1434, and the men of Darlecarlia rose in rebellion. By a strange coincidence, at exactly the same moment the envoys of the Hansa were negotiating a peace with King Erik, who had just won an overwhelming naval victory and was expecting very favourable terms. Of course, the rebellion of a third of his empire sank his hopes, and the miners of Bergslagen saved the Hansa in the eleventh hour. The miners and merchants were always in close contact, and the timing of the rebellion seems too neat to be wholly an accident.

The Swedes, however, did not regard themselves as pawns in anybody else's diplomatic game. They had risen to defend their ancient liberties against men like Josse Eriksson. The castles of some of the lesser stewards were burnt, preferably with the steward inside. The big castle at Vasterås surrendered, and the miners marched down from their own province into Uppland. As their leader, they chose a tough old knight called Engelbreckt Engelbrecktsson, whose family had originally come from Germany to help to open up the mines. He had already been the spokesman of Bergslagen before the king, but his request for lower taxes had not been a success. Within a month, the rebels had reached Stockholm, and the governor of the castle, Hans Kropelin, had been forced to sign a truce. There Engelbreckt was joined by the peasants of Norrland led by Erik Puke, and their united army moved southwards to engulf the castles at Örebro and Nyköping.

Engelbreckt's rebellion was entirely the people's, the miners', the farmers', the merchants'. Neither the lords spiritual nor the lords temporal knew quite how to react to it. Certainly they had causes for complaint against King Erik. Archbishop Olaf of Uppsala had been voicing them stridently from his exile in Basle. On the other hand, they understood the strength of the union their fathers had created. Many of them owned estates in all three kingdoms, and they had all paid their homage to Erik as king. The council had met at Vadstena when the rebellion began, and was still debating when Engelbreckt and his army arrived in the town. It was not an army to the council's liking. A German observer had already compared it to the Hussites who had besieged Danzig, and it had all the characteristics of a *jacquerie* or peasants' revolt. Engelbreckt burst into the council chamber and demanded that King Erik be defied. Nobody was keen to take the decision, and Engelbreckt impatiently seized the two nearest bishops and threatened to throw them out of the window to the soldiers. Faced with these tactics, the council agreed on a letter to King Erik setting out their complaints and demanding an answer in the impossibly short time of a fortnight. When the answer failed to arrive, they solemnly renounced their oaths to the king.

The circular deposing King Erik is an odd legalistic document. Although the nobles were far from satisfied with Erik's rule, the miners' rebellion had caught them unawares, and they were reluctant to be too closely associated with it. All the same, after Vadstena the rebel army contained some of the greatest names in the kingdom.

When the news reached him, Erik abandoned his now pointless treaty with the Hansa and sailed with his army to Stockholm. There was, however, no open warfare, and the two sides agreed to try to settle their disputes peacefully. The real winner in all this was the Hansa. To keep their monopoly of northern trade, they had to break the Union of Kalmar, but where they failed to defeat King Erik themselves, the domestic rebellion succeeded.

In Engelbreckt, the rebels had found a leader after their own hearts. He was like a father to them, and their loyalty to him was limitless. Years after his death, his friend Thomas, bishop of Strängnäs, made Engelbreckt the hero of his *Song of Freedom*, perhaps the finest patriotic poem in Swedish, and which opens every anthology.

> Freedom is the fairest thing,
> That man can seek the whole world round,
> For him who can his freedom carry,
> Will you to yourself be true,
> Then love freedom more than gold,
> For honour follows freedom.

In January 1435, the council met at Arboga. This *Riksdag* at Arboga probably deserves to be called the foundation of Swedish democracy, for not only was the council meeting for the first time completely independently of the king, but also the Commons were represented as a recognized party under Engelbreckt's leadership. Engelbreckt himself was made commander-in-chief over all the nobility.

That summer, the Swedes met their king again at Kalmar, and there followed a romantic reconciliation, where the rebels fell upon their knees to beg Erik's pardon and he then knelt to raise them up. It was not much else apart from being a romantic scene. King Erik promised to reduce taxes and to remove his unpopular bailiffs, but did neither. The leader of the aristocratic party, Karl Knutsson Bonde, was made earl marshal of the realm, but had set his sights even higher. Engelbreckt and Erik Puke were made members of the council, but the lot of their followers saw no real improvement.

A Street in the medieval Hansa town of Ystad

46

This unsatisfactory state of affairs lasted for less than a year, and in January 1436 King Erik was ceremoniously again deposed. This time, however, the rebellion was an aristocratic one. The council met at the monastery of the Black Friars at Stockholm, and there Karl Knutsson was elected regent by an overwhelming majority, against the protests of Engelbreckt and Puke.

The campaign opened well, but Engelbreckt had little part in it, for after the swift capture of several castles, he was struck down by rheumatism and had to retire, a crippled old man, to his castle at Örebro. The split between the two parties in the council had come to a head in a quarrel between Engelbreckt and Bengt Stensson Nattochdag, one of Karl Knutsson's close supporters, and a trial had been fixed in Stockholm. On 4 May, Engelbreckt left Örebro to sail through lake Mälaren to the capital, and that night he and his men camped on a little island. The others were gathering firewood when a boat drew up to the shore, so Engelbreckt hobbled down on his crutches to greet it, but from the boat leapt Magnus Stensson, and with his axe struck the old man to the ground. Then his followers shot the body full of arrows and fled. Such was the tragic death of one of Sweden's greatest national heroes. He fell like a martyr, and after his body had been buried at Örebro, there soon grew up tales of miracles wrought at his tomb, till he was remembered not just as a hero, but almost as a saint.

Engelbreckt's real enemy soon came into the open. In the *Chronicle of Karl Knutsson* there is a prophesy that Karl should be king, and his whole career was concentrated on that one ambition. He imprisoned his colleague, the *drots*, and then lured Erik Puke into a trap by means of a safe conduct, seized him and had him executed the following year. Meanwhile, open war had broken out between the peasantry and Karl Knutsson's men; but, deprived of their leaders, there was little the people could do and many were captured and burnt for high treason.

Negotiations began again with King Erik, and continued spasmodically until 1440; for among the councils of the three kingdoms, the opposition was not to the Union of Kalmar as such, but rather to the personality of the king, and the Swedes, in spite of their regent, sought to maintain the union itself. However, Erik's autocracy was beginning to anger the Danes also, and when he tried to force them to accept his Polish cousin Bogislav as his heir, they too deposed him. Instead, in 1440, the Danish Council elected his nephew Christopher of Bavaria as king, and next year the Swedes accepted him. Erik, however, did not acknowledge defeat. He seized the island of Gotland and established himself there in an excellent strategic position from which he could terrorize the whole of the Baltic as a pirate.

Christopher of Bavaria's reign was an insignificant interlude. He did not try to assert himself against the councils which ruled each kingdom, and in 1442 agreed to a new version of the laws which laid particular stress on the elective kingship. A famine in Sweden earned him the nickname, the 'Bark-bread King', and all the while Karl Knutsson consolidated his position. The *Chronicle of Karl Knutsson* makes Christopher out to be an evil and cruel drunkard who cheats Karl Knutsson of the lands he was promised.

When King Christopher died at Hälsingborg in 1448, there was no one left of the old royal house, and no candidate who could appeal to all three kingdoms. Yet no one waited for the joint elections. Instead, the Danes chose count Christian of Oldenburg as king. In Sweden, things were more complicated. The aristocratic party was split between the powerful Oxenstierna–Vasa families on the one hand and Karl Knutsson Bonde and his supporters on the other. At the news of Christopher's death, Karl Knutsson hurried to Stockholm from his fortress of Viborg in Finland; the election was held in a Stockholm filled with his troops, and the contemporary historian, Ericus Olavi, saw it as illegal. Karl Knutsson, however, was king, in spite of the mighty archbishop of Uppsala, Jöns Bengtsson Oxenstierna.

The Union of Kalmar seemed to have broken up. There was one king elected in Sweden, one king elected in Denmark, and both elected in Norway. Karl Knutsson's first move was to send his general Magnus Gren to capture Visby; but as was to happen time and again, he was then outwitted by Christian, who persuaded Erik of Pomerania to give him the rest of the island in return for a pension on which he could retire to Denmark. The Swedes then evacuated Visby, which Christian promptly occupied. The scene of the competition then moved to Norway. Karl had himself crowned at Trondheim in 1449, only to be driven out by the Danes.

Next year there was a serious attempt to restore the union. The two kings met at Halmstad and signed a treaty of eternal peace; the survivor was to become king of the whole North, and on his death twelve councillors from each kingdom were to elect the new monarch. There is no doubt that the delegates who worked out this detailed treaty were inspired by a real wish for union. So, indeed, were the two kings, only each wanted an immediate union under himself.

Inevitably, these two policies were difficult to reconcile. Just before Christmas in 1451, Christian suddenly attacked the great Swedish castle of Stegeholm, and so began a war that lasted for six years. It was a desultory affair. King Christian was by far the more powerful and used his wealth to hire well-armed German mercenaries. King Karl was without foreign allies, and at home he received no support from the Oxenstiernas. He fought a good defensive war in spite of his military inferiority, and, Sweden being the vast and inhospitable country it is, the Danes made slow progress. By 1457, Karl's position was hopeless. There had been a famine that winter, the Danes held all West Gothland, where they were joined by a constant stream of deserters, and in the spring archbishop Jöns Bengtsson and several of the council rebelled. Karl Knutsson understood that he was defeated, and laying his hands on all the treasure he could find fled to Danzig. Christian was accepted as king in Sweden and the archbishop duly made regent.

Christian's reign was short. He was buying out the other claimants t Holstein and required even more taxes than Karl Knutsson, and th original Swedish objection to the whole union was that it meant givii too much money to Danes. When the archbishop actually reduced taxe Christian put him in prison. At once, although it was the early January of 1464, the bishop of Linköping, Kettil Karlsson Vasa, rose to free his cousin and fellow priest. His army of peasants defeated King Christian's soldiers at Haråker and then besieged Stockholm.

Karl Knutsson was then invited back from Danzig to be king again, but he did not last long. His supporters were soon scattered and he himself was pensioned off to live at Korsholm on his Finnish estates, while Sweden was run by the two bishops. The authority of the Church did little to clear up the confusion.

The most powerful single force in Scandinavia was the Tott family. Old Axel Tott had four sons, Ivar, Erik, Laurens and Åke. Their estates stretched throughout the north and included the strategic island of Gotland, and Ivar himself married Karl Knutsson's daughter Magdalena. They sought to be the king-makers, and the mightiest vassals behind the crown. With Sten Sture, they stood as rivals to the Oxenstierna–Vasa group. Fortune's wheel had not stopped spinning round for Karl Knutsson; for, in 1467, the Totts fetched him back from Finland to become king again, but this time his real power was minimal.

Although most of his reign was filled by warfare, Karl Knutsson Bonde, whose family survives today, was more than just a soldier. He deliberately modelled himself on the late medieval ideal of chivalry, and in his court he copied the pomp and splendour of Burgundy. The literary monument to his reign is the rhymed *Chronicle of Karl*; it is really a work of political propaganda by his own minstrels, and pictures the king as a generous and noble knight. The balance of truth is restored in Ericus Olavi's *Latin Chronicle,* where the writer, being a clerk, gives the Church's not so flattering view. Karl Knutsson was one of the many mighty nobles of his century who, behind a façade of chivalry, pursued ruthless power politics, and he must be reckoned as one of the important kings of medieval Sweden. He was an intensely ambitious man, and his ambition was amply satisfied, since he ruled the country four times, once as regent, and three times as king, even though he was not a particularly attractive personality.

Karl's treatment of Engelbreckt was shameful. That cynical murder and the subsequent oppression of those men who had first risen to free Sweden is a stain that cannot be wiped out. However, he was not without ability, and perhaps in the long run his ideas turned out best for the country, for Karl Knutsson, though he never sat securely on his throne, irrevocably broke the Union of Kalmar, in spite of its later revivals. His reign decided that Sweden's destiny was to be an independent nation, not part of a Scandinavian union, so she did not share the history of Norway, which remained loyal to the kings of the union, and eventually sank for a long time to being nothing more than a Danish province.

In the spring of 1470, Karl Knutsson fell gravely ill, and realizing that death was near, he married his mistress, Kristina Abrahamsdotter, in order to make his baby son, Karl Karlsson, the legitimate heir. The only person of importance present at the deathbed was a young man called Sten Sture, the old king's nephew, and he had everything under control. To start with, he was the sole executor of the will, and so undertook to be guardian of the young prince. Once the king was dead, Sten Sture let it be publicly known that Karl Knutsson had wished him to be regent. As Sten Sture had married Ivar Axelsson's niece, the Tott brothers had little choice but to accept the *fait accompli,* particularly as he had promptly seized all the royal castles in his own name.

At last King Christian saw himself the only crowned king of Sweden, and proclaimed his intention of coming to take possession of his throne. The Oxenstierna family had been completely outmanoeuvred, and rather than see their rivals in power, they threw in their lot with the Danish king.

Next spring the usual truce was signed at Kungssäter so that a council meeting at Stockholm could try Christian's case. The king reached Stockholm in late June with the unexpected escort of a considerable body of fighting men, whom he encamped on the heights of Brunkeberg outside the town. At first it seemed likely that he would be accepted as king, but as the negotiations dragged on, the atmosphere turned unpleasant. Nils Sture left to go to Darlecarlia, and soon afterwards Sten Sture disappeared to Vadstena, where he raised the farmers against King Christian. Christian, for his part, began to fortify the camp on Brunkeberg. Meanwhile, inside Stockholm, the council was still negotiating for the perfect union.

At the beginning of October, the men of Darlecarlia and East Gothland joined forces south of Stockholm. They could not approach from the north, for the Oxenstierna family had summoned the soldiers from their own estates in Uppland to help King Christian. On the morning of the twelfth, as the fog lifted and the church bells rang for matins, Sten Sture's army advanced on Brunkeberg from the west, Nils Sture's from the north and Knut Posse's from the south. Although the Danes and their Swedish supporters were outnumbered almost two to one, their position was enormously strong. Time and again the Swedes charged up the hillside, only to be driven back. The brunt of the fighting came on the west, where Sten Sture led his men, and everywhere he went an East Gothland farmer, Björn the Strong, walked in front of him and cleared a way for the regent with his sword. King Christian himself had his teeth knocked out in the fighting. At last the Swedes seemed to break, and the royal troops charged down on to the plain by St Claire's convent. There the Swedes rallied, St Erik's sword was seen burning in the sky, and the Danes, overwhelmed by numbers, were forced to flee to their ships, many being drowned when the townsmen sallied out and destroyed the bridges before them.

Sture's victory was complete; for Christian had lost his army and was lucky to escape himself. During the winter, Älvsborg, which commanded

St George and the dragon in the Great Church at Stockholm, commissioned from Bernt Notke by Sten Sture

Sweden's only outlet to the North Sea, was stormed; Kalmar, Borgholm and Stegeholm all surrendered; and even the earl marshal of Denmark, Klas Ronnow, was captured. King Christian's hopes of conquering Sweden by force of arms were irrevocably gone, and at last the country could hope to enjoy a peace such as few men living could remember. Well might the Regent commission the magnificent statue of a knightly St George overcoming the Danish dragon to free the maiden Sweden, which still stands in the town church of Stockholm.

The battle of Brunkeberg is a landmark in Swedish history. It left Sten Sture undisputed master of the country to rule as he saw fit. Sten Sture the Elder, as he is known to the history books, was a most remarkable man. Although he was an excellent soldier, he must really be admired as one of the greatest diplomats Sweden has known, an equal to Axel Oxenstierna. He solved the question of who was to be king of Sweden by the simple expedient of perpetually negotiating about it without ever coming to a decision. These desultory talks lasted for the rest of Christian's lifetime, and were continued by his son Hans. Sten Sture's power was founded on his enormous popularity with the peasants and the townspeople. He was forever riding round the land, listening to their complaints and speaking to them on all important issues. This paternalistic government brought peace and prosperity, but it is interesting that, in the chronicles, Sten Sture is also presented as a pattern of chivalry, like Karl Knutsson, Nor did Sture neglect the other bases of power, for the old king's will had put the royal domains in his hand, and the young Karl Karlsson had been forgotten in convenient obscurity. He was also a shrewd businessman, always adding to his own estates, and he soon managed to edge his old allies, the Totts, away from power.

In 1477, the pope gave permission for a university of general studies to be founded at Uppsala, the first in Scandinavia. Hitherto Swedish students had been obliged to go to Paris, where there was a Swedish college, or even to Oxford or Prague, so the establishment of the university can be seen as part of the upsurge of national consciousness that followed the victory of Brunkeberg.

There was, however, one foreign problem that forced itself on the peaceful country, and that was the Russian expansion towards the sea. Ivan III had added Novgorod to his empire, based on Moscow, and was pressing against the borders of Finland. Sten Sture had already taken the precaution of forging the old peace of Nöteborg to give the Swedes a more easterly frontier, but Ivan was not interested in old treaties, forged or genuine. To meet the threat, Erik Axelsson Tott had built the castle of Olofsborg, which still stands unaltered, a grim and massive keep of stone dominating the empty woods and lakes, lost in the heart of Finland.

He had also fortified the town of Viborg, and it was here that the test came. In 1495, Knut Posse was the count of Viborg. All autumn, the cossacks had ridden through the countryside, and the Finnish farmers had sought refuge within the town's walls. By the end of September, Viborg was completely invested; and a sortie by the vastly out-numbered

Uppsala Cathedral and University. The students in the foreground are wearing their traditional white caps

garrison was a catastrophe. The commander of Olofsborg, Kylliainen, a real Finn not a Swedish settler, tried in vain to raise the siege. The Russian winter set in and the sea froze, cutting off the last link with the rest of Sweden, while the tsar's army made repeated assaults. Inside the town, famine spread. Sten Sture had sailed from Stockholm with a relief force in November, but his fleet froze fast near Åland and his men had to wait in their ships until the ice was strong enough to bear them. Meanwhile the Russians had made a last desperate attempt to storm the town, and the

Andreas tower on the wall fell to them, only to be fired by the garrison. Then, suddenly, the enemy disappeared; perhaps for the only time in their history, it was the Russians who were defeated by their own winter. The news reached the regent as he heard mass on Christmas Eve in the warm brick cathedral of Abo.

The threat to Finland was broken, but at home the regent's problems grew. The Tott family, whom he had supplanted, joined his rivals in the council and found a spokesman in the archbishop of Uppsala, Jacob Ulvsson. Sten Sture was often in conflict with the Church, and in 1497 he was excommunicated for the second time. The council consistently wanted the union revived; a weak king in Copenhagen was preferable to a strong regent in Stockholm, but it was impossible to tie Sten Sture down. Whenever there was an important meeting, his bad eyesight made it impossible for him to attend.

By March 1497, the council felt strong enough for the archbishop to tell Sten Sture to resign, but this he refused to do, saying that only the people who had elected him could depose him. The nobles then invited king Hans to Sweden, and with his troops defeated the Darlkarls near Stockholm. On seeing the defeat of his relief force, Sten Sture opened negotiations with the king for a compromise settlement. In November, Hans was crowned in Stockholm and promised to abide by the constitution of the Kalmar Recess. Sten Sture was fitly compensated, and although he lost a few counties in Sweden, kept almost the whole of Finland.

King Hans did not enjoy his new kingdom long. Sten Sture had for many years employed as his ambassador-at-large a close friend called Hemming Gadh, who had maintained the regent's widespread diplomatic contacts. In 1500, Gadh returned from Rome to become bishop of Linköping. It must have been an evocative contrast to come from the height of the Renaissance in the eternal city to a country filled with the turmoil and the flamboyance of the last years of the Middle Ages.

Bishop Hemming had learnt some political tricks during his years in Rome, however. He soon healed the breach between the old regent and the son of his erstwhile ally and later rival, Nils Sture. By 1502, the council had broken with King Hans and the Swedish army led by Svante Nilsson Sture captured the king's castles. Even Stockholm fell, three days before Hans's relief force arrived, defended for four months by his queen, Christina. Sten Sture was back in office. Next year, Sten Sture and Bishop Hemming escorted the queen back to Denmark. It was winter when they returned; and when the travellers reached Jönköping, the regent died suddenly. So a very remarkable career was ended.

It is fascinating to compare Sten Sture with Karl Knutsson Bonde. Both found themselves in very similar situations, but where Karl Knutsson's ambition drove him to seek the substance of power, and, by being crowned, to guarantee his own ultimate defeat, Sten Sture was content with its essence, and so held an impregnable diplomatic position. The regent was the complete *Realpolitiker*, and usually got what he wanted without having to fight for it; but he also took the responsibilities of his position seriously, and earned his popularity with the common people by his stable and prosperous government.

The regent's death threatened to upset everything. Bishop Hemming sent a secret messenger to Svante Nilsson to warn him of what had happened; meanwhile he hid the regent's body beneath a pile of skins and dressed up one of his peasants as Sten Sture to take his place in the sledge.

Svante Nilsson put the warning to good use, and within a month, just after the New Year, he had himself elected regent even before most people had heard of Sten Sture's death. He managed to get hold of a large portion of the dead regent's lands, and even forced the latter's widow to pawn a county to pay her husband's mercenaries. The inevitable meeting to discuss the union was then fixed with King Hans for 1505 at Kalmar. However, only the Danes turned up; so Hans was elected unopposed and duly began a war to reconquer his kingdom. In 1509, a compromise was worked out at the Peace of Copenhagen, whereby Hans was recognized as king, but, in return for an annual tribute of 12,000 marks, took no part in the internal government of Sweden.

By the following year the war had begun again, and thanks to the Hanseatic League, which changed sides, Bishop Hemming managed to capture Kalmar, where he led the siege in the spirit of a Renaissance cardinal. Then Svante Nilsson died, and at once those nobles who wanted peace, led by the old archbishop, Jacob Ulfsson, elected one of their own number, Erik Trolle, as regent. Svante's son, Sten Svantesson Sture, was reluctantly obliged to accept the *fait accompli*. Yet while the council was signing another peace with King Hans at Malmö, Sten Sture the Younger (as he is known) filled Stockholm with his soldiers and had himself elected regent too. To confound confusion, Hans died and was succeeded by his son Christian, who was to go down in history as Christian the Tyrant. Sten Sture worked swiftly to get the counties of Viborg and Nyslott given to one of his warmest supporters, Tönne Tott. The council then pulled off a counter-coup when the aged Jacob Ulfsson handed over the archbishopric to Gustav Trolle, Erik's son, who ignored Sten Sture and gave his allegiance to King Christian.

By 1517, the civil war was in full swing. Christian II made a proclamation to the Swedish people, and followed it up with an abortive naval attack on Stockholm. Meanwhile, the archbishop had been besieged at his fortress at Stäket, and forced to stand trial; he was sentenced to prison and Stäket was razed to the ground as a culmination to its long and violent history. A useful absentee Italian was elected archbishop, and Sten Sture's rule seemed secure.

Christian II was, however, made of a different mettle from his predecessors. Sweden, he considered, was his by right, and his it would become. Next summer he returned again to Stockholm, and again the siege was raised by a victory of Sten Sture's peasant army, this time at Brännkyrka. Christian offered to negotiate with the regent, who sent six ambassadors led by Bishop Hemming Gadh and a young Vasa, Gustav Eriksson. No sooner were they on board the Danish ships, than King Christian set sail and took them prisoner to Denmark. In the meantime, the Danes captured Älvsborg by surprise and, soon after Borgholm.

Christian had great success on the diplomatic front. Sten Sture was tried in his absence at Lund by Gustav Trolle, and the pope confirmed his excommunication. From this moment, Christian took his stand as the secular arm of the Church, which meant among its other advantages that he need not keep his word with condemned heretics. The war had been becoming more and more bitter, a genuine national struggle, and Gustav Trolle's role was that of traitor. That the archbishop of Uppsala should be the foremost supporter of the Danes earned the Church the contempt of the common people, and Gustav Trolle was in fact unintentionally preparing the ground for the Reformation.

With the new year of 1520, a huge Danish army, well-equipped and with regiments of mercenaries, invaded Sweden. On the frozen lake of Åsund near Ulricehamn, the knighthood of Sweden and their peasant levies stood to bar their way. At the very beginning of the battle, Sten Sture was mortally wounded by a cannon ball, and the superior numbers, and above all equipment, of Otto Krumpen's modern army overwhelmed the feudal Swedish troops. The Danes advanced up through Tiveden, where the Swedes made another unsuccessful stand. Sten Sture himself, fatally wounded as he was, set off for Stockholm to organize the defence, and died in his sledge on the way. The Danish advance continued. At Uppsala, several of the council yielded to Christian and were granted an amnesty; Stegeborg and Västerås both fell; only Stockholm held out. For in the Three Crowns, the great keep of Stockholm's castle, a woman commanded, Christina Gyllenstierna, the regent's young widow. Alone of the nation's leaders she did not accept defeat, but roused the burghers to defend their town against the Danish army; she led the defence in person, always at the point of danger, to maintain the lonely resistance in her conquered country. For four months the epic siege lasted, till the struggle became hopeless. The Danish troops were ruthless in crushing the leaderless risings in the countryside; and in September, Christina Gyllenstierna surrendered against an amnesty.

King Christian's victory was complete and he intended it to be final. For over a century the kings of Denmark had tried to assert themselves in Sweden, and Christian meant to settle with his rebellious province once and for all. He had a notable diplomatic success when he managed, for reasons still not clear, to persuade Hemming Gadh to change sides. Gustav Trolle was at last back in his cathedral, and there on 4 November he crowned Christian king, not by election but by inheritance.

For three days the feasting lasted at Stockholm's castle, and all the great men of Sweden from every party were assembled in peace. But Christian had prepared an orgy of treachery. He had already broken his word to Christina Gyllenstierna, and cast her in prison, dead to the world. On the fourth day, the nobles of Sweden, the bishops, the leading burghers and their wives met in the great hall; then the gates of the castle were shut, and King Christian mounted his throne. From the shadows, Gustav Trolle came forward and demanded the law's extreme penalty on all those who had raised their hands against him, the archbishop. The doors of the hall were opened and in strode the Danish soldiers; they led away the men whom the archbishop had named, and then returned each time for more victims, till at last only the women were left in the great hall, where dusk had now fallen.

Next morning a court met, a court composed only of priests. One by one the prisoners were tried and condemned for heresy, and with heretics no amnesty is binding. The same day the executions began. The first to die was the bishop of Strängnäs, then the bishop of Skara, then the great lords of Sture's party, Joachim Brahe, Erik Johansson Vasa, and many more; then it was the turn of the Commons, Anders Henriksson, the mayor of Stockholm, and the leading citizens of the siege. Over eighty corpses were piled up in the market-place, and on the top, torn from its grave, was thrown the body of Sten Sture. They lay there for a few days to let the lesson sink in, and then they were burnt outside the walls, as heretics.

'The Bloodbath of Stockholm' as it is called was over. In one fell swoop, Christian had wiped out all the important men who opposed him. In the rest of the country, his soldiers carried out similar executions in every town; and the people, without leaders, could do nothing but accept their fate.

5. Medieval Art

Sweden does not possess a great wealth of old buildings. In a country where wood was the standard material to use, only the very rich could afford to build in stone, and the natural life of the wood was made even shorter by the need to keep a big fire alight all through the long winter. Most Swedish towns were burnt down three times a century, twice by accident and once by the Danes or Russians. Most of the survivals from the Middle Ages are churches, for there were few great castles and these were usually rebuilt.

Even the first churches were built in wood, but the construction technique is one that has died out completely. Tree trunks were driven vertically into the ground like a palisade, and the carpenters often added a central tower, carried on posts, while the roof was made of birch shavings. Churches built this way are called stave-churches. There is only one surviving in Sweden, but there are several in Norway, whose fretted eves and dragons on the roof-trees look as ornate as Chinese temples.

The stave-church at Hedared in West Gothland is an anachronism, for it was built in the fourteenth century, but change came slowly in the depths of the country. It is a simple small room, and on the east wall are the faded ghosts of the original paintings. About fifty of the planks from the stave-church at Hemse on Gotland have been saved and are now at the Historical Museum at Stockholm. The logs have been cleft to preserve the curved surface, and this has been carved with the same twisted, tangled patterns that are found on runestones.

Most of Sweden's early medieval churches are to be found in the south, which, as a part of Denmark, became Christian a full century earlier. There almost every village can boast a Romanesque parish church, and at their head stands Lund, one of the most perfect Romanesque cathedrals in the world. When Ascer became the first archbishop in Scandinavia, he set about building himself a church worthy of his rank. Progress was rapid, for by 1123 the altar could be consecrated in the great crypt, and in 1145 the high altar itself; since when – apart from the two nineteenth-century towers at the west end – no significant changes have been made. We know the name of the original architect; he was an Italian called Donatus who died in Lund before the cathedral was completed. He was succeeded by a fellow-countryman called Regnerus, who had probably been working on the great churches of the Rhineland before he came to complete Lund.

Wandering round the outside, the Italian influence is obvious. The east end, with its round apse, recalls a cathedral like Pisa; the proportions are beautifully calculated, from the heavy blind arcade at the bottom up to the elegant open gallery with its slim columns that runs just below the roof. The north and south doorways retain their original carving, and the Samson and the lion in the north tympanum are definitely Lombard in style.

On entering the cathedral, its dignity and simplicity are striking, recalling another closely related Romanesque masterpiece, Speyer or the Rhine. Lund owes its restaint to Eskil, archbishop in 1138, who followed his old friend St Bernard of Clairvaux in banning all unnecessary decoration in God's house. The nave is designed with the beauty of a mathematical equation: it consists of four cubes defined by massive square pillars, and the aisles are also divided into cubes, the basic measurement of which is exactly half that of the nave. There is no triforium, just the plain stone walls and the clerestory windows. At the crossing, great flights of steps lead up over the crypt while the transepts have some superb pieces of Romanesque sculpture in the baldaquins over the altars: lions that carry the columns, and a superb six-winged angel from Isaiah.

The crypt is one of the glories of Lund; it is enormous, extending under the transepts as well as the whole east end of the church. Down here there exists a forest of low pillars decorated with strange patterns that seem

Lund cathedral

59

more the work of a wood-carver. One of them is grasped by a long-haired man, and at the next a woman squats with a child in her arms. The iconography is obscure, but the local people will tell you confidently that this is the giant Finn, his wife and child. Finn lived near Lund while the cathedral was being built, and the new sound of church bells ruined his peace; so he came in a great rage to pull the church down, but no sooner had he grasped the first pillar in the crypt than he was turned to stone, and his family with him. Near them is a well which probably dates from pagan times.

Lund deserves international fame; but the villages of Skåne possess a wealth of treasures equally old. A squat whitewashed church with a round apse and wide tower at the west end is the symbol of the province, and professional restoration this century has revealed a remarkable school of Romanesque wall painting. At Bjäresjö, the twelfth-century church is now the choir of its larger successor. Deep rich colours cover the

Font at Löderup

walls and the barrel vault. Directly above the altar, God the Father stares out with Byzantine fixity, between his knees Christ hangs on the cross, and on one of its arms is perched the dove of the Holy Spirit, all enclosed in a mandorla. On the north wall are two rows of scenes from the New Testament, and on the south two rows from the Old. The same subjects are to be found at other churches such as Övraby; for the order is traditional and leads back to the great churches of western France. It is a moving example of the universality of medieval christendom to see the glories of St Savin echoed in a little frontier parish like Bjäresjö. At the monastery church of Vä, the paintings have been less retouched by the restorers, and the Christ in majesty surrounded by the evangelists seems more austere.

Equally, an unexpected quantity of Romanesque sculpture has survived. The remains of the first cathedral at Dalby include the whole narthex at the west end, and the font with the baptism of Christ carved in low relief. The classic font which has given its name to the school is at Tryde; round the bowl reaching from its lip to the foot are four pairs of tall figures who have all the qualities of the saints around the old door at Chartres. Particularly fine is the font at Löderup, on which Christ and his angels have a unique rugged grandeur, and there, too, is a remarkable sarcophagus.

In the museum at Lund are fragments from the original west door. The Christ in glory has particular power. He is dressed as the high priest, long hair falling on his shoulders, and a great hand raises its fingers in blessing, yet the face wears an expression of profound pity, almost of fatigue. The angel beside is formal and stiff, even to wearing a Roman tunic.

Sigtuna today is a delightful town. Really it is no more than a large village, for there are no streets, the houses are scattered among the pine trees, and everywhere there is open grass, except on the little hill at the centre where there is only the bare granite underfoot. From the top of the hill the lake with its forest-clad shores seems endless, but down in the town it is hidden until you enter the hotel and find that the dining-room is a long terrace on the water's edge.

Yet, long ago, Sigtuna was the most important Christian centre of the North, the rival to the pagan might of Uppsala. Here missionary bishops preached and sometimes died for their faith, and here they built no less than three churches. They were symbols of the strength of the new religion, and also fortresses against the old; their towers were keeps and still bear traces of their battlements. Today these stark churches are all in ruins, and now the people worship in the warm, friendly brick church which the Dominicans built centuries later in honour of the Virgin.

One of the Romanesque churches is only a shattered tower, but the other two, St Per and St Olov, tell the story of the early missions to Sweden. Both were probably built by Englishmen, for both have the hallmark of the English cathedrals: a central tower at the crossing of the nave and transepts. St Per even has a second tower at the west end to strengthen its defences. The enormous walls needed to carry the central one have divided the church into five small rooms linked only by narrow archways, and the nave has a peculiarity quite common in old Swedish churches in that there is a row of columns down the middle so that it is practically impossible to see the altar.

To this group belongs the church at Old Uppsala. Little remains today of the ancient cathedral; the nave is gone, leaving the central tower at the west end, and vaults and paintings are gothic after a severe fire. By good fortune, however, the bishop's throne survives, its legs and back made with complicated turned patterns, probably the oldest surviving piece of wooden furniture in Sweden, perhaps the gift of St Erik himself. The church stands alone in the fields, forgetful of the violence of its youth.

England was not the only influence on Sweden as she became part of medieval christendom. One classic building inspired by the great contemporary churches of Germany, such as St Michael at Hildesheim, survives at Husaby in West Gothland. Husaby would be famous anyway, for Olof Skötkonung is buried there in a tomb with a standing stone at each end carved with Viking dragons. The oldest part is the wide west tower which was orginally built as a fortified keep; and the rest of the church was added in pure Romanesque. The west tower is now flanked by turrets and the three thin spires form a gable against the sky.

All these fortress churches prove how precarious was Christian life in Sweden at the beginning of the Middle Ages. Then, as the risk of being burnt in one's home by pagans declined, the original buildings were replaced. Yet in Småland, which has always been a hard, tough province, one example of the most common type of fortress church has survived almost unchanged. Hagby is simply a wide round tower with enormously thick walls and a small projecting round apse; originally there was a turret at the centre, rising from the floor, to provide a vantage-point for archers. Today it has a delightfully incongruous and rustic late eighteenth-century interior.

The island of Gotland is a treasure unknown outside Scandinavia. Even to the Viking poets it was the pearl of the Baltic. Magic had created it and magic protected it. Every evening the trolls sank the entire island beneath the waves, and every morning it rose again richer and fairer than before. Lying at the centre of the Baltic, the climate is so mild as to seem Mediterranean; Visby is called the city of roses, for they will flower there till Christmas. The summer winds blow in from the Russian steppes, and it is odd to see only blond boys and girls on those sweltering beaches. Much of the island is surrounded by tall cliffs facing the sea like city walls. Inland is a plateau of rich farmland turning to forest in the north and to heath land which is a botanist's paradise of rare flowers.

Gotland's great age began with the Vikings and ended when Valdemar Atterdag sacked Visby. Since then the island has slept like the princess in a fairy-tale and subsequent centuries have left untouched a remarkable wealth of medieval monuments. Visby has no less than twelve churches, eleven of them in ruins and only the cathedral in use. In the countryside, on the other hand, there are over ninety medieval churches in use. Furthermore, because of the great wealth brought by the island's trade, all are richly endowed with sculpture and paintings.

The great merchants lived on their farms, trade was a winter occupation. They had their own laws, among the oldest to survive, and their own poetry; even today their dialect is closer to Old Norse than any language except Icelandic. Several of their homes remain, like the peel-tower at Stora Hästnäs, just north of Visby, with its elegant gothic windows to warm the big living room with the sun; or like Katlunda in the south, where there is a complete medieval farm with all its outbuildings. Such prosperity shows that it was by no means hopeless for the islanders to take on the Hansa; but the saddest relic of their defeat is the hamlet of Västergarn. Here they had planned their own city to rival Visby, but the long earthworks only enclose fields. The substantial church was planned merely to be the chancel, and beside it are the grass-grown foundations of the intended keep.

The first pride of Visby is its city wall, which stretches in an unbroken arc from the beach inland beyond the cliffs that divide the town in two. To the north and east, the wall faces out over open country, and only in the present century did the town start to outgrow it. Down by the harbour is the Powder Tower, a square keep that is the oldest fortification, and beyond it, now opening on to the lawns, is a pair of water-gates by the site of the harbour. The walls were built as a protection against the yeomen of Gotland for the Hansa merchants, and, not being professional soldiers, they economized and built convenient stone houses into the wall. The towers are tallest and most clustered towards the land from whence the attack was expected, and a newer stretch to the south-east marks the breach through which Valdemar Atterdag made his triumphal entry in 1361. Within the walls is a little medieval city, with the great stone residences and warehouses several storeys high and the later picturesque cottages with colourful gardens. Narrow streets wind up the hillside, and when standing on the cliff looking out over the ruined churches, it is easy to imagine Visby in the days of its greatness, its towers and spires mirroring the masts of the ships in the harbour.

The cathedral is a stately building. Its east end is right up against the cliff, at whose foot a space opens on either side. Originally, this was the church of the German guild, and therefore the richest and grandest in the city. When the German merchants built their first church in the late twelfth century, it was only half its present size, a Romanesque building in the shape of a T. At the foot of the stem was the strong west tower, now capped by an incongruous Baroque spire; on the north side is part of the elegant open gallery which once ran the whole length of the church. Inside, the style is transitional with pointed arches rising from square pillars. Although it does not look it from the outside, the cathedral is a hall-church with nave and aisles of equal height, and under the steep roof, with its clerestory windows, is an enormous empty room. The Germans had, as a practical people, designed the top half of their church to be a warehouse, and standing on the cliff looking down one can still see the crane they built ending in a fierce lion's head, like a gargoyle. The entrance to the south is through a flamboyant Gothic door into the Swerting chapel, built in 1349. The contrast is striking. The carved leaves of oak and elm seem alive, and the high vaults are carried by dwarves and monsters.

For many visitors to Visby, the first ruin they remember is St Nicholas, for this is where the miracle play of *Petrus da Dacia* is performed amid the plain square pillars beneath the broken vaults. It was built for the Dominicans in the thirteenth century, using, like the rest of the city, the local grey sandstone; but on the west front the many lancet windows and two blind roses are picked out in red brick. The Franciscans dedicated their church to St Catherine, and it is probably the most romantic ruin in Visby. All twelve pillars of the nave still stand, and the ribs of the vaults leap like bridges across a chasm while the whole floor is open to the sky.

Below the cathedral is a remarkable pair of churches with matching façades: the Steward's (Drottens) and St Lars. The Steward's is of no great architectural interest, but St Lars is unique in Sweden. Its shape is a perfectly symmetrical Greek cross, and the choir is merely an apse added to one arm, the four pillars placed at each corner having once carried a dome that is now destroyed. It must be the work of an architect who knew the central churches of the Byzantine empire well, probably from journeys to Novgoród and southwards, and then applied the idea in his home town.

Perhaps the most original church in Visby is the double chapel of the Holy Spirit. It was built in the great age of the city at the beginning of the thirteenth century. On the ground floor, the nave is a perfect octagon from which a large choir opens, square-ended but with an internal apse; matching stairs behind a row of columns lead to an identical room above the nave with a hole in the middle of the floor and an arch at the east to give a view of the altar. Why this peculiar design was chosen remains a mystery.

The Gotland countryside being, as we have said, an amazing treasure-house of early medieval art, almost every village church has something outstanding on which the yeomen once lavished their wealth before it all came to an end with Valdemar Atterdag's sack of Visby in 1361. The psychological blow seems to have been even heavier than the material one, for work stopped everywhere.

At Stånga, massive blocks of superb sculpture, a flagellation, a deposition, have been stuck indiscriminately into the south wall after the spirit which had planned a monumental façade had been broken. Beside these fragments is a porch of almost Moorish ornateness, and the typical Gotland detail of a frieze of biblical stories which forms the capitals on either side of the porch. Inside, the vaults are carried on a single column in the middle of the nave. A crucifix hangs in the chancel arch with another typical motif, the circle joining the four arms, and at the west is a font with delightful carvings of the childhood of Christ.

Doorway at Stånga Church

Most churches have also kept some of their rich medieval painting. Iconographically, Dalhem is the most complete, but modern restorers have been too hard at work. The frieze of the porch's capitals and the majestic stained glass in the choir are more genuine survivals. At Gothem, one of the island's finest and biggest churches, the whole nave is painted with the childhood of Christ and the passion; on the north wall are the labours of the months and on the vaults little genre scenes.

The saints still watch from the walls of Lärbro's open interior, and the capitals of the porch beneath its strange octagonal tower tell the story of the nativity. The wall of the graveyard has a more serious purpose for it includes a peel-tower. The sculptures of Gotland are among the most valuable and undervalued treasures of European Romanesque, although mainly fonts but even capitals were exported throughout the Baltic region. The hard white sandstone lends itself to the naïve but deeply expressive style of the artists responsible. At Vänge, an emaciated Eve with lank hair hacks at the field after a serpent of Viking complexity has given her the apple at which she stares shocked. At Martebo, a tender Virgin cradles her child on the donkey that bears her in flight to Egypt. The skill that worked in stone also shows itself in wood, too; and the museum at Visby, Gotlands Fornsal, shelters a collection of remarkable sculptures. Probably the most amazing work on the island, which is worthy of international fame, is the crucifix at Oja, carved towards the end of the thirteenth century. A royal Christ hangs from an extravagently decorated cross, which is set inside a circle. In its lower segments, the tragedy of mankind is played out, the Fall and the Expulsion; but in the upper ones, the choirs of angels and the saved rejoice in the hope of the sacrifice.

Sweden does not have many great cathedrals, and among them the Gothic of Uppsala and Linköping must take pride of place. Uppsala is a wholly French masterpiece, the cousin of the great churches of the Île de France, although it was only built at the end of the thirteenth century. Linköping, on the other hand, has much of England in it and is a mixture of styles.

It was King Valdemar who decided to move the cathedral from the dying town of Old Uppsala to its thriving rival five miles away; but work began in earnest in 1287 when master Étienne de Bonneuil arrived from Paris, bringing with him many skilled workmen. The Frenchman designed a pure Gothic church for his northern patron, but it had to be translated into the Swedish idiom. The striking difference is that Uppsala cathedral is built in brick, and the expensive imported stone is reserved for the figurative carvings, with the inevitable loss of much of the designed detail. The basic plan is pure enough. The two west spires were completed in the last century, but it is internally that the French plan is most obvious, close indeed to the purest of all French cathedrals, Bourges. Nave and chancel are a single long space in which the transepts are marked only by a wider bay, and the round east end extends into a beautiful corona of three chapels. Everywhere there is an emphasis on height that seems so typically French. The sharply pointed arches of the arcade soar upwards, but above them there is no gallery, only a blank brick wall under the clerestory windows, which is typical of Gothic churches built in brick which obliges the architect to simplify. It is an ugly device, in spite of the painted gallery, and master Étienne has tried to break these empty spaces with a loophole in each bay.

He himself had returned to Paris by the end of the century, but work continued on the plans which he drew up. Above the west porch, his masons constructed the fine rose window, although the carvings with which they decorated the tympanum have mostly gone and a modern work has replaced the famous miraculous statue of St Erik. The north porch, which belongs to the earlier stage in the cathedral's building, has kept its French statue of St Olof, holding his warrior's axe and trampling on a troll. The south porch beneath its enormous window is the decorative masterpiece of Uppsala; it was probably donated by Archbishop Hemming (d.1351), whose arms, Sparre, match those of the cathedral. With its original painting and gilt, it must have stood out against the plain brick walls like a flamboyant reredos. The central St Laurence is medieval French, but most of the rest of the carving is native work. Directly above the door are the six days of creation, and the arch has a double row of apostles and prophets, all in a stone from Trondheim in Norway.

Inside the cathedral there are not many carvings. Only in the choir, after the French workmen had gone home, did masons from Gotland produce twelve superb capitals. They used typical themes from medieval iconography, interpreted in Gotland's heavy, solemn style. Particularly fine are the death of the Virgin, the feasting scenes, and – a favourite story in the North – Stephen the stable-boy, who saw the star of Bethlehem as he watched his five foals. Of the paintings which covered the walls of the medieval cathedral, only the remarkable suite in a chapel has survived, a fifteenth-century work telling the legend of St Erik.

When Gustav Vasa brought the Reformation to Sweden, he was ruthless in seizing all church property that could be turned into money, but he did not dare to take the reliquary of St Erik. His son, Johan III, who was even shorter of money, did melt down the reliquary, though he carefully preserved the actual relics, and later, when things were easier, had a new silver shrine made in the shape of a church, medieval in form but with Renaissance detail, into which the relics were placed. There they still lie: the saint's skull and Sweden's oldest royal crown.

Only in 1435 was the whole cathedral finally consecrated. It stands out above the quiet university town, but below the height which is occupied by the great Renaissance castle. One of the original gates of the close survives, and before the west front is the open market-place that has witnessed some of the most stirring events in Swedish history. Although the kings were mostly buried in Stockholm, Uppsala is the resting-place of many of Sweden's greatest men: soldiers like Baner and scholars like Linnaeus. St Bridget's parents, Birger Persson and Lady Ingeborg, lie there, beneath a tombstone with tracery like an English brass.

Apart from Uppsala, the only other church in Sweden which is directly inspired by French Gothic is the cathedral of Skara, and this has suffered two drastic restorations, one classical and one in nineteenth-century Gothic. (In the thirteenth century, Bishop Brynolf founded Skara College at the University of Paris, the deeds for which are still extant.) The choir, with its square end, is more English, but the nave is pure French, for

Skara even has the only triforium gallery in Sweden. Unfortunately, the proportions are wrong and the tall gallery squeezes the clerestory, so that the nave appears squat.

North of lake Mälären, surrounded by the deep green of the fir forests, is another great brick cathedral, Västerås, amid lawns and low wooden houses. The five aisles and the relatively low vaults give the church a pleasing open feeling, friendly and peaceful, which is a welcome background to the grave of the tragic Erik XIV; he now sleeps beneath a grand classical tomb of Italian marble, the gift of Gustav III, with its terse and elegant Latin inscription. Across the river stands the great castle.

Strängnäs cathedral has a lovely position on an arm thrust out into lake Mälaren. It stands on top of a hill, surrounded by lawns and old trees. Its solid square tower at the west end, capped by a Baroque lantern, is like a lighthouse above the water. Strängnäs has a particular charm. Built completely in brick, its walls have weathered to an almost golden colour. Inside, it is a hall-church with a wide low nave, and the shade of the brick pillars contrasts with the chalk-white Gothic vaults. The style is North German Gothic fetched from Lübeck, and the different parts date from between the end of the thirteenth century and the Reformation. There are several memorials of Engelbreckt's friend, the poet bishop, Thomas Simonsson, his tomb, his cope and his staff. The greatest treasure of the cathedral is the magnificent tryptych above the high altar. It was the gift of Bishop Kurt Rogge and was made in Brussels in 1490, one of the masterpieces of Flemish Gothic. The technical skill of the carving is amazing. There is perpendicular tracery of a delicacy one would only believe possible in stone, and the glittering colours have been well preserved. The whole work is alive with the extreme realism of the dying Middle Ages, brutal or humorous as the scene demands.

The bishops of Linköping tended to be so busy with politics that they had little time over for their cathedral. All the same, they were men of pride and power and their see was the richest in Sweden, with the result that several of them began ambitious, modern schemes, regardless of the work of their predecessors. Linköping is an amalgam of styles from the early thirteenth century to the end of the Middle Ages, yet the whole building has a marvellous feeling of unity. As it stands, it is one of Sweden's most beautiful churches.

Enter by the west door, and before you stretches a long avenue of pillars leading to the distant altar in front of the tall windows. This being a hall-church, the spacious aisles give more open proportions to its strong eastward drive. The ground-plan emphasizes the length, for it is not interrupted by transepts, the line of pillars simply curving round behind the altar. Yet, when you look carefully at the individual pillars, differences leap to the eye. Six massive square ones near the altar carried the crossing and transepts of the transitional cathedral, built by Birger Jarl's brother, Bishop Bengt. The nave was continued with lower aisles which can still be traced, but these were soon replaced by the hall-church. At the

Nave of Linnkoping Cathedral

beginning of the fourteenth century, the three westernmost bays were added in a very fine Decorated style similar to that at Lincoln. During the next century, although the work was often interrupted by the Danish wars, the east end was rebuilt with a lovely late Gothic corona of three chapels. The tower is of the nineteenth century, for the original church had none.

Linköping incorporates a superb collection of sculpture. All the way round the inside wall runs an arcade, which in the western bays is carved with cusps in the shape of human heads that rival the Decorated Lady Chapel at Ely. A hundred years later, when master Gierlac of Cologne was building the corona, his stonemasons filled the cathedral with grotesque human figures and carved the castle with soldiers on its battlements, in which the Host was kept. The finest tombstone, perhaps also the work of Gierlac, belongs to a bishop, the blessed Nickolas Hermannis, chaplain and confessor to St Bridget, author of the office containing the lovely hymn, 'Rosa rorans bonitatem'. In the ambulatory are kept some of the carvings from the tympanum of the elaborate Decorated south porch, among them a magnificent harrowing of hell. In the same style are the series of reliefs on the font, cast in bronze at Lübeck.

In the later Middle Ages, the most important religious centre in Sweden was not a cathedral but St Bridget's foundation of Vadstena. Its wealth was enormous; among the constant crowd of pilgrims, it welcomed kings as readily as peasants. Queen Margaret, the creator of the Union of Kalmar, became a lay-sister there. From its scriptorium came much of Sweden's surviving medieval literature; artists there could be certain of work, to the glory of God and the nation's greatest saint.

St Bridget had chosen Vadstena because it was on a visit there that Our Lord had appeared to her in a vision and told her the rule of her Order; but it is thanks to her daughter St Katherine that the enterprise succeeded. Katherine inherited all of her mother's energy and inspiration. She had accompanied St Bridget on all her pilgrimages, and had waited with her the long years in Rome. When at last the Order was approved by the pope, St Katherine became the abbess of Vadstena.

The Bridgittine Order is unique, for it assembles both monks and nuns in one house, under the rule of the abbess. The monks serve as chaplains to the sisters, and share the worship with them, but otherwise the two sexes are strictly segregated. We shall see that this had a profound influence on the architecture both of the church and of the conventual buildings.

The church of Vadstena convent is austere and soberly beautiful. The local stone has weathered to a clean slate-blue, so that to the people of East Gothland it is simply known as the 'Blue Church'. The plan is simplicity itself: three naves, all the same height and width, make it a hall-church, and the shallow vaults are carried on tall octagonal pillars of stone without capitals. Such plainness is unusual for 1430, but the ideals of St Bridget were stern and the magic of the Blue Church works in its proportions and its light-filled spaciousness.

Unhappily, scarcely anything remains of the unique organization of the interior demanded by St Bridget herself. To begin with, the church is back to front. The high altar is in the projection at the west end, and the only entrance is by two small doors on either side of the flat and bare east front. Originally the great altar of the Virgin stood in the middle of the east wall, opposite the high altar dedicated to St Peter. The whole floor of the church was open to the monks and the populace, but between the six easterly pillars was once a gallery approached by a catwalk, the door to which can still be seen high in the north wall. This gallery was the only part of the church to which the nuns were admitted. Their foundress did not believe in inviting temptation.

The other buildings were equally strictly segregated. The monks' lodgings form the core of the eighteenth-century range to the south of the church, while to the north was the nuns' cloister; only the foundations remain of the buildings where their quarters met at the west end of the church. Here were the precautions for such limited contact as was administratively necessary: a small window with a heavy grille between the two parlours, and a barrel set in the wall like a swing door for passing objects across. The chaplains talked to their penitents through the small peepholes in the wall behind the high altar. At the heart of the nuns' northern range is the hall of the original palace of the Folkung kings; it may well have been built by Birger Jarl himself, and is the oldest secular building in Sweden. At the centre is the handsome chapterhouse, with fragments of fifteenth-century paintings on the walls. On the other side of the classical doorway, added when the house was a home for old soldiers, is the King's Room with its damaged pictures of St Bridget and other female saints.

The Blue Church is practically a museum of medieval art. Two Swedish queens are buried there, Karl Knutsson's second wife, Catherine the Fair – Karl was a great patron of Vadstena – and Erik of Pomerania's English queen, Philippa, daughter of Henry IV, whose arms on her tomb carry the leopards and lilies. Near them lies the mighty Bo Johansson Grip and the hated Jösse Eriksson, steward of Dalecarlia. There are two magnificent tryptychs. The one on the south wall near the entrance was dedicated in 1459 to the patron saint herself; she sits at the centre, offering her revelations to the little kneeling cardinals, and on one of the wings are the stages of purgatory as she describes them. The artist, Hans Hesse, was a real bohemian, and the nuns had to pay him twice to get the job finished. On the high altar is a very fine tryptych from Brussels carved at the very end of the Gothic age. The nuns employed one of the great artists of the late Gothic style in the person of the Lübeck sculptor, Johannes Junge. His is the great triumphal crucifix, and his masterpiece the St Bridget in ecstasy; the whole figure is in movement, and the folds of her dress seem like running water; the saint's head is tilted back to gaze into the unseen world, and the right arm is raised, poised to write, although the hand is sadly lost.

While Vadstena is Sweden's most famous monastery, it is by no means the oldest. When Sverker the Elder's queen Ulfhild founded Alvastra, she was not to know that only a dozen miles away would rise St Bridget's monument. The setting of Alvastra is bucolic, while behind the ruins lowers the wooded mass of Omberg, its dark fir forests evoking the heathen past. The buildings at Alvastra add to Cistercian plainness the simplicity of a missionary church. On Gotland, the square pillars and round-headed arches of Roma are almost Roman, and well merited Linneaus' description of them as the finest stable in the kingdom.

Probably Vreta convent near Norrköping was founded in 1162 by King Karl Sverkersson; but the original church is older – built to house the tomb of King Inge, who had been poisoned there half a century before. The royal tombs were re-erected incorrectly by the antiquarian-minded Johan III. The nave is plain Romanesque, with heavy vaults and dark narrow aisles; the chancel arch is also strikingly narrow and leads into a gloomy transitional choir. Indeed, the only colour in the church is provided by the flamboyant Baroque funeral monuments of the Douglas family. On the south side is a remarkable little chapel, wrongly called Ragnald Knaphövde's, which is completely round, like a Templar Church. The ruins of the claustral buildings lie in a meadow of clover and foxgloves; the line of the cloister arcade is marked by a pergola of roses and clematis, while the garth is planted with herbs. On a hot summer's day, the peace of Vreta is numinous.

The great foundation of West Gothland is Varnhem, and even as the house of Sverker patronized Alvastra and Vreta, so the heirs of St Erik patronized Varnhem. A cell of Alvastra, it was first given to a French monk Henry, but the present church was begun in 1234 with the generous support of Birger Jarl, who lies buried there with his wife and son, beneath a remarkable but broken tombstone on which all three are carved. Varnhem has survived as an exceptionally pure transitional church, and this we owe to its second great patron, the seventeenth-century chancellor, Count Magnus Gabriel de la Gardie, who, having selected it for his resting place, restored it with a piety and a sense of history most unusual for his period.

Indeed, Varnhem can compare with Lund for the integrity of its style. The east end, with its fan of chapels supported by de la Gardie's massive buttresses, is a direct echo of the great Romanesque churches of the South. Inside, too, the choir takes pride of place, round arches being carried on enormous capitals, for the nave is as plain as at Roma, its arches hacked out of the solid wall and the vaults carried on clusters of colonettes with crochet capitals. The monastic buildings have been excavated and turned into a garden. The Englishman, used to houses such as Tintern, will be struck by their modest size, and when one remembers that Varnhem was one of the country's great monasteries, it becomes easy to appreciate the extent to which medieval Sweden was on the fringe of Europe.

At St Peter's in Ystad, part of the Franciscan house is now the town museum. Here we are in a different world, for when the friary was founded in 1267, Ystad was Danish, and all the buildings are in warm brick instead of cold stone. The interior is light and open, thanks to its tall windows, and the west front is a joy, filled by blind lancets and ending in a step gable. The burghers' church of St Mary has a sense of prosperity and sophistication which was lacking further north. It is a rich but strange building, for the whole western part, with its splendid Baroque spire in copper, was rebuilt when the old tower fell. Gothic vaults have been built haphazardly from the round arches, and a lively but very provincial seventeenth-century altar hides a complete ambulatory. In fact the church feels more Baroque than medieval. It has, however, a good tryptych and a moving early Gothic triumphal cross.

Ystad is a prosperous merchant town which has changed little over the centuries. Crooked streets of half-timbered houses lead to the market-place, where the Empire town hall stands with its medieval cellars, and behind it the green copper roof of St Mary's. There are even a couple of medieval private houses, built in the same brick as the churches.

This use of common brick for sacred buildings may seem strange to many, but in fact it is a technique which is widespread throughout Northern Europe, and in particular across the North German plain that stretches from the Dutch coast to Russia with scarcely a hill to break the landscape. There just is not any stone, but the sand and mud make excellent bricks, and so the great brick churches, in what the Germans call *Backsteinsgotik,* are found from Utrecht to Danzig and include such gems as medieval Lübeck. German merchants then spread the style around the Baltic as far as Stockholm and Riga.

The two important churches of old Stockholm are built in brick, the Great Church and the Riddarholms church. Riddarholm means 'Island of the Knights', and it lies just south of the larger island of the old town. The church was built by the Franciscans at the end of the thirteenth century. It was meant to be a hall-church with high and airy vaults, but only the north aisle was finished. However, the Riddarholm church had a grand history ahead of it, for it was to become the Westminster Abbey of Sweden, the resting-place of her kings. The first one to be buried here was its founder, Magnus Ladulås, though the effigy on his tomb dates from the Renaissance. Later on the church was extended westwards, so that part of the original façade is preserved within the present nave, and here proof can be found that the blind arches which decorate the façade of a brick church were originally painted with saints and prophets, as were the carvings in a stone church. What is even more exciting is the fact that, among the surviving pictures, are contemporary portraits of Magnus Ladulås and his queen, Helvig. The king is a dignified figure with a long cleft beard, and in spite of the painting's early date, there is considerable individuality about the face. He stands in front of a church, presumably Riddarholmskyrkan itself. Along both sides of the church are the funeral chapels of the different royal houses, but all the best monuments date from later than the Middle Ages.

The citizens' church at Stockholm is Storkyrkan, the Great Church, which is not in fact a cathedral. All the same, it has seen kings crowned and royal weddings. It stands on the highest point of the island of Old Stockholm directly behind the palace. The outside is rather unexciting, but inside the Great Church lives up to its name. It is a perfect rectangular hall-church: no less than five equal naves are carried on brick pillars and the ribs of the star vaulting are in naked brick. All the other surfaces are whitewashed in contrast to the warm rust of the brickwork, the whole taking on a clean, light atmosphere. The furnishings add gay splashes of colour; there are an ebony and ivory altar, stuccoed thrones, and Knotke's statue of St George.

It is surprising how little non-religious architecture there is left in Sweden from the Middle Ages. Most of the great castles have been so changed and rebuilt that they now belong to later periods, and only on

73

Gotland were the ordinary citizens wealthy enough to build in stone instead of wood.

The greatest of all Swedish castles was Tre Kronor in Stockholm, founded by Birger Jarl. Its heart was the enormous circular keep of the 'Three Crowns' (Tre Kronor), which dominates the city in old paintings. The keep was built late in the twelfth century, and was destroyed in the catastrophic fire of 1697.

This idea of a single tower of refuge, with thick stone walls and the entrance on the first floor, governs Swedish military architecture right through the Middle Ages. Only at the now completely ruined royal castle of Näs on Visingsö and at Stockholm were there simplified versions of the great castles of England and France, with their many baileys and barbicans. The oldest such keeps are called *kastells,* like the Powder Tower at Visby, which is now incorporated into the town wall. The finest of the survivors is at Hälsingborg. The massive square tower stands on a mound in the centre of the town, and looks across the narrow sound to Elsinore. It was probably build by Erik of Pomerania in order to control the trade of the Baltic with the outside world.

The most usual fate of the medieval castle was to be incorporated into its Renaissance successor. Both at Kalmar and at Varberg, the old keep forms the core of the present castle, though it needs an archaeologist to identify it. Nyköping, with its bloodthirsty history, is now a ruin. Here, was the famous 'Guest Night' of 1317; at the bottom of the keep is a round dungeon, hewn from the living rock, where King Birger's brothers died, and in one wall there is a hole where, it is said, the dukes, in the desperation of hunger, tried to dig their way out with a boar's tooth.

These keeps were designed exclusively as places of defence. In times of peace, people actually lived in the surrounding buildings, which were often of wood. Only towards the end of the Middle Ages were the ideas of fortress and residence combined in Sweden. In the fourteenth century, a cousin of St Bridget, Junker Knut Nilsson, built himself a seat on the shore of lake Mälaren. Wiks Hus is simply an enormous rectangular stone house, originally nine storeys high, standing on a steep slope above the water. It has an ordinary roof between step-gables, and at each corner an archer's turret rises from the upper storeys. Unfortunately, the inside was radically altered by General Gustav Horn in the 1650s. In spite of being militarily a rather unsophisticated building, it proved an excellent fortress; for, in Sten Sture's wars, it was held for King Christian and was besieged by the Swedes for eighteen months.

During the fifteenth century, Skåne was spared the incessant civil wars in the rest of Sweden by being part of Denmark, and her nobles were able to build themselves fitting homes. Some, like Tosterup, with its lovely painted church beside the moat, are still lived in; but the finest of them all is now a museum. The plan of Glimmingehus is just the same as that of Wiks Hus, but here the original five storeys have survived unchanged inside, the dark wide rooms having low vaulted ceilings and narrow windows set in the eight-foot-thick walls. The moated tower stands in the fields like a giant's runestone, and from it on a clear day one can see the island of Bornholm floating in the Baltic.

Glimmingehus was begun at the very end of the Middle Ages in 1499, and like its neighbour, Bollerup, is equipped with ports for cannon. The builder was the Danish admiral, Jens Holgersen Ulfstand, governor of Gotland, and his architect Adam van Düren, who had worked at the cathedrals of Lund and Linköping. After him it was owned until this century by the Rosenkranz family, one of whom figures in *Hamlet*. The entrance, covered by a turret, is from the courtyard, and the interior is designed to be defended floor by floor. Ulfstand himself is portrayed between his two wives above the entrance, and in the great hall there is another carving of a knight in armour with Ulfstand's shield, and the confident inscription, 'I am a warrior strong and great, from Gotland I to Skåne came 1487.'

Sweden, like Britain, hides a wealth of art and history in its parish churches. Stop in almost any village, and the tidy whitewashed church with its red roof may well prove to have a Romanesque font, Gothic paintings and, almost invariably, a colourful Baroque pulpit. To the art-lover, the greatest appeal of these village churches is the exceptional number that still have their medieval wall paintings. Nowhere else in Northern Europe has the iconoclasm of reformers and the neglect of centuries done so little damage. Many of these churches are now literally as their builders left them, except that the garish colours have been muted by time.

It took at least a hundred years for Gothic to penetrate into the depths of the Swedish forests, and so the late thirteenth-century church at Dädesjö in Småland has still the youth and freshness of a new style. Only the nave of the abandoned church is left. The wooden roof is covered by a pattern of small roundels, and in each one is painted a single scene, just as in an early stained-glass window. It tells the story of the nativity. On the walls are two rows of arcades, running right the way round the church like stone work, with damaged stories of the crucifixion and the resurrection. The figures have been copied from an illuminated manuscript, but this has succeeded in making them come alive in a way that makes their charm something more than merely age and provincialism. The font is older than the church, for on it Viking dragons fight beneath round arches. On the altar stands a statue of St Olof, the saint seated on his throne, trampling beneath his feet the giant Skalle and the confident strength of his expression belonging to a Christian soldier.

The little wooden church of Södra Råda dates from 1323, a work of peace in a land at war. The paintings have faded to grisaille, rows of serious statuesque figures in Gothic recesses, among them Peter, the contemporary bishop of Skara. On the eastern wall is the Trinity flanked by John the Baptist and the Virgin, at whose feet cower two little figures, probably the artists. On the opposite wall is the glorification of the Virgin, and the soft limp gesture with which she sinks into death is a superb piece of Gothic expressiveness. The artist must have been a local man copying a manuscript, and no scholar; he thought that Genesis in Latin was a prophet!

By the next century, the cultural mood of Northern Europe was set by the splendour and chivalry of Burgundy, and Karl Knutsson deliberately modelled his court on that of Charles the Rash. Bright blues and greens dominate the church at Tensta, whose walls seem hung with tapestry. The whole church was painted in 1437 by Johannes Rosenrod, who signed himself humbly, 'With the help of Him who made the world from nothing.' The western part tells the story of St Bridget with unique legends, and on the north wall of the choir kneels the patron, Bengt Jönsson Oxenstierna, father of the famous archbishop, Jöns Bengtsson.

Many of the artists were, like Rosenrod, Germans who had wandered north from commission to commission, bringing with them the fashions of Flanders. So, by the second half of the century, the idealized art of Burgundy was being replaced by the harsh realism of the dying Middle Ages. A certain Peter was expert at these goliard scenes. At Osmo he painted the devil tempting a revolting old hag to lust, and at Sala death saws down a tree into which a terrified young man has climbed, an image taken up by the film director Ingmar Bergman in *The Seventh Seal.*

The outstanding painter of the period was Albertus Pictor. He was a well-known citizen of Stockholm, where he also ran an atelier for embroidery, and he must have been a good businessman, for the records of 1509 note that he paid more tax than any of his colleagues. His great talent lay in his draughtsmanship, in the grotesque realism of his faces and in the skill with which he composed his groups – as in the betrayal at Härkeberga, where the monstrous head of Judas is wedged between the heads of Christ and a helmeted soldier. Most of Albert's work is in

Wallpaintings at Härkeberga Church

76

Uppland. At the porch of Härnevi is a striking allegory of piety and worldliness. The broken body of Christ with the instruments of his passion dominates. To His right the pious man kneels in white gazing on the crown of thorns; to His left the worlding in red jacket and blue trousers looks over his shoulder to his house and the gold within.

Albert's masterpiece is the church of Härkeberga. It is, in effect, an anthology of medieval iconography. In the porch is an imaginative wheel of fortune, where the minstrel plays his drum for the man who rises, and death grabs at the one who tumbles down. Inside the church is the Last Judgement, and while the fate of the damned is gruesome, Albert succeeds in the more difficult task of making the blessed look convincingly pleased. Above the altar, the Trinity and the worshipping angels swim in a sea of purple. On the walls of the nave are three rows of pictures like a tapestry, whose scenes are taken from the *Biblia pauperum*.

More than four hundred churches have significant remains of wall paintings. All the work was done *al secco*, and as a result time and whitewash have dimmed the original colours. Other church furnishings to have survived include the magnificent fourteenth-century wooden choirstalls at Lund, which are Gothic at its freshest and most attractive; the north side has vivid scenes from the Old Testament, and the labours of the months on the south can rival the work in stone of any great French cathedral. Lund also has some very rare brasswork, such as an enormous seven-armed candelabra, and a most ingenious astronomical clock, featuring the Zodiac and knights and heralds who sound the hours.

The sculpture has inevitably suffered more over the years, but there are few old churches in Sweden that cannot show some piece, albeit broken, of medieval wood carving. The master of the Burgundian style was Johannes Junge, whose work has been mentioned at Vadstena. Bernt Knotke was the most outstanding sculptor of the late Middle Ages; and he, too, came from Lübeck but settled in Stockholm. His work can be shamelessly realistic, as in his fine statue of the kneeling king Karl Knutsson at Gripsholm, whose ugly face and snub nose show no hint of flattery.

Bernt Knotke deserves fame above all for his St George in the Great Church in Stockholm. It has been called the finest equestrian statue north of the Alps, and makes an interesting contrast to the near-contemporary Colleoni monument in Venice. The St George is without doubt one of the greatest works of late Gothic sculpture. The young St George, his horse and the dragon form a pyramid whose base is the writhing dragon with its strange lobster-like wings that contrast with the firm outline of the horse. The knight, for all his elaborate armour, is bare-headed as he raises his sword to strike. On a separate plinth, the princess kneels in prayer for her rescuer. This is, of course, also a political monument, for the princess is Sweden, whom Sten Sture rescues from the Danish dragon at the battle of Brunkeberg.

Sweden's art during the Middle Ages reflects the country's political and economic place on the fringe of Europe. Even in that international age, it must have seemed strange and remote. The only native style was inherited from the Vikings, and this gave Swedish Romanesque sculpture a unique beauty; but after this tradition died out, it was replaced by the influences from the mainstream of European culture. These influences were interpreted in Swedish terms. The use of brick in building, and the consequent development of wall painting rather than stone sculpture, and the wealth of sculpture in wood are all specifically Swedish.

Culturally, medieval Sweden was bound to be provincial, but it has left such remarkable treasures as Lund and Visby which are part of the heritage of all Europe.

6. Gustav Vasa and His Sons

Among the six hostages with whom Christian the Tyrant had sailed off after his first invasion of Sweden was a young Vasa called Gustav Eriksson. He was related to Sten Sture and had fought as a squire at Brännkyrka. Once in Denmark, he was lodged with some distant cousins in an easy captivity, from which he escaped in the autumn of 1519 to Lübeck; and there he lived as a welcome guest for almost a year. Every ship that called brought news of Danish victories; and, at last, the twenty-four-year-old Gustav set out to join his aunt Christina Gyllenstierna, who was defending Stockholm.

However, young Gustav Vasa never got as far as the capital, for on the way he was met by the news of the Bloodbath of Stockholm; and rightly deduced from the executions of his father and two uncles that he was also on the death list. Instead, he made his way to Darlecarlia, which has so often been the centre of resistance to invasions.

Everywhere he went, Danish soliders were hunting and killing prominent nationalists; for Christian intended to break Swedish resistance for good, and that meant eliminating every possible leader of a rebellion. Gustav himself wandered from farm to farm, disguised as a peasant. In later years, his friend Peder Svart told in his chronicle the story of Gustav's many and narrow escapes: how a cook beat him in front of the Danish soldiers to quell their suspicions; how he stayed with Arent Persson at Ornäs, and while Arent was fetching the enemy to betray him, his wife helped Gustav escape across the frozen lake. When he reached Isala, the pursuers were hot on his trail; so his host Sven Elvsson hid Gustav in a sledge-load of straw and drove him past the Danish guards. The soldiers ran their spears through the straw to check that there was no one hidded there, and wounded Gustav in the leg; as Sven Elvsson drove on, blood began to drip on to the snow, so the resourceful farmer stopped and cut his horse in the fetlock to explain the trail of blood.

By Christmas 1520, Gustav had reached lake Siljan, the heart of Dalecarlia. Outside Rättvik old church he tried to call the congregation to arms, but they refused to act alone. So, on Christmas Day, Gustav Vasa took his stand on a mound outside the church of Mora. South of him lay lake Siljan, its summer beauty a memory beneath the snow-covered ice, and from its shores the black forest stretched over the hills. This was the heart of Sweden, and the last hope of her freedom.

When the congregation came out from the Christmas service, the young nobleman addressed them. He told them of the Danish victories, of Christian's treachery and the Bloodbath of Stockholm, and he offered himself, Sten Sture's nephew, to lead them. The men of Dalecarlia heard the unknown youth in silence; and when he described the horrors of the Bloodbath, refused to believe him. The last hope had failed; and so, putting on his skis, Gustav Vasa set out for Norway and a life of exile.

Next day Lasse Olofsson of Mora came home from Stockholm. His news was the same as Gustav Vasa's; and it ended with the information that there was not one leader of good blood left free in Sweden. The men of Mora had let the last Vasa go away unheeded. At once the villagers chose their fastest skiers and sent them off along the day-old trail through the forests to bring Gustav back. The race lasted fifty-six miles to the last village before the frontier, Sälen, and there they caught him up. The event is still commemorated today, and every year the *Vasaloppet* is run again by hundreds of young Swedes.

Back in Mora, Gustav Eriksson Vasa was elected captain of Dalecarlia. In February, with a few hundred men, he captured Falun and its copper mountain. Everywhere he went, his firey oratory armed the farmers and the townsmen; the spirit of Engelbrekt swept through the north once again. Lasse Olofsson reached the coast to make contact with the privateers of Finland. Throughout the country, young men left their homes at night, or fled from Stockholm by boat, and daily Gustav's army grew.

That spring at Dalaborgen, the charge of the Danish cavalry was held and the infantry routed. Sture's friend, the old lagman Nils Vinge, raised Värmland; in Småland, Klas Kyle, who had fled from the Bloodbath, was fighting an obstinate guerrilla war. In vain Archbishop Trolle recalled an unpopular bishop from Västerås, and offered other popular concessions. In July, the lagman of West Gothland, Ture Jönsson Tre Rosor, made up his mind to defy King Christian; and Bishop Hans Brask of Linköping joined him soon after. The rebellion spread to Finland, where the king's man in fright even executed their ally, Hemming Gadh. Only the great castles with their Danish garrisons held out; and on 23 August Gustav Vasa was elected regent by the *Riksdag* at Vadstena.

However, so long as the Danish admiral, Sören Norby, controlled the sea, the key fortresses of Stockholm, Kalmar and Älvsborg could not be captured. Now was the time for Gustav to use the friends whom he had made at Lübeck. The policy of the Hansa had always been to keep Scandinavia divided; and Gustav Vasa had fulfilled their highest hopes; so the city fathers, led by Herman Iserkel, Gustav's former host for a year, were delighted to supply the young man with arms, mercenaries and limitless credit. To command this private army, Gustav was able to hire a German mercenary general called Berend von Melen, who had last been employed by Christian himself, and let him invade the Danish territory of Blekinge.

In the meantime, the Danish nobility, after seeing what had happened to their Swedish cousins, became somewhat suspicious of Christian's

Gustav Vasa, by an anonymous contemporary painter

autocracy; and in 1523 they deposed him in favour of his cousin Frederik of Holstein. Christian's empire had shrunk to Gotland, which the loyal Sören Norby still held in his name.

Gustav's blank cheque on Lübeck reached the horrifying sum of 114,500 marks, and the city fathers began to get a little worried about the security of their investment. Discreet pressures were brought to bear, and at Whitsun 1523 a *Riksdag* met at Strängnäs, attended by Herman Iserkel, which elected Gustav king of Sweden. The first act of the new king was to guarantee his debts by granting Lübeck's merchants most favourable trading privileges. Indeed, the treaty practically made Gustav a vassal of the Hansa. Next year, the Council of Lübeck completed the defeat of Christian by bringing together his two successors at Malmö to sign a treaty by which the Danes recognized Gustav in return for Gotland.

The young king's first year brought every possible difficulty. The treasury was empty and everything that he did depended on the goodwill of the Hansa. His general, Berend von Melen, tried to seize Kalmar for himself and had to be driven out by force. The Sture family were furious to see the fruits of their long struggle against Denmark fall into the hands of a Vasa, and Christina Gyllenstierna made no secret of her opinion that it was her son Nils, still a boy, who should have been king. Sten Sture's old councillor Peder Sunnanväder, the bishop of Västerås, started to stir up trouble in Dalecarlia, where the farmers were not pleased to discover that their young protégé seemed to need even more taxes than Christian. Gustav acted swiftly; he won back the Darklkarls by his speeches; and when Sunnanväder was captured, he was made to ride into Stockholm dressed as a clown before being executed.

Energetic and forceful as he was, the young man who found himself ruler of Sweden had undertaken an almost impossible task. His threats to resign may well have been more than simply emotional blackmail. In spite of his violent temper, Gustav Vasa was a brilliant natural administrator; he took charge of a bankrupt country, loaded with debts, of an economy weakened by a century of war and of a society whose feudalism was utterly inadequate to cope with the Renaissance world. Yet, by the time he died, he had introduced into Sweden a new order which was to last in its fundamentals until the nineteenth century.

Gustav's overriding problem was money, and for any sixteenth-century ruler there was one obvious solution to this particular problem. Although he was personally uninterested in religion, Gustav's political background was anti-clerical. He continued the Stures' policies of getting his own candidates elected bishops, and claimed tax from the monasteries. Next he forced the monks of Mariefred at Gripsholm to surrender their monastery, Sten Sture having founded it without the consent of his heir, Gustav's father. The Swedish nobles were quick to take the legal hint. The crown then took over the tithe as an emergency measure, and demanded large loans from the richer institutions as patriotic gestures. At the end of the Middle Ages, the Church owned just over 20 per cent of Sweden's agricultural land; and on this significant proportion the Crown received no tax at all. The Crown itself owned a mere 5 per cent. The logic was inevitable: the only way Gustav could hope to pay his debts and give his government financial independence was by expropriating the wealth of the Church.

The mood of the nation was ready for an attack on the Catholic Church. Years of political involvement, culminating in the infamous career of Archbishop Gustav Trolle, had lost the sympathy of the people and given the Church a reputation for being unpatriotic and pro-Danish. Martin Luther's Theses were well known in Sweden. A young Swede from Örebro, called Olavus Petri, had studied at Wittenberg under Luther himself, and returned home afire with the mission to reform the church, from his post of schoolmaster at Strängnäs. The dean of Uppsala, Laurentius Andreae, used his powerful position to help the reformers. A new archbishop, Johannes Magnus, was sent from Rome specially to repress heresy, but soon saw which way the wind was blowing and left the country. The defence of the Church was left to Gustav's old ally, Bishop Hans Brask of Linköping.

Gustav had laid his plans with care. When the *Riksdag* met at Västerås in 1527, the king made a speech attacking the bishops for not helping the crown when it was in such desperate need of money, and his listeners remembered Laurentius Andreai's declaration that the wealth of the Church belonged to the people. Finally, Gustav put to the *Riksdag* the question of where the necessary money was to come from. He had already put the answer, and the nobles enthusiastically worked out the details for nationalizing church property. Gustav's speech at Västerås is the masterpiece of a very great orator; he presented his case with only one possible conclusion, accusing his opposition of ingratitude and skilfully bribing or threatening his supporters.

All the same, the attack on the Church had been fundamentally economic. There was no dramatic breach like the one in England, for Gustav was not concerned with titular supremacy, or any of Henry VIII's other difficulties; all he wanted was the cash. The Church in Sweden did not officially espouse Lutheranism until much later, and in theological matters the Reformation came very slowly; so slowly, indeed, that for a long time nobody was quite sure to which camp Sweden belonged. The final break with Rome was recognized very quietly after the king's Erastian policies had made it a *fait accompli.*

It is important to remember this distinction between Gustav Vasa's political Reformation and the religious one, for it gave the new Church in Sweden a unique position. In theology, the Swedish Church, like the Church of England, remained deceptively close to Roman Catholicism. Calvinism never found a following until the growth of the 'chapel' sects in the nineteenth century. Sweden kept her bishops, who even claim an unbroken apostolic succession through Bishop Peter Månsson.

Politically, however, the Church in Sweden is entirely subordinate to the state. It is only recently that anyone who did not belong to the established Church could be eligible for any official post, and even today, when, for most Swedes, religion is a mere formality, a Catholic is regarded as a suspicious eccentric. The clergy are civil servants, paid directly by the government, and are still the only official registrars of births and deaths. And, of course, until the present century, they were usually the only teachers, too. In the remote forest parishes, the priest was often the only representative of authority; and, as a result, the parson has always played a very important role in Swedish society, especially since there was often no squire in the northern villages. His farm, the *Prästgården*, was open to important travellers, perhaps to the king himself. In any crisis, the parson, being its only educated man, was the natural leader of the community; and the clergy dominated academic life as well.

Although he was far too diplomatic to quarrel unnecessarily with Rome, Gustav Vasa made it clear where his sympathies lay. In his speeches, he talked of the privileges and the greed of the churchmen. Olavus Petri was allowed to conduct a virulent pamphlet campaign in favour of his tutor, Luther. His brother Laurentius was made the first Protestant archbishop, in spite of there already being two archbishops in exile. Gustav also chose Laurentius Andreae, a known reformer, to be his chancellor. Increasingly, church services were held in Swedish. Olavus Petri found time to translate the New Testament, and he wrote several popular hymns which are still sung in the churches today.

Naturally there were many, especially in the deep countryside, who were horrified to see their old faith callously destroyed, their church bells melted down for the king's treasury and the monasteries pillaged by taxmen.

Early in 1527, a young man had appeared in Dalecarlia claiming to be Sten Sture's son Nils. The Darlkarls, who were notorious for their aggressive independence, had begun to feel that Gustav Vasa was getting above himself and rallied enthusiastically to this new Catholic leader –the *Daljunker*, as they called him. Who he actually was is an unsolved mystery, for the real Nils Sture died quite genuinely of plague in Stockholm that winter; but the *Daljunker* managed, with Norwegian support, to capture the whole province. The king reacted quickly. Taking his private army to Dalecarlia, he summoned the people to meet him, trained his cannon on the crowd and then executed the leaders on the spot. The *Daljunker* himself had to be extradited from Germany, but he, too, was executed.

On 8 January, Gustav Vasa was finally crowned king. The delay is significant; Gustav had become king solely by his own efforts, for his hereditary claim was no better than that of many of his fellow nobles, and was weak enough in any case. To the outside world, he was only a successful adventurer, the client of the merchants of Lübeck (facts of which he was always conscious). So Gustav had not dared to take the decisive step of a coronation until he was certain of his power; and that power had to be absolute, so he forgot to swear in his coronation oath to support the Church and the aristocracy.

Next year the officer in charge of the surrender of Nydala monastery was murdered and the whole of Småland rose to defend the old faith. This time the rebellion was joined by many of the great nobles, by the marshal Ture Jönsson Tre Rosor, and by the bishop of Skara. However, it lacked wider support and soon collapsed, while those leaders who escaped had to join Bishop Hans Brask in exile.

At last King Gustav was secure on his throne. The first part of his reign had been a constant struggle: against the Danes, against the Swedish nobles, against the old-fashioned peasantry; now they had all reluctantly agreed to accept him. It was time also to think of a wife. It was important for Gustav to marry into a ruling house, for that would represent a tacit acceptance of the upstart; and in 1531 he won the hand of the eighteen-year-old daughter of the Protestant prince of Sachsen-Lauenburg. The young Katherine was thoroughly unhappy and frightened with her violent husband; and had she not fallen at a dance four years later and died of a miscarriage, she might well have fled from him. She had had time though to give birth to a son and heir, Erik, in 1533, and in the year after her death the king, having had enough of political marriages, took the Swedish lady Margareta Leijonhuvud as his new wife.

During these years, contact with Germany was close. The only available administrators and soldiers came from Germany, and with them they brought such political concepts as royal absolutism and the cultural influence of the Renaissance. Gustav himself felt very bitter at not being invited to join the Schmalkadian League of Protestant German princes. The debts to Lübeck were steadily repaid, until the city began a desperate war with the Dutch, when Gustav, not wholly without justification, repudiated the rest. The pattern of trade had been steadily moving away from Lübeck, and it was an irony that the collapse of the Union of Kalmar was followed by the decline of the power of the Hansa.

Foremost among these German advisers was Konrad von Pyhy, a typical Renaissance adventurer, a good scholar and lawyer, who had been in the service of the Habsburgs. Gustav made him his chancellor to organize Sweden on German lines; but he overstepped himself on an embassy to France by letting Francis I draw him into an alliance against the emperor. On his return, he was impeached for embezzlement, which King Gustav, being an economical man, regarded as a very serious offence. Gustav always treated his ministers rather ungently. Late in his reign he was known to chase them round the audience room with a naked dagger. When Laurentius Andreae and Olaus Petri quarrelled with the king about the independence of the Church. Gustav had no hesitation in casting them both into prison.

Even after the meeting between Gustav and Christian III of Denmark at Brömsebro in 1541, when Gustav chose other allies, the influence of Germany remained. Architects like the Pahr brothers from Augsburg built the new royal castles, and the education of Queen Margareta's three sons, Johan, Karl and Magnus, with their stepbrother Erik, was entrusted to a German scholar, Georg Norman, who had been recommended by Luther himself. Norman himself eventually became superintendent of the Swedish Church.

Gustav's rule was efficient and prosperous, but it was also strict. The authority of the crown was stronger than the Swedes had ever known it, and the Reformation was forced on an unwilling country people. Dalecarlia had been cowed by the ruthless repression of the 'Bell Rebellion', but in 1542 an even more serious revolt broke out in Småland. Its leader was a yeoman called Nils Dacke, who gave his name to the rebellion. He defeated the royal troops sent against him at Kisa, and by November Gustav was obliged to sign an armistice with Dacke that left him ruling the whole of Småland, except Kalmar, from Kronoborg. Dacke took the unwilling Stures as his emblem, and was negotiating with the emperor when the royal troops decisively defeated him at lake Hjorten. Dacke himself was later shot in his forest refuge. His rebellion had no other policy than to put the clock back; but it came closer to success than any of the others, and made Gustav modify his policies.

In the history books, Gustav Vasa is known as the 'father of his country', and it is an honour that he fully deserved. It would be difficult to overstate his achievement; and his reign has as much significance for Sweden as the Norman Conquest had for England. The national feeling that moved Engelbreckt and Sten Sture the Elder was confirmed in Gustav Vasa. He gave his country unity and independence, the foundations on which the later glories of the Swedish Empire were built.

Gustav ruled his land as if it were his private estate, and since he was a brilliant organizer, his rule brought wealth and peace. No detail was too small for him, from the price of iron to the date of the harvest. Trade expanded rapidly, and in due time the economic dominance of Lübeck was broken. It is worth remembering that the only wars of his reign were internal rebellions, for Gustav was at heart a man of peace. When the Union of Kalmar broke, Sweden was war-racked and impoverished and the crown was effectively bankrupt. The great nobles, enfeoffed with whole provinces, were almost independent rulers. But by Gustav's death, the country was more prosperous than it had ever been before and a modern centralized state had been created. The source of all this was the wealth of the crown. Abroad, Gustav's riches were fabulous, as was his meanness.

As a man, Gustav Vasa is a likeable figure, in spite of his ruthlessness and his notorious temper. His personal tastes were remarkably simple, and in his dealings with his family as much as with his country, he behaved as a kind and loving father. He knew, too, how to handle men, and the force of his speeches shows he had the style of a demagogue. Portraits of him display a burly man of strong features, with, of course, his famous sandy beard. As a family, the Vasas had a streak of genius. Of Gustav's sons, three became kings, while in the fourth his

Vadstena Castle on Lake Vättern, a typical sixteenth-century fortress

heredity led to madness. The life of the most gifted of them all, Erik, became a tragedy.

In a family of such strong personalities, strains were inevitable. Disregarding Norman's pious sermons on brotherly love, Erik and Johan grew up as rivals, and their father was not the man to share power with anyone. The most famous family row was the scandal of Vadstena. Gustav's eldest daughter had been married to a German, and after the wedding the guests continued their celebrations at the grand new castle of Vadstena. There the bridegroom's brother was seen several nights climbing in through the Princess Cecilia's window. When the news got to Erik, he stormed into his sister's room to catch Count John in his shirt but no trousers and promptly arrested him. Gustav was livid at this lack of tact. Erik did not make matters better by telling his father off for pulling his erring daughter's hair during the subsequent moral lecture.

In spite of such incidents, father and sons remained close. Erik as the heir remained in Sweden to act as his father's deputy. He was given the provinces of Kronoborg and Öland as his appanage, and at his residence of Kalmar he established a splendid Renaissance court. Johan was placed in charge of the frontier province of Finland, towards which the Russian of Ivan the Terrible had begun to be a threat.

In the Baltic States, the rule of the Teutonic Knights was collapsing and Johan saw an excellent opportunity to extend Sweden's territory. Erik's political interests were directed westwards, to the Protestant powers of Europe. His hope was to marry the Princess Elizabeth of

87

England. Gustav approved of neither of these schemes, so the brothers duly helped one another. Johan even went to England, where Lord Cecil found him a 'good fellow'.

Gustav himself reigned in peace. In 1551, Queen Margareta died, and next year the lusty old man married her sixteen-year-old niece, Katarina Stenbock. No wonder his enemies compared him to King David. Death came to him in 1560 after a long and full life. Knowing the end was near, Gustav read his will to the *Riksdag*. Erik was his heir to the throne, and his other sons were left large dukedoms on the German model, as befitted king's sons.

Erik XIV was a Renaissance prince, whereas his father and brothers were men of the Reformation. His coronation was celebrated with a flamboyance rare in the North. Foreign diplomats were amazed to watch Lapps herding their reindeer in the procession. To add lustre to his court, Erik created the first orders of nobility in Sweden; there had been no real titles since the last of the jarls till Erik made his counts *greve* and barons *friherre*.

The old king, in his wish to see each of his sons fittingly provided for, had in fact come close to destroying his own life's work. The independent dukedoms of the younger sons made nonsense of the centralized royal authority, and Erik faced his half-brothers and allied to them the powerful lords of their mother's family, including Sten Eriksson Leijonhuvud and Svante Sture. It was an opposition to be feared, but the new king asserted his rule at once. By the Article of Arboga, accepted by the *Riksdag* in 1561, the dukedoms were made subject to the royal authority, and the other rights of the aristocracy were curbed.

The rivalry between the brothers was not ended. Duke Johan, who ruled in Finland like a free prince, had the mortifying experience of seeing his brother take over his Baltic ambitions and become the protector of the city of Reval and parts of Estonia. Johan countered this by a brilliant match. In 1562, he married Katherine Jagiellon, the sister of King Sigismund Augustus of Poland, and received as dowry the Polish castles in Livonia. For a subject to make such a marriage without his king's permission was an open threat, and Johan's father-in-law forced the issue by demanding that Duke Johan declare himself independent ruler of Finland from his court at Åbo. However, the Finnish nobles remained loyal to Erik. Henrik Horn and Herman Fleming fled to Stockholm with details of Johan's plans, and after a weak resistance Johan and his wife were captured and imprisoned at Gripsholm.

As these years saw the foundations of the Swedish Empire laid, it is essential to examine the situation on the Russian frontier in some detail. The importance of Russian trade had been growing steadily, for she was almost the monopoly supplier of certain luxury goods; and the Hansa, the Danes and the Swedes sought to control this wealth. The clearing-house of this trade was Narva, and in 1558 it fell to Ivan the Terrible. It was this shock that made the citizens of Reval offer to become Erik's subjects; Sweden thus held both sides of the Gulf of Finland and could at last blockade Narva, although she had no power over the newly opened Arctic ports. These strategic territories were the prize in any free-for-all; once Klas Horn had occupied Reval, it was clear that the Swedes had won, so the losers, Denmark, Poland and Lübeck, at once combined to attack them. Ivan the Terrible was prepared to remain neutral; but he suggested that a reasonable reward might be for Erik to hand over Johan's wife, Katherine Jagiellon, for he never knew when the Polish king's daughter might come in useful.

The war that began in 1563 is known as the Northern Seven Years War. It opened badly for the Swedes with the Danish capture of Älvsborg, but the Danes did not follow up their victory. Instead, there was a desultory and indecisive campaign each summer. Erik's theatrical nature delighted in warfare, but he also showed himself a remarkably efficient and competent campaigner in the field, except when his unstable nature made him give way to fits of despair. Gustav Vasa's new army of trained levies received its first test and acquitted itself well against the German mercenaries employed by the Danes. Trondhjem and Varberg both fell to the Swedes, although they failed to recapture Älvsborg; and then in 1565 Nils Boije captured Halmstad and held it in spite of the Danish victory of Svarteå. At sea, the Swedish fleet under Klas Kristersson Horn won two great victories off Öland and Bornholm, after which Sweden, not normally a naval power, successfully ruled the Baltic. Admiral Horn's ensign was a golden cross on a blue field, and these were the battles where Sweden's national flag received its baptism of fire.

The Danes were fortunate in their commander. Daniel Rantzau was an extremely able general, but he lacked the resources to bring the war to an end. After the Swedish defeat at Axtorna, he pressed deep into East Gothland and burnt Linköping, but was unable to consolidate his position.

Against this backcloth of war another more dramatic tragedy was being played out: that of Erik XIV. In him his father's qualities had been exaggerated to extremes. Old Gustav's furious temper had developed into a murderous rage that could turn to melancholia within hours. His culture had grown into genuine creative gifts. Erik believed without question in his divine right to be an absolute monarch; and he saw his kingdom as the field for the expression of his own personality. His court brought a breath of the Italian Renaissance into the North by its splendour and by the intensity of the king's talents.

This life is preserved for us in Erik's own diaries. These fascinating books are filled with thoughts on politics and philosophy, with astrological calculations, with vivid drawings of people and castles, even with snatches of music, for their author was a gifted composer. When Erik's plan to visit Elizabeth of England was frustrated by a violent storm, he wrote her an elegy in Latin on his misfortune, which that equally gifted queen much appreciated. His heated blood loved the calm of his beautiful country, to be rowed out on lake Mälaren during the warm summer nights and there to sing or play the lute. In his short reign, he gave his father's austere castles a veneer of elegance that brought Sweden back into contact with Europe's art.

By nature, Erik was a lonely man, and the political ambitions of his nobles only intensified this characteristic. He ruled through his first secretary, the low-born Göran Persson, whose ruthlessness was balanced by his loyalty. Though Erik might award Roman triumphs to his generals, he never really trusted them, and he modelled his rule on that of Machiavelli's Prince. Suddenly, in the spring of 1567, Erik moved against the great nobles. Their leaders, including Leijonhuvud and Svante Sture, were arrested and imprisoned at Uppsala. Svante's son Nils had been awarded a parody of a triumph. They were condemned for high treason before Erik's High Court, which he used as a Star Chamber, but no final decision was taken.

This was followed by one of the most horrifying events of Swedish history. Erik went down to the dungeon where Svante Sture was confined and begged him on his knees for his friendship. The reconciliation was only a few hours old when the king, his cloak hiding his face, entered Nils Sture's cell and thrust his dagger into the young man. Disregarding the prisoner's cries of innocence the guards then finished him off. A massacre of the noble prisoners followed at Erik's orders. Meanwhile Erik himself vanished, and for four days was lost in the forest. The madness that was on him lasted for six months, during which time he refused to have anything to do with the government of his kingdom, the only entry in his diary from this period concerning the casual execution of a cook called Christopher.

During these desperate months, Erik married. His suit with Elizabeth had foundered on the English queen's virginity, and faded into an elegant flirtation. Instead, he approached the landgrave of Hessen, the head of the German Protestants, for the hand of his daughter. While the negotiations were in progress, Erik sent a letter to Elizabeth lamenting that, since the lady of his heart would not have him, he must turn to Hessen. The Danes captured the letter and naturally forwarded it to the landgrave, which closed the question.

The woman to whom Erik forced the old archbishop to marry him in secret was his mistress, Karin Månsdotter. Erik had first seen her as a child of fourteen, selling nuts in the market-place of Stockholm, and struck by her beauty had had her taken to the court. She had already borne him a daughter, and their son Gustav was born the year after the wedding. Karin herself was a peasant girl, a sylph from the woods, and her innocence made her the saddest victim in this royal tragedy.

Meanwhile, a Council of Regency had been formed under Sten Leijonhuvud and Per Brahe, and their first action was to release Duke Johan. By 1568, Erik was well enough to resume the government of his kingdom, and he confirmed his wedding by a splendid ceremony in Stockholm's Storkyrka. Both his brothers were invited, but neither came. Instead, while Stockholm feasted, Vadstena castle surrendered to Karl's troops. Civil war spread as the dukes neared Stockholm; the nobles abandoned Erik and his capital was betrayed. The defeated king was cast in prison; and Göran Persson, refusing to incriminate his master, was broken on the wheel.

Erik's last years were cruel. He was moved from prison to prison by the fearful Johan, for he was popular with the common people and a plot to rescue him by his friend Charles de Mornay came very close to success. His gaoler was an old enemy who once struck his prisoner, breaking his arm, and the ill-healed bone was found when the royal tomb was opened in recent years. He was never allowed to see his wife and children again, and his son died obscurely in Poland. The moving record of this period has survived in Erik's papers, tortuous syllogisms to prove that he is still king being interrupted by drawings of Karin Månsdotter, snatches of music being jotted down in soot in the margin of books. He saw his madness as the work of black magic, but, as his disorder grows, his diaries contain fantastic instructions to the oceans and mountains. Death released Erik in 1577, and the rumour ran that he had been poisoned by arsenic in his pea soup.

The *Riksdag* officially deposed Erik in 1569, and Duke Johan became King Johan III. The new king was not as ruthless or as forceful as circumstances made him appear; these were far more the qualities of his brother Karl. He began his reign by rewarding the nobles with lavish privileges for their support; and he had to allow their leaders, like Hogenschild Bielke and his brother Duke Karl, considerable influence on the government.

The war with Denmark was ended by the Peace of Stettin in 1570, for the simple reason that neither side had the energy to continue it. Frederik renounced his claim to Sweden, and Johan his to Norway, Skåne and Gotland; the Swedes ransomed Älvsborg once again. For the rest of his reign, Johan kept the peace.

After Erik's fall, Duke Karl was established as an almost independent prince. His dukedom covered Södermanland, Värmland and Närke, and was extended to Livonia; in his own lands he ruled supreme, and the taxes he paid to Stockholm were more loans than dues.

By nature, Johan III was pious and scholarly. A lover of pomp, he was a high churchman by nature, and under the influence of his deeply religious Polish queen, Johan's sympathies drew him towards Rome. His genuine desire to see Christendom reunited made him welcome a Jesuit school to Stockholm and give his support to the surviving monasteries. Gustav's Reformation had been essentially financial, and Erik, although brought up in a Calvinist background, was not interested in religion; so the theological position of the Church in Sweden was far from clear.

The fruit of Johan's beliefs was the *Red Book*. This was a liturgy, Catholic in form, infused with the spirit of the Counter-Reformation; and in 1576 he tried to enforce its use throughout Sweden. Many pastors refused to use it, and when they were evicted Duke Karl offered them a refuge in his lands, where he had forbidden the use of the *Red Book*. Johan's son Sigismund was brought up as a devout Catholic. His tutor, Erik Sparre, belonged to the old faith, and at Johan's court there were constant visitors from south of the Alps, and twice even the grand master of the Jesuits himself. The sympathies of the common people, however, were Lutheran; and Duke Karl unscrupulously exploited them to win support for himself.

On the eastern frontiers, a permanent war with Russia smouldered on, until Pontus de la Gardie was made governor of Estonia. He was a French adventurer who had been captured in Danish service and took a job with the Swedes instead; he was also a fine soldier. In 1581, the year after he took office, he finally solved the problem of Narva's trade by capturing the town.

In 1587, the king of Poland died, and at the election of the new king the successful candidate was Sigismund, heir to the Swedish throne. The political implications were profound; for the young man would one day rule two separate kingdoms, one of which was Protestant and the other Catholic, and both of them fearful for their freedom. At Kalmar, a series of articles was drawn up to cope with the situation after Johan's death. By these articles the equality and independence of Sweden were affirmed; Duke Karl was forbidden to be regent.

When Johan died in 1592, everyone was prepared for a crisis. The Swedish clergy met at Uppsala, and officially accepted the Augsburg Confession as the basis of their belief. Only the authority of the Bible could be acknowledged; the *Red Book* was declared a 'Lamentable delusion', and no one save the Lutherans might hold a public service. Meanwhile the nobles and Duke Karl prepared a seried of constitutional demands which Hogenschild Bielke presented to Sigismund. Sigismund, for his part, fully intended to rule Sweden in his own way; and when he arrived in Stockholm almost a year later, he was openly accompanied by his papal nuncio. The governor of Finland, Klas Fleming, remained conspicuously loyal to his king.

There followed a long wrangle, which ended indecisively when Sigismund had to return to Poland; but Duke Karl and the nobles of the council were effectively left to rule Sweden. At Söderköping, a *Riksdag* met at which the Commons confirmed Karl as regent and Vadstena, the last monastery, was closed down. The nobles disapproved of such provocative action, and their uneasy alliance with Duke Karl began to give way. Karl was himself as gifted a demagogue as his father, and in his speeches he stirred up the people to look on him as their only leader. With his encouragement, the peasants of Finland rebelled against Klas Fleming and Sigismund. Duke Karl's ambitions were becoming obvious to all, and several members of the council, including Erik Sparre, left for their own safety to join Sigismund in Poland.

It was 1598 before Sigismund took the inevitable step of bringing military force to bear against his uncle. He captured Kalmar, seized by Karl the year before, and, accompanied by some of the greatest names in the council, advanced into the country. Duke Karl had meanwhile roused the people to resist the Polish invader. At Stångebro, near Linköping, Sigismund's troops were defeated; at which the king gave up the contest, leaving his supporters to be captured and ruthlessly eliminated by Duke Karl. Sigismund's motives are a mystery. Perhaps he simply could not bear to see civil war in the land of his youth; for although he reigned in Poland till 1632, he never made another attempt to reconquer his other throne.

Duke Karl showed his true colours in victory. He systematically and savagely destroyed all opposition. Throughout Sweden and Finland, Sigismund's friends were lynched by the mobs stirred up by Karl's vicious propaganda. The loyal Klas Fleming had died too soon for Karl's revenge; but with his own hands the duke struck the body where it lay in state at Åbo. Using the same crowds as his weapon, he broke the power of the council and the aristocracy. At Linköping, in 1600, he stood its most prominent members before his court, and each one was condemned to death and executed for his loyalty to the rightful king. Among the victims of the event which came to be known as Linköping's Bloodbath was Hogenschild Bielke, who was so old and frail that he had to be carried to the executioner's block.

Although the Estates hailed him as king of Linköping, Karl did not take the title until 1603, and it was confirmed in his heirs at the *Riksdag* next year. His government, however, recalled that of Gustav Vasa. Indeed, he was in many ways the one among the brothers who was most like their father; although he lacked Gustav's charm, he had the same gift for handling the common people, the same pragmatism in religion, and he was even meaner than the old king.

To his credit he was an excellent administrator. The real achievements of the reign of Karl IX are the iron mines and gun foundries of Värmland, and the new towns like Karlstad and Karlskoga. His greatest monument is Gothenburg, on the shore opposite Älvsborg castle, which received its charter from his son Gustavus Adolfus, answering Sweden's age-old need for a port on the North Sea. Karl IX is also remembered for reforming the Swedish legal system, often developing his brother Erik's ideas. There are many stories told about the 'Grey Cloak', as he was affectionately known, when he rode unknown through the country to see that justice was impartial and that the poor were defended against the rich.

As far as foreign policy was concerned, Karl IX was inevitably at war with Poland, and he sensibly moved the theatre of operations to the enemy's territory, where the Swedish exiles from 'Butcher Karl' had gathered in Danzig. These desultory campaigns lasted several years, until, at Kirkholm, the Polish cavalry utterly routed a Swedish army three times their own number. After this defeat, Russia seemed more interesting. There the heirs of Ivan the Terrible had died out, and the whole empire seemed to be falling apart. Karl was delighted to fish in these troubled waters and he gave his support to one of the factions, who, in return, proposed his son, Gustavus Adolphus, as tsar. A Swedish army under Jacob de la Gardie, the son of Pontus, captured Moscow in 1610, but was unable to hold the city. Then the invaders were defeated by

Michael Romanov, and the existence of Russia was saved by one of her greatest sons.

The same year Karl IX had a stroke, but he lingered on, partially paralysed, until 1611. His heir, who was to become famous throughout Europe as Gustavus Adolphus, was by now a boy of sixteen, who accompanied his dying father in the business of government. To Christian of Denmark it seemed too good an opportunity to miss. The last news that Karl received was that the Danes had invaded his country, and in a strange desperate gesture from his deathbed he challenged King Christian to single combat.

So died the last of Gustav Vasa's sons, leaving his country facing the same circumstances that had existed when his father first won the throne: a Danish invasion. It was, however, an immeasurably different Sweden that faced this new attack. The Sweden that broke away from the Union of Kalmar had seemed to the world to be a mere Danish province, but during the century in which the country was ruled by Gustav Vasa and his three sons, Sweden grew to be a nation, conscious of its individuality and independence. It faced Denmark and Poland as an equal, and was accepted as such.

The age of the Vasas brought to Sweden both Reformation and Renaissance. The new nationalism in politics was also to be felt in the country's intellectual life. Ironically, its first and perhaps finest advocate was Uppsala's last Catholic archbishop, Johannes Magnus, for, after he had been thrown out of his see, he retired to Italy and devoted his declining years to his mammoth *Historia de Omnibus Gothorum Sveonorumque Regibus*. The Vasas found that their historians worked better in exile or in prison. Olaus Petri wrote his chronicle of the long wars with Denmark after he had narrowly escaped with his life for claiming that the Church was independent of King Gustav. Karl IX sent Messenius to Lapland to complete his great work of scholarship on the history of Swedish culture since earliest times.

The Vasas were an intellectual family, and their court set a good example to their rather primitive countrymen. Indeed, with the fall of the Catholic Church, it became the only serious patron of the arts, and the arts in turn became secular, castles replacing churches and history hagiography.

The most gifted of the Vasas was undoubtedly Erik XIV. His court at Kalmar was full of foreign intellectuals; his closest friend, Charles de Mornay, was one of the classic Renaissance adventurers, equally soldier and scholar. Erik owned an organ, still a rarity in those days, on which he used to play and compose, and he also kept an orchestra. During his short reign he was constantly building and embellishing his palaces. This was the age, too, of the great Danish astronomer, Tycho Brahe, the ruins of whose cabbalistic observatory can still be seen on the island of Ven in the Sound, and Erik, like so many of his contempories, was fascinated by astrology.

His brother Johan was, by contrast, scholar rather than artist. Where

Erik read Machiavelli, Johan read Serlio and Vitruvius; his passion was architecture, and he once wrote in a letter that building was his greatest pleasure. Johan was also an antiquarian. He restored Riddarholm Church and gave Magnus Ladulås a new tomb; and, at the convent of Vreta, the burial place of the old East Gothic kings, he built monuments for all those shadowy figures of legend. Johan's love of art inevitably drew him back towards the Catholic Church (in contrast to the third brother, Karl IX, whose sole hobby seems to have been left-wing theology), and he repaired much of his father's iconoclasm.

It is illuminating to compare the surviving portraits of different members of the family. The most famous picture of old King Gustav by the German painter Jacob Binck has been lost, but there are several contemporary copies, the best of which belongs to Uppsala University. It shows the king as a middle-aged man, dressed in a sumptuous embroidered velvet cloak which fills the frame in a manner that recalls many of Titian's portraits. The face is strong and confident above a thick, short, square beard – the face of a commander and a leader, 'the breaker of the tyrant's yoke'. At Gripsholm Castle, which serves as the national portrait gallery of Sweden, there is a full-length relief of Gustav by the architect Willem Boy. It hangs near a fine portrait of his son Erik, painted as a present for Elizabeth of England. Here Mannerism has replaced the style of Titian, and the eye is caught by the loud contrasts of red and green. This picture is very different from another portrait of Erik in the National Museum at Stockholm. In this the king is dressed in black and wears a plain square cap. Against this sombre background is set his pale handsome face with its dark eyes and cleft beard. It is a moving portrait, ominously prophetic of the tragedy of its sitter.

The art of sculpture also flourished in the service of its royal patrons. The Renaissance tombs in Uppsala cathedral are among the finest in the North. In King Gustav's chapel, the sarcophagus stands in the middle of the floor; on its lid recline the figures of the king with crown and sceptre, and of his first two wives, one on each side of him. The effigies are carved in a light red-veined alabaster, as are the four elegant obelisks which stand at the corners. In another chapel, are buried King Johan and his queen Katherine Jagiellon. The walls are covered with lavish stucco strapwork, framing landscapes of the consorts' two home cities, Cracow and Stockholm. The picture of Stockholm is particularly interesting since it shows the old castle of Three Crowns, which was destroyed by fire. Queen Katherine lies on a plain tomb beneath a superb Tuscan arch, decorated with the arms of Poland and Sweden. Against the opposite wall, Johan III's tomb is virtually Baroque. It was ordered by Sigismund after his death; and when Sigismund was deposed, it got stuck in Danzig because nobody was prepared to pay for it. It only found its rightful place in 1782. It has the form of a baldachin, beneath which the king lies in full armour, resting on his right elbow; around him stone putti bear his arms and emblems.

The finest of these Renaissance tombs is at Vadstena. There, opposite

Erik XIV, by S. van der Meulen, 1561

the door, is buried Duke Magnus, King Gustav's fourth son, in whom the hot blood of the Vasas took the form of incurable madness. The effigy is supported by arcades of elegant colonettes, and the unhappy prince is shown in full ducal robes. He died at Vadstena in 1595, and the tomb is the work of Bernt van Münster, one of the architects of the castle. Karl IX is buried at Strängnäs, suitably beneath a slab of plain marble.

The true monuments to the Vasas are their castles. At each important and strategic point about the country, such a fortress was rebuilt or founded. From the outside, the blank walls and massive towers look medieval, only larger and heavier; but the flamboyant spires and gables hint at the interiors, where there are concealed the splendid rooms of a sixteenth-century palace.

In the Middle Ages, Sweden's best protection had been its vast area and its wild forests. Once King Gustav had secured his throne, he set about organizing a scientific system of defence. As soon as it fell into his hands, he began to reconstruct Stockholm's old castle, and pulled down the choir of the Great Church to enlarge the defences. At Uppsala, he began a new castle to defend his country's second city; and at Gripsholm he built, on land taken from the suppressed monastery, the finest surviving castle, to command lake Mälaren. For these castles served as centres of administration and as rallying-points where an army could be assembled and from which it could be supplied. Vadstena, which was founded on a virgin site, is the perfect example of this. An invader from the south would have to pass to the east of lake Vättern, and the first open country he came to after the forests was the rich plain of East Gothland. Here a defending army based on Vadstena could bring him to battle in favourable conditions. Were he to choose the other route, and pass between lakes Vännern and Vättern, the defence would be based on Älvsborg, King Gustav's fortress on the North Sea. Strategically, Älvsborg was the most important of all these castles. There is little left to see on the small rocky island, past which the ships sail on their way in to Gothenburg; but, in those days, it commanded Sweden's only lifeline to the west, and more than once it had to be ransomed at enormous cost. On the other coast, Kalmar had been the frontier fortress of Sweden for as long as records have been kept, but the sixteenth-century reconstruction was so thorough that no trace remains of the medieval castle. Across the water is Borgholm, the last of the Vasa castles surviving in Sweden and the key to the island of Öland. However, there are others in territories no longer Swedish: Åbo in Finland, and Reval in Estonia.

Amid all this military building, only Johan bothered about religious architecture. His most important church, designed by William Boy and situated in Stockholm, is dedicated to St James. It is a rather uninteresting building, whose Gothic windows seem out of place with its classical details.

Work began at Gripsholm in 1537; the castle lies on the low ground at the water's edge, so that it seems to float like a ship on lake Mälaren, and the view of its domed, copper-clad towers rising out of the waves is one of the most beautiful and well-known in Sweden. Today one enters through a pleasant courtyard formed by the eighteenth-century stables; but King Gustav's castle is an irregular hexagon with four great round towers at its salient corners. These towers are linked by the living quarters, which give direct on to the outside wall. The blocks are seven storeys high, so that to stand in the central courtyard feels like being at the bottom of a deep well.

Gripsholm was understandably a favourite country residence of several kings, and different generations have furnished and decorated it and added to its superb collection of portraits. The rooms nearest the entrance have retained their original Renaissance character. In the first tower is Duke Johan's Chamber, where, by tradition, Sigismund was born while his father was imprisoned there by King Erik. It is a lovely room, the walls and the deep windows clad with wooden panels which are master-pieces of marquetry, flowers, shields and even figures being represented by the different-coloured woods. In the top storey of the same tower is a grim, plain room, known as Erik XIV's prison. The story goes that this unhappy king paced the floor so often that his footsteps had worn away the oak.

Kalmar, too, lies on the water. A deep creek of the Baltic separates the impressive silhouettes of the castle and the new town with its port. The whole building is surrounded by seventeenth-century earthworks and gun emplacements; once past these, the visitor is faced by a perfectly symmetrical façade with round towers at either end and a great square gatehouse in the centre. On the other three sides, the Renaissance order has failed and irregular turrets and walls are jumbled together in a charming confusion. In its present form, it is mostly the work of the Pahr family, four Italian brothers who were all employed by Johan III on his various building enterprises. Dominicus Pahr designed the delightful well head that stands in the centre of the courtyard: an elegant hexagon of Doric porticos which suggests the temple of Vesta.

The main staircase, paved with old gravestones, leads up to the great halls, which are now bare and empty; but the panelling of the walls makes one forget the fact. In between the Doric columns, themselves of wood, are panels of marquetry which defy adequate description. Using a dozen different woods, the carpenters have made, not just complicated patterns, but, as at Gripsholm, whole scenes and landscapes. It was the great age of such craftsmanship, and Kalmar is richer in it than any other Swedish castle. In one of the towers is a perfect sixteenth-century room on which no expense has been spared. It is called King Erik's Chamber, though it was decorated for him before he mounted the throne, and it is a surprisingly small room for such a display of virtuosity. The lower part of the walls is panelled even more ornately than is the hall, with Corinthian columns, and a fireplace supported by caryatids. The space between the panelling and the coffered ceiling is filled by a frieze, brightly coloured and in deep relief. Its subjects are hunting scenes from Öland, a bear savaged by dogs and a wild boar being struck down by the huntsmen.

Of all the Vasa castles, Borgholm on the island of Öland has the most

Interior at Gripsholm Castle

Kalmar Castle

dramatic position. It stands on its cliff above the Baltic, facing the mainland across the waves, and in the summer sun the white limestone walls
gleam like polished bone between the green heath and the blue sky.
Indeed, Borgholm is like a skull; for it was completely burnt out at the
beginning of the last century and now only the empty walls remain, too
thick for the fire to shake. The logic of the plan is pure: a perfect square
with an enormous central courtyard and massive round towers at each
corner. The original spires, built by Johan III, did not last long, and during
the next century the architect Nicodemus Tessin gave the whole castle a
classical façade to make it a fit residence for Prince Karl Gustav von Pfalz.
The details on the empty doors are the legacy of this rebuilding; but the
bones remain the proud work of the Vasas.

Only Vadstena was founded on a completely virgin site; and the castle
there shares with Borgholm the distinction of perfect Renaissance
symmetry. The original design was by a Dutchman, Arendt de Roy, but
progress was slow and Johan III had his father's plans altered and an extra
storey added. Like Borgholm, Vadstena is a square with a round tower at
each corner; but the *corps de logis* extends only along one side, joining two
of the towers, and in the middle of it, above the gate, is a broad square
tower that dominates the surrounding plain for miles. The detail at
Vadstena is all Renaissance, the magnificent portal of the entrance and
the rows of logical windows; but, unexpectedly, the Middle Ages reassert
themselves in the high Gothic windows of the central tower, to remind us
how new the classical columns then were. The later history of Vadstena is
typical of these castles. It sank slowly from being a royal palace to a
barracks, and finally was used as a distillery. The inside has been
completely stripped and only the dignity of the rooms remains.

Of the halls of state, as opposed to more intimate rooms, the finest
survivor is without question the great hall of Uppsala. The castle itself has
been much altered, but, flanked by its typical round towers, one wing still
crowns the hill above the town and the cathedral. The hall, which is a
magnificent room, has recently been restored, but the most striking
feature of it is its sheer size. There is room for a football pitch on the floor,
and the high roof is carried by gigantic beams. It is a fitting setting for such
stirring events as Queen Christina's abdication.

When one looks at these severe fortresses and compares them with the
elegant palaces that kings were building themselves no further south
than England, it is necessary to remember that they might easily be
required to face a siege. The other arts could find few patrons apart from
the royal house, for the general level of culture was, even among the
nobility, low. We must wait for the next century to remedy this, when the
victorious Swedish armies looted the artistic treasures of Germany, and
were introduced in that way to the standards of the rest of Europe.

7. Lion and Minerva

'If I could but speak, gentlemen, what would I not say to you.' His body broken by a stroke, Karl IX raved at his own helplessness, while the Russians harried Finland, and Karlmar and Borgholm surrendered to Danes. In the field, his armies were led by a broad-shouldered, fair-haired boy of sixteen; for Sweden's neighbours left the young Gustav Adolf no time to be with his dying father. He had to win his crown before he had even inherited it.

Such was the youth of one of the greatest soldiers of European history. Gustavus Adolphus loved the rough and tumble of battle. His cure for flu was to fight Per Brahe with sabres in the great hall of Uppsala Castle; but he also had to take the responsibility of supreme command at an age when his contempories were still cadets. His character was as tough and as obstinate as his father's. As a boy, he once made his noble companions play at Linköping's Bloodbath, in which several of them had lost relations; but where Karl IX had been mean and suspicious, Gustavus Adolphus was frank, expansive and trusting.

When the old king died in 1611, Gustavus Adolphus had halted the Danish advance. The next year he recaptured Borgholm. It was a young man's war; many of Gustavus' officers were of his own age, and they fought with an adolescent carefreeness. That spring the young king rode through the thin ice and had to be pulled out of the river by one of his future marshals, Johan Baner. At Karl IX's deathbed, another young man had taken command in the palace. Axel Oxenstierna, scion of one of the country's oldest houses, was chancellor of Sweden at the age of twenty-eight. He at once made the council declare Gustavus Adolphus of age; and so began the life-long partnership of two outstandingly able men.

The Danes had not intended to fight a long war; and by 1613 they were prepared to sign peace at Knäred. This did little other than restore the *status quo*, but the Swedes had to ransom the vital fortress of Älvsborg, which guarded their one outlet to the North Sea at Gothenburg, for the astronomic sum of one million riksdaler to be paid over four years. Everyone, from the queen mother selling her jewels in the palace to the cottager in the forests, had to pay, and the Ransom of Älvsborg has entered folklore as a bitter duty. Even then it would have been unpayable, as Christian of Denmark expected, if he had not made the mistake of quarrelling with the Dutch, whose wealthy bankers were thereupon delighted to give Sweden a bridging loan.

To the east, Russia was passing through her time of troubles. At the

Peace of Stolbova in 1617, Sweden annexed Kexholm and Ingermanland, with the important commercial centre of Narva. Russia was now cut off from the Baltic, and the Swedes had achieved their ambition of controlling all the trade from the east down into Europe. Only then, when life was quieter, did Gustavus have himself crowned.

The first need of the nation as the new reign began was reconciliation, an end to the bitterness accumulated between Karl IX and the Swedish nobility; and this was achieved by the leaders of the two political camps, Gustavus Adolphus and Axel Oxenstierna. By the Charter of 1612, Oxenstierna re-established the power of the council, but in the event it was never used. Instead of running an independent policy, the nobles were employed by the crown as officers and administrators; and the government of Sweden took the form of an aristocratic bureaucracy. With the new generation, the exiles at Sigismund's court in Poland began to return, until at last even Erik Sparre's son Johan was readmitted to the Council.

The characters of the king and his chancellor complemented one another perfectly. Gustavus Adolphus was a true Vasa, hot-tempered and impulsive, often reckless for the consequences of his actions and alive with an inexhaustible and irresistible energy. Oxenstierna, on the other hand, was a supreme diplomat. He is the only man ever to have got the better of Cardinal Richelieu. He was also a great administrator, and so ran the country that its limited resources were enough to place Sweden among the great powers of Europe. There was a famous exchange at one council meeting when the king lost his temper with Oxenstierna and yelled at him: 'If we were all as cold as you are, we would freeze!' to be met with the reply: 'If we were all as hot as Your Majesty, we would burn!' The two men were close personal friends, and it is really only right to look at their achievements as one whole.

The Sweden they ruled was potentially a rich country, although its economic development lagged behind its natural resources. The traditional mineral wealth grew in importance as Western industry consumed more iron ore, and, more especially, quantities of copper which was essential to the casting of cannon and was also widely used in coinage. Further, the Baltic nations had almost a stranglehold on the navies of Europe, since they were practically the only source of timber for masts, of tar and pitch, and of hemp and flax for sail and ropes. From the eastern coast of the Baltic were shipped large quantities of grain and furs. However, Sweden in particular was short of capital, and found a ready supplier in the Dutch. Dutch merchants were welcomed, and indeed Gothenburg was full of them. There are many old Swedish families who originally came from Holland. The most famous immigrant was the banker, Louis de Geer, who built himself an enormous commercial empire by organizing the fragmented copper-mining industry. It was the development of this latent wealth that enabled Sweden to set her armies in the field.

Although his favourite occupation was undoubtedly fighting,

Gustavus Adolphus was well educated and something of an intellectual. He spoke five languages comfortably and understood more; while technical problems fascinated him. He even designed a new light cannon which radically changed the use of artillery in the field. Oxenstierna, too, was a fine scholar, and used to regret not having more time for such pursuits. As a young man he had travelled widely before entering politics. Most other Swedes of the period were insular boors.

As part of the reformed administration, Gustavus Adolphus founded several gymnasia on the German model. Being a practical man, he planned an education for laymen as well as for priests with a broad and modern curriculum. The first gymnasium was founded at Västerås under Rudbeckius, a fiery preacher and a good scholar who produced the 1618 version of the Bible in Swedish. His statue (by Milles) stands outside the cathedral there. Uppsala university had been reduced to a shambles by the swings of the religious pendulum in previous reigns. Gustavus re-organized it, with generous endowments from the crown and creating the first Chair in Law. He also made such able men as Rudbeckius and Messenius professors; and when these two had quarrelled enough, he sent Rudbeckius to govern Estland, where he is remembered for reform-ing the barbarous state of the peasants. In his stead he installed his own old tutor, Johan Schroderus, another fine scholar, as chancellor and ennobled him as Skytte. Nor was all this useful activity confined to Sweden itself. Schools were equally founded in Finland, and universities

The House of Lords, Stockholm

103

at Åbo, and even at Dorpat and Reval in the newly won provinces east of the Baltic. Indeed, Sweden enjoyed perhaps the most advanced and democratic educational system in seventeenth-century Europe.

Inevitably, there were political changes too. Gustavus Adolphus was one of nature's leaders rather than rulers, and his enthusiastic and generous character prevented him from becoming a despot like his father. On the other hand, under Oxenstierna's diplomatic guidance, the council ceased to be the king's rival and returned to its original role as the king's advisor. The nobles, instead of just living on their estates and hatching plots, became soldiers and administrators. Meanwhile Gustavus, as his daughter Christina would do even more during her own reign, expanded their numbers beyond recognition. The new men were commoners, performing the work Gustavus expected of his nobility: scholars like Skytte, soldiers like Wrangel, and as many as a quarter of them were foreigners; Dutchmen like de Geer the banker, scores of Scots and German soldiers of fortune, like Hamilton, Douglas or Königsmarck. The *Riksdag*, which included the other three Estates, clergy, burghers and yeomen, was summoned only for special occasions and had nothing to do with the decisions of day-to-day administration.

It is important to appreciate that this system of administration was standard throughout the Swedish empire, and that the provinces were treated as an integral part of the country. The mayor of Riga, which Gustavus himself had captured, was bound to attend the *Riksdag* and vote. The postal system established in 1636 covered the whole Baltic. Indeed, the century of Swedish rule was probably the most civilized and most prosperous in the unhappy history of the Baltic states.

Although Gustavus Adolphus had shown what he could do in a pinch, the Swedish victories in Germany during the Thirty Years War could never have been won with the unorganized amateur rabble that he had led against the Russians and the Danes. These almost feudal levies were abolished, and the soldiers and officers were properly paid so that they did not have to look to loot for survival. The basic unit was the regiment, raised, as in Britain, from one county, like the famous Småland dragoons, but the most renowned of his troops were the brigades, known by their colours, blue, red and green. Sweden is, indeed, the only country apart from the United Kingdom that has kept the regimental system, and a Swedish mess is very like an English one. The soldiers were armed with new muskets and pikes, made in de Geer's smithies to designs which the king himself had improved. The same foundries in Dalecarlia made the light cannon he had invented, which could be drawn by one horse instead of a team of ten or more. As their firepower was unreduced, the effect of this extra mobility on the battlefield was literally devasting.

The Swedes, for all their glorious military history, have never been great sailors, unlike their Danish cousins. However, if the Baltic was to be a Swedish lake, a navy was essential, and under the admiral Klas Fleming it was built up till it could more than hold its own.

For a heroic figure, Gustavus Adolphus had an extremely attractive personality. He was spontaneous and impulsive, and his outbursts of temper were always bounded by his sense of fairness. He was liked and admired by his officers and worshipped by his men. To treat war like a sport was really irresponsible rashness, but the king would rush to join in any scrap. He was severely wounded twice and carried a bullet in his shoulder for his last years. Indeed, he was so reckless that he was bound to be killed sooner or later. The great love of his youth was Ebba Brahe, the sister of one of his friends. The story of this romance is a part of folklore, for the queen mother, who was a dominating woman, would not tolerate the waste of such a political asset as the king's bed, and in the end Gustavus had to be content with giving Ebba a diamond necklace for her wedding to Jacob de la Gardie. He had only one bastard, Vasaborg, who after a distinguished career as a soldier came to be buried in the Riddar-holm Church.

In the end, both royal brother and sister made political marriages. Visiting Germany in person, Gustavus won the hand of Maria-Elenora of Brandenburg-Prussia. The elector needed allies, but his wife strongly disapproved of the suitor; so Gustavus went off sight-seeing incognito, leaving behind him a girl desperately in love. As the Thirty Years War spread, the elector's point of view won and the pair were married. However, they had only one child, their daughter Christina, and she was born late. The marriage of Gustavus' sister Catherine turned out to be more significant in the long run; for her husband, Johan Casimir von Pfalz, lost his lands in Germany, and it was his heirs living in Sweden who eventually continued the line.

This being the seventeenth century, one is obliged to try to analyse the religious beliefs of Gustavus Adolphus and, *cuius regio eius religio*, those of his people, although they are inextricably and not entirely cynically confused. Perhaps only a Chinese historian could do this impartially. The king of Sweden for the rest of us is either the Lion of the North, the hero of Protestantism who saved Europe from the tyranny of the Inquisition, or else a fanatical barbarian who reduced Germany to a wilderness. Which-ever he was, his short active career brought him into the popular limelight to a degree none of the other important actors achieved. Whether in panegyrics or in abuse, he is the foremost subject of contemporary propaganda, which is racy reading even by twentieth century standards. Gustavus had been brought up in his father's fundamentalism, but fortunately did not share his ruthless intolerance, and his fervour was tempered by his natural good humour. All the same, it burnt quite as strongly as in the Englishman with whom he had so much in common, Oliver Cromwell. His sense of mission against the Catholics was in-disputably genuine. However, Gustavus was also an Erastian, and here his motives become confused. The Church he regarded as a body within the state, and hence Catholicism became synonymous with treason.

When the Thirty Years War began in Prague, it seemed to have little relevance to Sweden. Far more serious was the threat from Poland, where the elderly Sigismund still claimed the throne he once held, and the frontiers touched in the disputed lands east of the Baltic. Karl IX had been constantly and unsuccessfully at war with Poland. His son was a much better soldier.

Waiting until Sigismund was busy fighting the Turks, Gustavus invaded Livonia in 1621 and besieged its capital, Riga. The Swedish army was just learning its new drill and its new weapons; the king was out digging trenches in person, and Prince Radziwill's outnumbered Poles had no hope of saving the city. Riga, the market for a vast hinterland and inhabited mainly by German merchants, soon surrendered, and Livonia was left at Sweden's mercy. Gustavus promptly integrated it into his empire. It is interesting that, while he forbade the practice of Roman Catholicism, the Orthodox Church was left with full religious freedom.

The chief Swedish objective was to conquer the Polish coast, thus controlling the trade of the interior and making the Baltic a Swedish lake. In 1626, Gustavus' new army inflicted a crushing defeat on the Poles at Wallhof. However, the politics of Europe were reaching northwards. The year after Wallhof, the first of Wallenstein's regiments was sent to help the Poles; and in 1629, under the auspices of France, Sweden and Poland signed the Truce of Altmark. Gustavus kept his conquest of Livonia, and almost more valuable, Sweden was granted for six years the tolls of the whole Polish littoral, and it was with this source of ready money that Gustavus financed his entry into the Thirty Years War.

By 1629, the German Protestants were waiting for the *coup de grâce*. The Protestant cause had gone from weakness to weakness ever since the Catholic victory in 1620 at the battle of the White Mountain in Bohemia at the beginning of the war. The Emperor Ferdinand had in Wallenstein and Tilly two superb generals against whom the Protestants had no equals, and Protestant Germany had been slowly but inexorably overrun. In France, the country which had the most to fear from the growth of Habsburg power, Richelieu did not dare to intervene openly in a religious war against the Church of which he was a cardinal. Of the Protestant powers, neither England nor Holland was prepared to get too involved, while Christian of Denmark's intervention in 1626 ended with his disastrous defeat by Wallenstein at Lutter.

All seemed lost; the Holy Roman Empire would follow Bohemia in becoming a hereditary possession of the Habsburgs, whose realm would stretch from America and Spain to Hungary and the Baltic. One could plausibly speculate that Europe was on the verge of becoming a single political unit. Germany certainly was, and it would also have been fiercely and tyrannically Catholic. One man alone, Gustavus Adolphus, changed the direction history was taking. He saved the Protestant religion and broke the Habsburg ambition of a German empire; but at the cost of thirteen fresh years of horror for Germany.

By 1628, Wallenstein had cowed the whole of northern Germany and was preparing to launch his ships on the Baltic. But when he demanded the port of Stralsund as his base, the citizens defied him. Instead, they welcomed the Danish and Swedish ships into their harbour, and

Germany during the Thirty Years' War

although it was now besieged, there remained one free Protestant city on
the German mainland. Foiled at Stralsund, Wallenstein occupied Jutland
and forced Christian of Denmark to make peace.

For the Protestants there was only one possible saviour, one hope
awaited like a Messiah. In June 1630, the Swedish army landed on Rügen,
and at its head was the king of Sweden, the Lion of the North. Above the
disembarking men and horses and guns raged a thunderstorm, and soon
the news was spreading that, as he set foot on German soil, the king of
Sweden had fallen to his knees to ask God's blessing on his just cause.

His soldiers, too, brought fresh faith to the increasing cynicism of the
war. Every man carried a hymn-book in his kit, and prayers were said
morning and evening. Discipline was strict and morale high; the
Germans were amazed to see provisions paid for and looters hanged.

Such chivalry had been forgotten amid all the barbarity of the preceding years; but, as long as their king was alive, the Swedes were a unique example to all others.

The army itself was small, about 13,000 men, divided into 16 troops of horse and 92 companies of foot with a highly professional unit of artillery-men. But this Swedish nucleus was vastly expanded by regiments of mercenaries, who were, much to their surprise, subject to the same exhilarating but unrewarding discipline.

Although the Protestant people welcomed Gustavus, their rulers, after years of defeat, were more cautious. The two Protestant electors, Brandenburg and Saxony, were reluctant to commit themselves; so Gustavus used his first months in Germany to consolidate himself in Pomerania. However, one man did commit himself. At Bärwalde, in January 1631, Gustavus signed a treaty with Richelieu's envoys; under this the king of Sweden promised to keep an army of 30,000 men and 600 horse in Germany to fight the Habsburgs at the expense of France for an annual consideration of 20,000 talers. When it came to diplomacy, the bluff soldier king had outwitted the French prelate: He had bid up Richelieu's original offer of 15,000 talers, and had forced him to publish a treaty he would rather have kept secret. Now politics had irrevocably taken over from religion in the Thirty Years War; French Catholic money was supporting the Protestants, and Gustavus, although his faith was utterly genuine, fully intended his principles to be profitable to his country.

It required a gesture to make the Protestant princes take up arms; and this gesture came tragically with the fall of Magdeburg. This wealthy city, in a strategic position commanding the Elbe, had surrendered to the imperialists; but on the news that Gustavus had landed, the citizens threw out the Habsburg garrison and declared themselves free. They were soon besieged by Tilly's army, and on 10 May, before Gustavus could reach them, the city fell by storm. The sack has become a byword for horror. The imperialists were looting ferociously to make an example, when suddenly fire broke out and, within a few hours, the city was nothing but a smouldering ruin. Of 30,000 inhabitants, only 5,000 survived, and for weeks afterwards the bridges downstream were clogged with corpses. The news shook all Europe. Within weeks, both Brandenburg and Saxony had joined the Swedish alliance. Then Gustavus and John George of Saxony led their joint armies to recapture Leipzig from Tilly. However, instead of waiting in the fortress, Pappenheim, the hot-headed general of the imperialist cavalry, provoked a battle, and on the morning of 18 September 1631 the two armies faced one another at the village of Breitenfeld.

Tilly's army of 32,000 veterans was outnumbered by the 22,000 Swedes and 17,000 Saxons; but the Saxons ran away almost at once, so that the odds turned in the imperialists' favour. On the Protestant left, the Saxons seemed ordinary enough, but the rest of the line must have been a strange sight for the veteran army. Instead of the traditional formation with the infantry in the centre and the cavalry on the wings, Gustavus had mixed them both up in small squares like the pattern on a chess-board. The result was so flexible that the enemy found himself punching a cushion where he expected to break a wall. This brilliant tactical invention won the day; but it was much helped by Gustavus' other original technique, for it was he who invented the drill for the infantry whereby the front file fired while the back files reloaded. The rapid fire of the Swedish musketry was twice the speed of anything known before, and its effect on Pappenheim's cavalry was devastating. Again and again Tilly tried to overwhelm the Swedish lines with mounting losses. At last, when the afternoon came, Gustavus, wearing his plain buff coat and plumed hat, led his reserve to the attack, splitting up the enemy cavalry from the foot. The result was a rout. Of Tilly's proud army nothing remained.

The whole of Europe resounded with the news. In Vienna the Emperor Ferdinand walked among the other penitents through the rain to beg for God's help. In Holland, staid burghers danced in the streets, and every Protestant church echoed with hymns of thanksgiving. The menace of Catholic domination was gone irrevocably. In its weakest hour, God had sent a saviour to Protestantism, and with the victory of Breitenfeld Gustavus enjoyed a prestige among ordinary men never rivalled by any of his contemporaries.

The emperor had no army in the field to oppose him, and Gustavus marched unhindered down the Rhine to Frankfurt. From all over Germany, from Holland, from Scotland, men flocked to serve beneath his standards. Soon he had almost 80,000 men under arms and was, for all practical purposes, the ruler of the whole of northern Germany. To Frankfurt he summoned Oxenstierna, who calmly undertook the enormous administrative responsibility.

In Paris, a bewildered cardinal was wondering how to regain control of his tool. Gustavus had broken Austria as the dominant power in Germany according to plan, but the plan had intended that the empty place be filled by France not Sweden. Gustavus was drastically reorganizing the conquered territory and instituting other reforms. He tried to reconcile the Lutherans with the Calvinists, and then to unite all the Protestants in a *Corpus evangelicorum*, of which Sweden would have been the senior member. It was even rumoured that Gustavus wished to be elected emperor, but this he was probably too much of a realist to consider.

There was only one man who could now save Austria, and that was Wallenstein, who had been disgraced a couple of years before. After considering surrendering Bohemia to the Swedes, Wallenstein yielded to the letter written in Ferdinand's own hand and started to raise an army.

Meanwhile, Gustavus' plan for the 1632 campaign was to attack Vienna from the west down the Danube. Donauworth was captured in a superb artillery battle by Lennart Torstensson, the gunner from Breitenfeld; then Gustavus forced the passage of the Lech, where the Finns built a bridge of boats under heavy fire, and Tilly's new army was swept aside.

At Augsburg, Gustavus danced with the prettiest girl of the town, and was given a musical box now in Uppsala university. Munich surrendered and paid a vast fine, and then the news came that Wallenstein was threatening the Protestant city of Nuremburg. Wallenstein's attempt at a diversion worked, and Gustavus, instead of pushing on to an undefended Vienna, hastened northwards. Wallenstein occupied the heights above the city with 50,000 men, while Gustavus had only 20,000. For two months the armies faced one another, and then, when Oxenstierna arrived with reinforcements, the Swedes made a determined effort to dislodge the enemy. For two days they stormed the hillside, but in vain. This was a serious defeat, and Gustavus decided to cut his losses and return to his original plan of marching on Vienna.

Wallenstein, however, turned northwards, and Gustavus was drawn back by forced marches to defend his Saxon allies. The year was old when he caught up with the enemy, and on 16 November the armies again faced one another, this time outside the village of Lützen. On the evening before the battle, the king is supposed to have sat in his tent writing a hymn that the Swedish army still sings today, 'O little band, do not despair'. It was an ominous testament.

The autumn mist was already thick over the flat fields when the Swedish army paraded before Gustavus for the prayers before battle on 16 November. There were 16,000 Swedes facing slightly fewer imperialists under Wallenstein's direct command; but, summoned by desperate couriers, Pappenheim with another 12,000 men was hastening to his commander's aid. Gustavus himself led the Protestant right wing, and soon broke the cavalry opposite him. Meanwhile, on the left, Bernhard of Saxe-Weimar was barely holding his own with the Green Brigade blinded by the smoke from the burning Lützen, which Wallenstein had set on fire; and Gustavus himself rode to his relief, although already wounded in the arm. What happened then in the smoke and the fog is a mystery. It might have been something as banal as dropping his glasses, for Gustavus was very short-sighted. At all events, just after noon, the king's horse, bleeding and riderless, was seen careering across the fields. At the same moment Pappenheim arrived and threw his men on to the Swedish right, driving them out of the positions they had captured.

From both armies men shouted that the king was dead. The enthusiastic Catholics were pressing back the Swedes, who seemed numbed with the fear that the news was true. Soon panic was spreading, till it was halted by the black-dressed figure of Fabricius, the royal chaplain, who, prayerbook in hand, summoned all around to go forward with him to find their master's body. Like a rising tide, troop after troop of grimly silent soldiers advanced on the imperialist lines, moving inexorably forward and searching each foot of ground as it was captured. On the left this fanatic charge recaptured the corpse-filled ditch, while the gallant Pappenheim, shot in the lung, was carried off to die in his coach. On the right, trying to control his desperate men, Bernard swung them round to capture the pivot of Wallenstein's position, and Wallenstein himself, raging impotently, watched his army break and flee into the night.

The same foggy night could not smother the host of torches as the Swedes searched for their king. It was Stålhanske who found him, stripped naked beneath a pile of corpses near the disputed ditch, savaged by many spiteful wounds.

They laid Gustavus in the middle of his army, but every man knew that his part was over. There had been three brief years of idealism and glory, but now the war resumed its old course. Lützen might be a victory, and Wallenstein withdraw to Prague, eventually to be murdered, but nothing could replace the loss of Gustavus.

His epitaph in English was well written by one of his own officers, Alexander Leslie, later to play a major role in the British Civil War:

> So are we to our unspeakable griefe deprived of the best and most valorouse commaunder that evir any souldiours hade, and the church of God with hir good cause of the best instrument under God, we because we were not worthy of him, and she for the sinnes of hir children.

Another anonymous Briton wrote a history of the German campaign of Gustavus Adolphus which shows how much he meant to the Protestants of Europe. *The Swedish Intelligencer* may be propaganda, but it glows with genuine faith and its hero was an inspiration to his cause.

Meanwhile, all the politics of Europe were about to change. Well might Oxenstierna pass the only sleepless night of his life when he heard the news of his king's death, with its weight of private grief and public responsibility. 'There is now no king his like in the world,' he wrote. The Swedish armies were left in Germany, tactically strong but without a strategy. At home the king was succeeded by his little daughter Christina, a girl aged only six.

It must have seemed that Sweden was finished, with all that that implied; but such a view had not taken account of the genius of Axel Oxenstierna. He carried his country through sixteen more years of war to a peace that left her the most powerful country in the North, completing on his own the work of Gustavus Adolphus. The basis of his power was the Council of Regency, planned in discussions with the king, in which, apart from Jacob de la Gardie, the marshal, and Gyllenstierna, the admiral, all the members were Oxenstiernas.

Yet it was to be four years before the regent could return home. His first task was to save the Protestant alliance from disintegration. Next spring the Protestant leaders of Germany met at Heilbronn, and there, encouraged by Richelieu's ambassador, made a treaty with Sweden known as the League of Heilbronn, which established Oxenstierna as the head of their cause. It was, however, a rescue operation, for the Protestants were shattered by the death of Gustavus and the initiative passed to the Catholics. The Protestant armies were now mainly mercenary, and the Swedes were long served by Colonel George Fleetwood's English regiment.

In 1634 came the battle of Nördlingen, which placed the Protestant cause as severely in jeopardy as it had been when Stralsund was invested. It was autumn when the Catholics army of some 33,000 men laid seige to the small Swedish garrison of Nördlingen in the Black Forest. To relieve it, the Swedish general Gustav Horn and Bernhard of Saxe-Weimar could only raise a joint army of 25,000 ill-equipped troops. Even so, they attacked, Bernhard facing the enemy to draw their fire while Horn tried to outflank them through the woods to the right. Against him the Spaniards had entrenched themselves on a steep hill; with almost insane gallantry, the exhausted Swedes attacked the stronger army again and again. Fifteen times Horn launched their narrowing ranks up the slope; only to fail. Then, as he retreated, Bernhard's gunners broke. The imperialists charged and the Protestant retreat became a rout, Horn was captured and the army annihilated.

The Spanish and Bavarian armies advanced unopposed through the Protestant territories, till, in southern Germany, only Augsburg remained free. Richelieu seized the opportunity of the Swedish defeat to try to make himself the supreme leader of the anti-Habsburg forces. Yet, surrounded by disaster, Oxenstierna coolly played for time.

When the treaty between the two allies was finally signed at Compiègnes next April, France recognized Sweden as an equal ally, while neither would make a separate peace and Sweden would be compensated for her sacrifices with German territory. Then France solemnly declared war on Spain. With that the steady metamorphosis of the Thirty Years War from a religious into a political struggle was completed. The Catholic French fought the Catholic Habsburgs for the mastery of Europe. The Swedes had landed in Germany to save the Reformation, but now their goal was an empire of the Baltic.

The situation remained serious. Augsburg fell after a long siege and the Swedish general Baner had to admit that his mercenary troops were in open mutiny. He could do nothing till his army was reinforced by fresh troops from Sweden in 1636. By then the Saxons had gone over to the Habsburgs as the more successful side; but, by a brilliant series of manoeuvres, Baner kept their armies apart and cut off the larger imperialist army at Wittstock where they had dug themselves in. Although the Swedes had marched all night, Baner attacked at once. In a daring gamble he personally led half his men in a frontal assault, while the rest of his army raced to outflank the enemy. For a long time the bait in the trap seemed doomed, but Baner's nerve held. After noon, Leslie's Scots went into action on the left, but so much stronger were the enemy that the relief was only temporary. Slowly the Swedes were driven down the hill in pockets. Only as the sun was setting did Stålhanske's guns open fire to the rear of the enemy. Attacked on three sides, the enemy fled, leaving the exhausted Swedes to sleep on the battlefield.

The war continued its desultory and destructive course, for neither side was strong enough to win. In 1641, Baner died and Oxenstierna appointed Lennart Torstensson, the gunner, to be commander-in-chief.

Torstensson is one of the great personalities of the war. Tough, obstinate, unwaveringly loyal, he restored the army's morale by sheer willpower and led it to a series of victories worthy of Gustavus himself. His mercenaries, devils who feared neither God nor man, soon went in terror of him. Discipline was savage, and the enemy was treated ruthlessly. The Finns, for instance, were famous for cutting the ears off every Catholic priest they caught. Torstensson was crippled with gout and, when he could not ride, had to be carried about the battlefield in a litter.

In 1642 he brushed aside the Saxons at Schweidnitz, and marched due south on Vienna. He was within twenty-five miles of the imperial capital before the Austrians could put an army against him, and in face of their stronger forces he withdrew.

At Breitenfeld, Torstensson halted. One feels that any imperialist should have been reluctant to fight on that particular site which had witnessed Gustavus Adolphus' brilliant victory eleven years before, but they came rashly on. At dawn, Torstensson's right wing charged the imperialists through a murderous cannonade, and swinging inward rolled up their larger army till it was surrendered. The archduke lost half his troops and only just escaped himself.

Meanwhile, Christian of Denmark was moving towards joining the Habsburg side, providing another example of how the war had lost its religious character. He had been intriguing with the Swedish queen mother against Oxenstierna; and then he struck a severe blow at Sweden's trade by raising the tolls on the Sound.

It was September 1644 before Oxenstierna's orders reached Torstensson. He at once marched northwards into the winter, and by January had occupied the whole of Jutland to the helpless amazement of the Danes. The army which the emperor sent to attack Torstensson in the rear was promptly overwhelmed and destroyed at Aschersleben.

At the Peace of Brömsebro next year the Danes had no choice but to surrender the islands of Gotland and Ösel, from which they had dominated the Baltic, and, on the Scandinavian peninsula, the provinces of Jämtland, Härjedalen and Halland. Hereby Sweden finally and conclusively replaced Denmark as the dominant power of the North, and Denmark's hold on the Baltic, which had lasted since the Middle Ages, was broken.

Meanwhile the various belligerent powers had at long last got round to a peace conference, which met at Münster. It was, however, exceptionally dilatory and took four years to reach a conclusion; and all this time the agony of Germany continued. Torstensson had eventually got himself recalled for ill-health, and was replaced by the admiral, Karl Gustav Wrangel. Wrangel was another of Gustavus' extremely able officers, and he managed by his skill to keep for Sweden an equal authority with France, to which her resources did not entitle her. He and the French marshal Turenne together conquered Bavaria. Another Swedish army under Königsmark invaded Bohemia and attacked Prague; they soon captured the castle and the city west of the Moldau. The Swedes were trying to storm the Charles Bridge against the citizens' heroic resistance when the news of peace arrived; and so the Thirty Years War ended in the city where it began.

The Peace of Westphalia confirmed Sweden as the foremost Protestant power and the military leader of northern Europe. Yet, measured in concrete terms of land and wealth, the reward was not really up to her efforts; she received, as fiefs of the empire, Western Pomerania, the port of Wismar and the bishoprics of Bremen and Verden, which meant strategic control of the three great trade rivers of north Germany. To all intents and purposes, the ambition to make the Baltic a Swedish lake had been realized. Yet the supreme importance of the Thirty Years War to Sweden lies elsewhere. At its beginning, Sweden had been an insignificant country on the fringes of Europe; by its end, she had become the arbiter of the Holy Roman Empire and the first military power of the continent. To the Swedes themselves, it was their first experience of the outside world, even for many of the officers. Their eyes were opened to the culture of the rest of Europe, and the soldiers who returned brought with them a cosmopolitan breath of the wide world. It seems to us a contradiction that war might have a civilizing influence; but, from the sacked cities of Germany, a stream of treasure poured home to Sweden: furniture, pictures, jewellery, whole libraries and collections. Every Swedish home surviving from that period contains such plunder. Imperial power also brought with it a host of foreigners who settled in Sweden, and these were by no means just soldiers of fortune, but industrialists, bankers and artists, who continued the process of education.

Indeed, Sweden even joined the colonial powers for a short while. In 1638, a settlement called New Sweden was founded at the mouth of the Delaware river, based on Fort Christina, where Wilmington is today. However, the Dutch captured the colony in 1655, and they, in turn, lost it to the English. Louis de Geer's African Company also kept a slave-trading fort on the coast of Guinea.

The outstanding personality of these years of peace and education was the young queen Christina. She would undoubtedly have been a remarkable woman in any age and whatever her rank. Given the prestige of the daughter of Gustavus Adolphus and the might of her empire, she established herself for a short while as the intellectual arbiter of Europe. She was also a very odd character.

Gustavus had naturally hoped for a son. He left instructions for Christina to be brought up as a boy, and her earliest memories were of soldiers and cannon firing salutes, which she loved. When the king was killed, her mother, who was a silly woman at the best of times, broke down completely. She locked herself in her suite, which she had entirely decorated in black, and gave herself up to hysterical mourning. Her wretched child was forced to share this seclusion, as well as all her fads, which included being forbidden to drink anything.

The moment Oxenstierna returned he put a stop to this nonsense.

Instead, he started to give Christina a comprehensive education, which included riding, shooting, German, French, Latin, Spanish, Italian, Greek, mathematics and other useful subjects. Fortunately Christina was highly intelligent. In statecraft, she had the best teacher in Europe, Oxenstierna himself, although she forgot his sad warning, 'If only you knew with what little wisdom the world is governed.' Her teachers were all delighted with her brilliance; but the only human kindness she knew came from her father's sister Catherine, who was living in exile in Sweden.

The result was bound to have its eccentric aspects. Christina had become queen at the age of six; all her life she regarded herself as belonging to a different order of humanity, and this was reinforced by her being intellectually head and shoulders above any of her companions. The only person she was afraid of was Oxenstierna; whenever he came for an audience, she would rush around shrieking with rage while the old man calmly waited outside the door. Emotionally, too, she was extremely potent. This virile tomboy had a passionate schoolgirl crush on her playmate, the gentle Ebba Sparre, and this lesbian streak was to recur later in her life. She then had a stormy liaison with Magnus Gabriel de la Gardie, son of her father's old flame, Ebba Brahe, and the gilded youth of his day. She forced Oxenstierna to make him ambassador to France, and at his wedding to her own cousin, Maria Eufrosyne, told the bride, 'I give you him whom I may not have myself.' Then her attentions moved to her male cousin, Karl Gustav. He was absolutely infatuated with her, but she obstinately refused to marry him.

Christina regarded her throne as a stage for her personality. Hence she had few political objectives. She wanted peace because war absorbed too much money she could spend otherwise, and she wanted to be independent of Oxenstierna. On her father's death, power had gone to the council, dominated by the great chancellor and representative of the old families of the high nobility; against them was the royalist party, centred round her German uncle and supported by many of the newer nobles like the de la Gardies. At the negotiations at Westphalia, she forced the ambassador, Oxenstierna's son, to be accompanied by the low-born but very able Salvius, each with a practically independent policy.

Christina treated her kingdom as her private estate; her extravagance was astronomical. At the beginning of her reign the court expenses absorbed 3 per cent of the royal revenue, by the end they absorbed 20 per cent. The country was progressively impoverished, and towards the end there were open riots. She was equally lavish with titles, and the old Swedish aristocracy was swamped by her new creations and by the soldiers of fortune from the war.

In other ways she used her money well. Her collections were a wonder of the age, for she had those two often separated qualities: taste and wealth. Her generals had orders as to which works of art to loot for her in Germany. Her favourite painter was Raphael, and she also owned several Titians. Later Bernini was to make her an annual present of a drawing.

Unhappily, she took almost her entire collection with her when she left the country. Of the little left in the country is the superb series of Cranachs in the National Museum, originally looted from Munich. Her library, too, was exceptional; its pride was the *Codex argenteus,* the first written work in a Germanic language, a translation of the Gospels made for Theodoric the Great at Ravenna in the sixth century and written with silver on purple parchment. It then disappeared to Holland, when Magnus de la Gardie bought it back and gave it to Uppsala University, where it is now. Also left in Sweden is the magnificent silver throne made for her coronation, and it is still used today by the king when he opens the *Riksdag.*

At the court there was a remarkable gathering of intellectuals. Chanut, the French ambassador, helped Christina in her interests, and it was he who persuaded Descartes to make the long journey to Stockholm. The breadth of the young queen's knowledge impressed the old philosopher profoundly, but the relationship came to a sadly abrupt end when Descartes died of pneumonia during his first Swedish winter. She corresponded with Pascal, who dedicated his calculating machine to her, with the flattering words, 'Régnez donc, incomparable princesse, d'une manière tout nouvelle, que votre génie vous assujettisse tout ce qui n'est pas soumis á vos armes. Pour moi, n'étant pas né sous le premier de vos empires, je veux que tout le monde sache que je fais gloire de vivre sous le second.'

Another of her close friends was Cromwell's ambassador, Bulstrode Whitelock, and this urbane Puritan was captivated by her ability. There were many other considerably less desirable acquaintances, the inevitable con-men attracted by her generosity, like her doctor, Bourdelot, who dominated his patient.

Christina was bound to be fascinated by religion, but as an intellectual problem, certainly not as a revelation. Equally, she soon found the metaphysics of Catholicism more interesting than the dour Protestantism of her countrymen. Discreetly she made known her wish to be instructed in the Catholic faith. The pope secretly sent to her two professors, one of theology and subtly one of mathematics, Malines and Cassati, disguised as diplomats. Under their teaching, Christina resolved to change her faith.

The daughter of the saviour of Protestantism thus sought to renounce his creed. Such dramatic news needed preparation. Obviously Christina could not retain her throne. She had already succeeded in forcing the acceptance of Karl Gustav as her heir. Then, in 1654, she announced her abdication. It was an emotional moment. The establishment, exasperated by her bad government, was not sorry to see her go; but to others it seemed a tragic loss. The marshal, Brahe, refused to take the crown from her head, but Christina removed it herself for her cousin. That night she left the country secretly.

Although she had abandoned her throne, Christina still expected to be treated as a queen. She made a triumphal progress through Europe, entering Spanish Brussels amid wild merrymaking, until she reached Innsbruck. There Christina of Sweden was officially received into the Roman Catholic Church with pomp and ceremony, and the whole Catholic world rejoiced at the conversion of its greatest enemy. Yet there were already doubts about her sincerity, and she is supposed to have remarked on seeing the plays laid on that evening, 'It is right the cardinals should entertain me to a comedy, since I have just entertained them to a farce.' At Rome, where she intended to settle, she scandalized the pope by wearing the scarlet of the courtesans for her first meeting with the Holy Father.

Christina was lodged in the Farnese Palace, where she seems to have lived a life of utter hedonism, admittedly on a high intellectual level, exploring antiquities in the afternoon and giving debauched parties in the evenings. Her extravagance was notorious; she had already forced the Swedish exchequer to grant her an allowance which the country could ill afford. In Rome, she spent her income on a series of disreputable lovers and dishonest servants, as well as on artists and musicians.

Christina then took herself to France, where, after making a sensational first impression, she outstayed her welcome by trying to dabble in Mazarin's politics. When Louis XIII had tactfully dismissed her to Fontainebleau, she caused a scandal by having one of her servants, Monaldeschi, who had forged some letters, stabbed to death in front of her. When the assassins complained that the victim was wearing mail, Christina coolly told them to slit his throat. Unwelcome in France, she made a couple of abortive attempts to return to Sweden, where her reputation had been irrevocably ruined; and then settled in Rome, where the embarrassed pope sent a brilliant and well-born cardinal, Azzolino, to take charge of his errant daughter. She proceeded to amuse herself by intriguing for the throne of Naples.

There at last Christina mellowed, devoted to society, alchemy and archaeology, and the writing of rather pretentious aphorisms. She was undoubtedly a remarkably talented woman who dazzled her contemporaries by her wit and eccentricity, but she also shocked the urbane southerners by her coarseness. Against these talents there have to be set her utter irresponsibility and her self-indulgence, which cancel them out. Her reputation has been given some lustre by the early feminists, who saw in her disregard for convention and her love of male dress one of the heroines of their cause. One must admire her unusual policy of maintaining peace in an age that loved war. On the other hand, her personal extravagance brought her country to the verge of bankruptcy and impoverished it for a generation – a price out of proportion to the cultural benefits of her reign.

Christina was not alone in her wish to civilize the rough Swedish aristocracy. Even as busy a man as Axel Oxenstierna had wide intellectual interests, and Magnus Gabriel de la Gardie was a gifted dilettante. While the tone was set by the court regrettably little remains, for most of the objects of royal patronage were either removed by Christina when she

Queen Christina, by C. W. Heimbach, 1667

abdicated or else were destroyed in the disastrous fire at Stockholm's palace.

The great nobles were fit patrons of the arts. Most built for themselves magnificent houses in Stockholm, where they resided in preference to their country estates so as to be close to the court. At the south end of the royal palace, opposite the half-moon forecourt, stands the Oxenstierna palace. Unfortunately, only one wing is complete, but the dignified façade, carried on a heavily rusticated ground floor and decorated with classical windows against the terracotta stucco, would not have been out of place in Michelangelo's Rome. The splendid palace which the political theorist Count Rosenhane built for himself on the Riddarholm is now aptly occupied by the Swedish Ministry of Finance; and the Foreign Office now resides in Lennart Torstensson's palace opposite the Opera. It is now renamed after the heir-apparent, but if, after facing its elegant

Palladian façade, you walk down the narrow street on the north side, the tough old general's home is as found as he left it. The rendered façade is absolutely plain, and in the centre is the most magnificent, massive Baroque portal. The carving is done by a German, Diederich Blume, and shows Torstensson's and his wife's arms supported by two lions and surrounded by cannon, drums and the full panoply of war. The most famous such palace was built by Jacob de la Gardie, governor of the Baltic provinces under Gustavus Adolphus, but no trace of it remains. It was called Makalös or Nonsuch, and old prints show an ornate building with turrets and gables in the style of the late Renaissance in southern Germany.

One of the most beautiful buildings in Stockholm is, without doubt, the Riddarhuset or House of Lords. It lies on the waterfront beyond a formal garden, and is splendidly colourful, for the white pilasters of the Palladian façade are set against the red brick and carry a heavy, curved green roof. It was begun by Simon de la Vallée, who was then killed in a duel by Colonel Erik Oxenstierna. The exterior, which has the most lovely proportions, is the work of a Dutchman, Justus Vingboons, but its grandeur is patrician rather than Dutch. The broken roof is typically Swedish and was designed by Simon's son Jean, who crowned it with giant allegorical figures. Above the porch, Minerva and Mars flank a medallion proudly inscribed 'Arte et Marte'.

It was a wealthy age, and the burghers of Stockholm did quite as much to honour their town. Seventeenth-century Stockholm must have been very like Amsterdam, and even today the Old Town on the island is a uniquely preserved city of that age. The narrow streets, often too small for motor-cars, are deep gullies between the tall houses with their peeling stucco. The merchants who built them combined shop, home and warehouse all in one. In those dark lanes, façades would have been invisible, so instead they spent their wealth on the doorways; everywhere you go, there are lavishly decorated Baroque or Mannerist portals, with pilasters and volutes exaggerated by the northern imagination. The best known is the double porch of the Petersenska House on Munkbron, but a stroller will discover many more. After a century of being a slum, the Old Town is now going the way of Chelsea in London. Many of the houses have been lavishly restored, but it seems impossible to destroy its charm, and the pastel washes on the rendering brighten up the old streets and pick out details of the architecture which had become hidden beneath centuries of dirt. Even though the antique shops are opening up in the dark vaults on the ground floor, there are other courtyards where dingy pubs are hidden away full of bricklayers or sailors from the ships that even today anchor at the shore a hundred yards away. The next lane may have a tobacconist selling hard-core pornography, photographed with typically Swedish efficiency and attention to detail. The charm of the old town is this boisterous aliveness, born in the days when it was the capital of an empire.

Out in the country, many of the nobles rebuilt their homes with the loot from the Thirty Years War. At Läckö in West Gothland, the work of the de la Gardies has fortunately survived, although the building's great interiors were criminally stripped of all their furnishings and fittings in the last century. The castle stands on a promontory jutting into lake Vänern. Its light-grey walls and towers are reflected in the water against a background of dark-green forest; inside, the sense of desolation is even stronger, in spite of the praiseworthy efforts of the custodians, for these magnificent halls are as empty as an old grave. The rebuilding was begun by the general Jacob de la Gardie, but most of the work belongs to his son Magnus Gabriel. He made it into a fit palace for the regent of Sweden. The façades are plain, broken only by the asymmetrical towers and the imposing portals. Inside there are two main courts, the greater having a grand Italian arcade, open to the weather. The chapel in the big tower is provincial Baroque with its pulpit and altar. The altar used to have famous silver panels which general Jacob came by in Russia. On each side of the windows are niches containing the twelve apostles, carved by Johan Werner, displaying realistic faces and theatrical gestures.

Everywhere there are the most splendid stone fireplaces. In the guard-room are the giant portraits of Gothic heroes from the fictitious history of the time. The great hall is in the west wing, complete with an elegant musicians' gallery. Its panelled walls were originally filled with paintings of Swedish victories; but now there only remain the sieges of Wohlgast and Frankfurt-an-der-Oder, and the capture of Munich. The rest of these lively battle scenes with the named portraits of field-marshals and generals have gone to Karlberg, the Swedish Sandhurst, to inspire a more pacific generation. Karlberg is itself another of de la Gardie's palaces. It has a beautiful position on lake Mälaren, its long white façade stretching out on the shore. The architect was Jean de la Vallée, and one recognizes his lush Baroque style, with the massive swags and arched roofs. The central pediment and pillars seem to be hacked out of the stucco like brutal sculpture. Inside is an enormous stateroom, well suited to passing-out balls.

Among his other intellectual interests, Magnus de la Gardie loved history. He continued Johan III's restoration of Varnhem church, and built his own funeral chapel to the south; there are the life-size lead statues of his father Jacob as a Roman general, and of Magnus himself as a senator, surrounded by their banners and coats of arms.

More surprising is the fact that so busy a man as Field-Marshal Karl Gustav Wrangel had time to build himself such a palace; but Skokloster, not far from Stockholm, is a worthy rival of Läckö. The Wrangels came from Estonia; but were soon assimilated into the Swedish empire. Karl Gustav, after a glorious military career, ended as a Swedish count. The architect to Skokloster was Jean de la Vallée, but Wrangel himself took a personal interest in the designs. Here, too, the plain but beautifully proportioned white façade looks out over the waters of lake Mälaren, and it was originally surrounded by a vast formal garden. The palace is exactly square, with a central courtyard. The entrance is a vast hall the width of the building, carried on four pairs of columns in Italian marble. On the main floor the long gallery displays the portraits of twenty of Wrangel's senior officers, in an atmosphere of universal hero-worship. Every room has magnificent fireplaces; in the dining-room there is even a *trompe-l'oeil* painting instead of the grate; beside each of them is a typical Swedish tiled stove that would burn through the whole winter night. The stucco ceilings, by a German, Hans Zauch, are superb; one shows the four continents (no Australia, of course) in droll allegories. In Wrangel's own bedroom, the ceiling is covered with sabres and muskets; perhaps the silence of the forest kept the old soldier awake. The charm of Skokloster lies in the fact that the family have kept all the fine old furniture, so that one can visit a complete seventeenth-century home. It also houses an enormous collection of contemporary weapons, spoils of Wrangel's campaigns or an armoury for his regiment.

On the shore of lake Mälären Axel Oxenstierna built himself a country seat at Tidö, which is one of the best preserved of houses from the period. The style is a splendid Dutch baroque. In the courtyard a double flight of steps leads to the great porch. The interiors are remarkable for the quality of the panelling and the amazingly detailed inlay. With its chapel and galleries it was a fit home for the man who was ruling half Europe.

Skokloster

121

In the other arts also the victorious warriors brought back the Baroque from the south. Except for the extravagantly decorated south porch of Stockholm's St James's Church by Heinrich Blume, practically none of the work was ecclesiastical. The funeral monuments are concerned with glorifying man and have little reference to God. In the Great Church in Stockholm, another German, Heinrich Wilhelm, carved the impressive statue of Hope above the grave of Salvius, the upstart scholar whom Christina ennobled and made a member of the council. At Uppsala cathedral, Gustav Baner's tomb with its flight of sorrowing angels was carved by a Dutchman, Claezon. One of the finest such works is in Västerås cathedral, where Magnus Brahe and his wife lie in alabaster on a black marble tomb, prepared for eternity by Jost Henne. At Skokloster chapel, General Hermann Wrangel, Karl Gustav's father, not only lies upon his tomb but also rides forth from the stucco landscape of the wall as a soldier leading his men.

The only paintings that are left from the period, as befits an age of individuals, are portraits or else a few battle scenes. There are two really good collections to visit, at Gripsholm and at Skokloster. The first court painter was a Dutchman, David Beck; his work varies in quality, but at its best shows much of Rembrandt's influence. His portrait of Axel Oxenstierna, privately owned, is outstanding. Against a dark background, the great chancellor is painted in a plain black suit: nothing reveals his rank and power except the face, caught in a Rembrandesque light with its strong, straight mouth and penetrating eyes. Beck's portrait of General Gustav Horn at Gripsholm shows another type of man: the tough simple soldier. He also painted of Queen Christina, a portrait now in the National Museum, when she was twenty-four. The pose is allegorical, but the face is realistic enough, at once intelligent and arrogant. The deep colours of the dress and the veil blowing in the wind are reminders that Beck had studied with van Dyck.

Christina's favourite artist was the Frenchman, Sebastian Bourdon. One of his portraits of her is in the National Museum; but undoubtedly the most famous is in the Prado at Madrid; it shows Christina on a prancing horse, dressed in strange male clothes, attended by a page with dogs and a falcon. As an expression of the queen's personality, it is superb, catching her defiance of convention, her courage and manliness. Ehrenstrahl painted the poet, Georg Stiernhielm, blending, in a dignified pose, the humanist, civil servant and scientist. Stiernhielm's great work was an epic *Hercules,* the paragon of all the ideals of an heroic age. Although he wrote in hexameters, his language is fresh and natural, not, as one might fear, heavy with Latin words. His subject is derivative, but the words are his own, and justify his being called the 'Father of Swedish Poetry'. He was a scholar, too, and as such was one of the few Swedes to shine at court.

It was an uphill struggle for Christina to civilize her countrymen. Stockholm had never seen an opera till she summoned an Italian troup in 1652. Natives as gifted as Stiernhielm were few, and most of the court were foreign, a fact which must have influenced her abdication. Regret-tably most of her expenditure was on those intangibles which the age loved, such as masques and pageants which leave only a few engravings behind. Christina's achievement is proved more simply by the fact that, after her reign, Sweden's cultural life never again fell into abeyance.

8. The Caroleans

Karl X was very different from his intellectual cousin Christina; it is just as well she refused to marry him. He was by profession, a soldier, and by nature an adventurer, but also an extremely able and ambitious man.

He inherited from Christina a financial chaos. Luckily, he was an excellent administrator, and within the first year of his reign he had forced a reduction through the *Riksdag* whereby a quarter of all crown land recently acquired by the nobles was returned. Another way of keeping Sweden's large unemployed army quiet was to enter into a fight.

In 1655, Karl invaded Poland enthusiastically. Politically, there was considerable logic to making the Baltic a Swedish lake and regaining the tolls from the Prussian ports; and anyway, it was a consolation for the king who had been just too young to enjoy the Thirty Years War. Of fighting he certainly soon had his fair share. The war was a series of marches and counter-marches, during which he captured Cracow once and Warsaw twice. The second time was in a battle against heavy odds which lasted for three whole days. However, Poland was far too big a country to occupy, and the threat to the balance of power was attracting her allies.

All was not going well, and in the summer of 1657 Frederik III of Denmark declared war. Karl was delighted at the excuse to disentangle himself from Poland, and with his talent for doing the totally unexpected, marched his entire army along the shore of the Baltic and into Jutland. There he trapped the surprised Danish troops in the fortress of Frederiksodde, which was stormed by Field-Marshal Wrangel at the end of October. Then winter set in, leaving the Swedish king with his army trapped in a foreign country.

Now follows one of the greatest technical feats in military history, the equivalent of Hannibal's crossing of the Alps. The winter of 1657/8 was savagely cold, and between the Danish islands the sea began to freeze. A young engineering officer called Erik Dahlberg rode over to the island of Fyn to reconnoitre, and his report was promising. On 30 January the whole army marched out on to the ice to cross the Little Belt; the men could feel how the ice bent beneath the weight of the guns, and soon they were marching knee-deep in slush over the solid ice. The king's sledge was lost through a crack minutes after he had left it, and in another place the ice broke to swallow up two squadrons of cavalry. The rest of the army crossed safely, and Fyn was occupied. Yet the more serious obstacle of the Great Belt remained. Fortunately, the cold grew worse. The French ambassador, who accompanied the campaign, thought it was horrible: bread had to be cut with an axe and the wine froze in the barrels. Dahlberg's reconnaissances were again favourable, and a week later the army crossed more than ten miles of ice to Laaland, where the fortress of Nakskov surrendered from shock. The way to Zealand and Copenhagen was open. 'Now, brother Frederik, we shall talk in plain Swedish,' said Karl with satisfaction. There were no troops to defend Copenhagen, and the Danish envoys, offering peace, ran into Karl himself reconnoitering as near as Køge.

The Peace of Roskilde which followed is the greatest disaster of Danish history; it irrevocably broke Denmark as a great power. The terms were harsh, but the whole country lay at Karl's mercy. Denmark had to surrender her richest province Skåne, Blekinge and Bornholm, while Norway lost Bohuslän and Trondhjem. Sweden itself had at last gained an ocean frontier and in doing so had broken the Danish control of the mouth of the Baltic; more lasting a benefit, the rich cornfields of Skåne meant that famine was no longer an annual threat up in the North. With this peace the Swedish Empire reached its widest territorial extent.

However the adventurer in Karl was not satisfied. Soon he regretted the mere survival of his enemy, and began to negotiate with Oliver Cromwell to partition her, England getting Jutland and Sweden getting Norway and the islands. Unpredictable as ever Karl suddenly invaded Zealand again that summer, determined as he said not to do madness by halves, and laid seige to Copenhagen. Denmark rallied in her darkest hour. 'I shall die in my nest,' was Frederik's message to his citizens; and himself he led the epic defence of Copenhagen. There were few soldiers in the city, but bands of apprentices and students held the redoubts against the famous Swedish infantry, and even beat off a general storm. Meanwhile the diplomats were active. The prospect of a united Scandinavia under Sweden would unbalance the balance of power in no uncertain terms; and soon England, Holland and France were all bringing pressure to bear. In the midst of everything Karl X died, of pneumonia.

With a regency in Sweden there was an outbreak of peace in Northern Europe. A series of treaties ended the hostilities, leaving Sweden with all her gains except Trondhjem and Bornholm.

Karl X had married Hedvig Elenora of Holstein-Gottorp; it was a political marriage, designed to encircle Denmark from the South. There was only one child, a boy called Karl, who was four years old when his father died; so once again at a crucial stage in her history, Sweden was in the hands of a regency, nor was there a man of Axel Oxenstierna's stature to take command.

The old nobility saw the regency as a marvellous opportunity to regain power. Its head as Chancellor was Magnus de la Gardie, Christina's old favourite, a charming and civilised man but a bad statesman and a worse soldier. The Council sacked from the regency Karl X's brother Adolf Fredrik and Herman Fleming who had organised the reduction; instead all the other regents and their friends had their hands in the till collecting

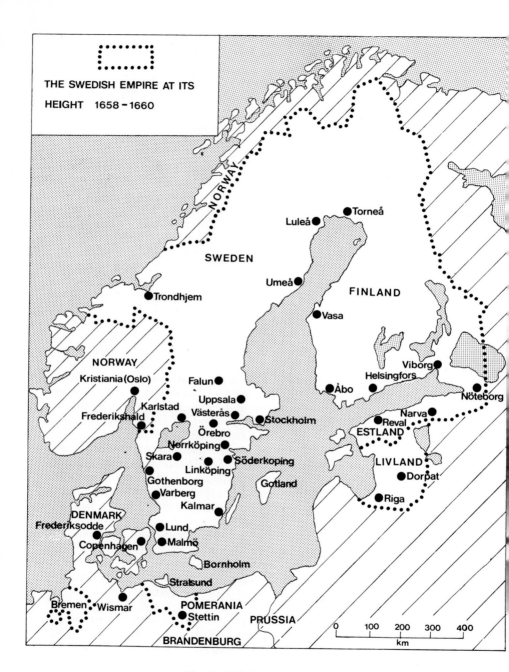

NORWAY

Torneå

Luleå

SWEDEN

Trondhjem

Umeå

FINLAND

Vasa

NORWAY

Kristiania (Oslo)

Falun

Viborg

Helsingfors

Karlstad

Uppsala

Åbo

Nöteborg

Frederikshald

Västerås

Stockholm

Narva

Örebro

Reval

ESTLAND

Norrköping

Skara

Söderkoping

LIVLAND

Linköping

Dorpat

Gothenborg

Gotland

Varberg

Kalmar

Riga

DENMARK

Frederiksodde

Lund

Copenhagen

Malmö

Bornholm

Stralsund

POMERANIA

Bremen   Wismar

Stettin

PRUSSIA

BRANDENBURG

0   100   200   300   400

km

The Swedish Empire at its height

estates and pensions. The Treasurer Count Gustav Bonde tried in vain to economise. One of his measures was nationalising Palmstruch's Bank in Stockholm, and thus creating the first central bank in Europe. He did not get on with de la Gardie; and it is significant that his successor, Nils Bielke, who even recommended another reduction, was even less popular.

Abroad, Sweden had many enemies, all waiting to have a nibble at her empire, and de la Gardie's foreign policy was aimed at keeping peace. Fears for the balance of power drew him into the Triple Alliance of 1668 with England and Holland to resist the ambitions of Louis XIV. However, it was not difficult for that autocrat to detach de la Gardie, who had always been a Francophile, from his shop-keeping allies. When Louis attacked Holland six years later, Sweden had returned to her traditional role of joining France to encircle Germany.

Meanwhile, the young Karl XI was growing up. It was a rather neglected and unhappy childhood; his mother, Queen Hedvig Elenora, was more interested in playing cards than anything else, his tutors were easy-going and their work was not encouraged by the king's word-blindness; all through his life, his handwriting and spelling remained atrocious. The only aspect of his education that left a permanent mark was the contemporary brand of god-fearing Protestantism. Fortunately, Karl was an out-door boy. The Palace Museum still displays his toy cannons, and he grew up to love hunting and the life of the camp, although he lacked his own son's passion for actual fighting.

The same year that he came of age, Sweden signed a military alliance with France, and soon she was drawn into the Dutch war by a hard-pressed Louis XIV. In spite of the French subsidies, the Swedish army was disgracefully ill-equipped. Wrangel, who was now governor of Pomerania, was forced to invade Brandenburg in 1675, and there, at Fehrbellin, he was defeated by a smaller Prussian army. Although the battle was a mere skirmish, its psychological effect was enormous, for the legend of Swedish invincibility, built up during the Thirty Years War, was broken; and all her enemies plucked up their courage to attack. At once the unsound basis of the Swedish empire became obvious, and with it the criminal incompetencè of the regency that had done nothing to make it more secure. A joint fleet, the Danes commanded by Admiral Juel and the Dutch by Van Tromp, entered the Baltic and sent the best part of the Swedish navy to the bottom off the southern point of Öland in 1676; and so Pomerania was cut off, and slowly mopped up by the Prussians, while the Danes invaded Skåne and the Norwegians chased de la Gardie in West Gothland.

Fortune's wheel had turned so far that now it was Sweden that was threatened with annihilation. The country was saved not by its elder statesmen but by the courage and energy of its young king, whom the world had regarded as a stupid nonentity. Realizing that he could not hope to win a war of attrition, Karl decided to stake everything on one battle, and marched with all the troops he could raise down to Skåne. It was October, and the Danes had reasonably assumed that the fighting season was over. Instead, they were visiting their cousins in the re-captured province. Karl's army was ravaged with plague, and the winter campaign taxed even such able staff officers as Erik Dahlberg and Gyllenstierna. On 3 December, however, he attacked the Danish lines outside Lund across a frozen river. Karl himself led the right wing, fighting with desperate courage, for as he told his officers, if this battle were to be lost he did not wish to survive it. The Danes before him broke and fled, but the rest of their army had surrounded the Swedish centre and left wing. It was only in the eleventh hour that Karl found a gap in the enemy lines and broke through to relieve them. Under the shock of his attack, the rest of the Danish army fled to leave the Swedes with the field.

Next year, Karl completed his campaign to drive the Danes out of Skåne. The enemy armies left behind them a flourishing resistance movement, drawing its strength from the wild and deserted forests along the northern borders of Skåne and Blekinge. These guerrillas were called *Snapphanar*. Peasants and woodmen carried on their struggle against the invader long after the Danish armies were withdrawn, and later romantics have woven round them stories worthy of the outlaws of Sherwood. Across the sea, after a gallant defence by Königsmarck, Stralsund, the last Swedish fortress in Germany, was captured.

Further south, the war had gone unexpectedly well for France. Turenne's and Condé's victories soon enabled Louis XIV to dictate peace at Nijmegen to his enemies, not only on his own behalf but also on behalf of his less lucky ally, Sweden. The Scanian War was ended by the Treaty of Fontainebleau, signed in 1679, under which Sweden's reconquest of Skåne was confirmed, and almost all her lost German provinces were returned to her.

Karl XI had had to fight for his inheritance, and having won it, he devoted his life to making it strong and secure. This is therefore perhaps an appropriate time to look at the Swedish empire at its height. It had not quite achieved its goal of making the Baltic a Swedish lake; for between Pomerania and Livonia, both Prussia and Poland had corridors to the sea. The precious naval supplies of timber and tar were, however, a Swedish monopoly, as were the enormous wheat harvests of Livonia. The merchants of Stettin, Wismar, Riga, Narva, Åbo, Stockholm and Malmö all sailed beneath one flag. Administratively, the empire had two parts. First, there was Sweden proper, which included Finland and the Baltic Provinces, all of which was governed from Stockholm and fully inte-grated with the original country. All the cities of this area sent their representatives to the *Riksdag* as equal members, and the Finnish, Estonian and Latvian nobles enjoyed the same rights as their colleagues across the sea. These were prosperous years for the Baltic States, and the Swedish rule there is fondly remembered. There is in Latvia, unless it has been cut down by a superstitious commissar, an oak-tree of which the legend is that it will not fall before Swedish rule returns. As a result of the great expansion of the Russian empire, particularly during the present

128

century, it is very difficult for most Europeans to realize that Riga and Dorpat were once cities as Western and as civilized as Oslo or Stockholm; nor are their inhabitants Russians, since their languages were German, Finnish or Swedish. The second part of the Swedish empire was its German provinces. These were never absorbed in the same way, but were left with their own constitutions beneath a Swedish governor; for their cities were rich ports which paid their taxes direct to Stockholm.

His martial successes had given the shy Karl XI some much-needed self-confidence. His first priority was to call the regency to account for the condition of his inheritance. Already prejudiced against the great nobles by his upstart friends, like the Wachtmeisters, Karl did not have to seek far for examples of their incompetence. Once peace was agreed, the inquisition of the regency began. One of the new nobles sneaked to the king a remark of de la Gardie's about him: 'We must get that young lout abroad, for damn me he does no good at home' – a comment that rings true from an arrogant intellectual on the subject of a boorish youth. The inquisition was, however, bloodless. Karl was a practical, not a cruel man; he simply made the regents responsible for all financial losses the country had incurred. These crippling fines reduced even de la Gardie to comparative poverty, and helped to fill a very empty exchequer.

Karl also resurrected his father's policy of reduction. The return of royal land alienated over the years was a slow process; but, by the end of his reign, perhaps 30 per cent of the country had been given back to the crown. The reduction caused most bad blood in Livonia, where the estates were either recent gifts to soldiers or else dated from before the Swedish rule, and many of the Latvian nobles were reluctant to see their peasants given the same rights as in Sweden. The opposition was led by Johan Patkul, one of the old German junkers; eventually he was charged with treason and fled into exile to devote the rest of his life to weaving plots for Latvian independence.

In Skåne, the problem was another one, for here was an unwilling province to be absorbed into the nation. At first Karl was so incensed by the *Snapphanar* fighting that he proposed to ship the entire population across the Baltic. Fortunately, his governor of Skåne, the soldier Rutger von Ascheberg, dissuaded him from a policy of terror; instead, he succeeded in separating the *Snapphanar* from the civilian population till they were reduced to the level of bandits. Ascheberg ruled his province by conciliation. In 1668, Sweden got its second university with the foundation of Lund, so that the students of Skåne, forbidden to go to Copenhagen, did not need to make the long journey to Uppsala. The first task was to change the language. Fortunately, Swedish and Danish are very alike, and it was comparatively easy to hold church services in Swedish and to oblige all schools to teach in Swedish. Even today, the people of Skåne speak with a heavy accent that is quite individual. Thanks to Ascheberg's humanity, Skåne provides the most remarkable example of the assimilation of a conquered province, and the Danish traditions were forgotten completely within a century.

As part of the reconciliation with Denmark, Karl XI married a Danish princess, Ulrika Eleonora. The wooing was complicated, and Count Brahe in Copenhagen even had to buy her engagement present, which Karl was too mean to pay for; and, in Stockholm, the queen mother, Hedvig Eleonora, continued to take precedence over her daughter-in-law. However, the marriage turned into a love match, for Ulrika Eleonora was simple, kind and universally popular. She bore her husband three children who survived: the future hero Karl XII, and his sisters Hedvig Sofia and Ulrika Eleonora. When she died, only thirty-six years old, the whole country mourned her.

These years of peace were also, thanks to Karl's economies, years of comparative prosperity. There were major artists in every field working in Sweden, but architecture was particularly favoured, and it produced one masterpiece of world rank.

If you take the boat from Stockholm to Drottningholm, it sails for about two hours through a typical northern landscape: along every shore there stretches the dark green line of unbroken forests of fir and pine, and everywhere on the lake are little islands of bare, polished granite; then suddenly, beyond an island, appears Drottningholm palace. It is as if a magician had taken a *château* from the Loire and dropped it, complete with gardens, into this Arctic background. The magician's name was Nicodemus Tessin the Elder. He was born in Stralsund, and as a young man had worked for Axel Oxenstierna at Tidö, then travelled in France and Italy. On his return he was given the task of building a completely new palace at

Drottningholm Palace

Drottningholm, which Queen Hedvig Eleonora had just bought from Magnus de la Gardie.

The palace stands on the very edge of the lake, its lawns leading down to the water, its white façade commanding the view while the wings disappear among the trees. Originally, this was the front, plain but elegant. Nowadays, the garden aspect is what everyone remembers. There the central *corps de logis* stands at the head of a long ride. The façade is decorated with statues and a monumental entrance at the head of a flight of steps, the roof is curved and, on each side, the wings spread out till they are closed by cupolas. The tourist enters a magnificent Baroque hall with a double staircase. At every corner of the balustrade is a statue, a series of Apollo and the nine Muses by Nicolas Millich, splendid life-size figures in sweeping draperies. Everywhere there are superb stucco ceilings and doormantles by the Italian Carove, one of the best being in the guardroom. Beyond this is the most sumptuous room in the palace, Hedvig Eleonora's bedroom. The bed itself is in an alcove framed by two Ionic columns, and above it stucco putti play with extravagant swags of flowers; there is gilt everywhere. On the walls are paintings of the fates in traditional classical landscapes by David Ehrenstrahl, fine works in the style of Poussin; more charming is an allegory of Hedvig Eleonora with putti holding the plans of Drottningholm.

Sweden's military fame is not neglected. Karl X Gustav has his gallery, the walls of which are covered with battle-scenes by J. P. Lemke of his Polish and Danish campaigns, and there is also a forceful and aggressive bust of him by Millich. Karl XI's gallery has an equivalent series of paintings, and also a fine allegorical ceiling and three superb Swedish chandeliers. The other interiors were changed in the next century, for the Swedish royal family still uses Drottningholm, as Windsor is used in England. The gardens have been preserved in the style of Versailles. They are filled with statues, all stolen, most of them from Wallenstein's palace in Prague, including the centrepiece, the famous Hercules fountain by Adrian de Vries, and the rest from Fredriksborg in Denmark.

Among the other nobles who commissioned country houses from Tessin was Erik Gyllenstierna, the governor of the Baltic provinces. His home, Eriksberg, is both imposing and friendly, with its yellow-washed walls and white details and it became the model for many lesser homes, using its heavy curved roof and its two wings attached at right angles to the main house. The baroque porch stresses the centre with its lush stucco work; inside, again Carove gave the rooms their fine plaster ceilings.

The cathedral at Kalmar is Tessin the Elder's other great masterpiece. The whole town had been moved by Karl X to protect the castle, and a completely new cathedral was needed. Tessin, who was already working on the restoration of Borgholm's Vasa castle, planned a late Renaissance Roman church. It is perfectly symmetrical about the axes, but the nave/choir is longer than the transepts; so it is the west front, facing a square, that appears to be the principal façade. Indeed, it is more like a palace than a church, with its central pediment, flanking turrets and plain windows. The interior is dignified and calm. It has been left white, which stresses the details, and the only colour is the maginificent altar with its deposition by David von Krafft. At the Riddarholm church, Tessin added a fine Baroque mortuary chapel for the Carolean kings.

Karlskrona is another new town. Karl XI founded it to give his navy an ice-free base on the Baltic. There, among the dockyard buildings, is the Admiralty church, touchingly named Ulrika Pia after Karl's queen. Tradition has it that it was designed by Erik Dahlberg; and it is only a simple wooden structure in the shape of a Greek cross, but the proportions are perfect and its poverty becomes the Carolean heroes who worshipped there. Karlskrona's main square feels almost southern, with the towers and the Baroque façade of the Frederick's church balancing the long, classical town hall, and in the background the temple-like dome of the German church.

Dahlberg spent his years of peace travelling round the country, sketchbook in hand. The result is an outstanding set of 469 engravings, published under the title *Svecia antiqua et hodierna,* which can rival Piranesi's views of Rome. Dahlberg was interested in everything, from the ruins of Sigtuna to the newly finished Skokloster. He went down Falun mine, and shows how the silver was won; copied runic letters, and recorded romantic ruins like Alvastra. He also illustrated military history, as in his engraving of Lund, where the cathedral appears through clouds of smoke from the guns.

When Tessin died he was succeeded as royal architect by his son Nicodemus Tessin the Younger, and his masterpiece was to be the palace in Stockholm. On the instructions of Karl XI, he built a new north wing like a screen to the rambling medieval castle, the Three Crowns. The style he used was the Roman Baroque he had learnt on his grand tour, simple to the point of plainness, no central feature, just rows of windows like soldiers on parade, but with an unerring sense of proportion. Inside, however, all is pomp and splendour. Karl XI's gallery has survived unchanged, lit by a row of windows facing mirrors, and from the richly decorated ceiling hangs a matching row of chandeliers.

In the Great Church at Stockholm, Tessin the Younger has also designed the pair of royal thrones. They blaze with colour inside the church; above each is an enormous gilded crown from which falls in folds of stucco a mantle of deep blue strewn with golden crowns. They were a remarkable family, the Tessins, and on a near-by pillar is a modern monument to three generations.

One of the greatest Swedish painters is David Klöckner, later ennobled as Ehrenstrahl. He was born in Pomerania and first worked for Wrangel, the governor-general. There is a very fine portrait of his patron at Skokloster. Then Ehrenstrahl left for Italy, and brought back from his grand tour the glories of the Baroque style which suited the Swedish empire. His portraits use all the typical props of Roman togas and the allegories of peace and war and the muses that belong to the monumental and laudatory art of the period. However, this all retains its strength, never becoming insipid, thanks to the painting of the sitters themselves. Uppsala University has an excellent portrait of Erik Dahlberg, dressed in armour and leaning against a column, with his intelligence and his courage clearly written on his face. Ehrenstrahl's best portrait is perhaps of Karl XI at Gripsholm. The king has a traditional pose on a rearing horse with his sword drawn, the dark blue uniform contrasting against the white mount. The ground is covered by trampled snow, and in the background are banners and marching men against a troubled sky. Ehrenstrahl also painted some beautiful landscapes and still-lives, like the black grouse in the National Museum.

The most important of Ehrenstrahl's disciples is David von Krafft, but

Karl XII, by David von Krafft after J. D. Swartz, 1706

his work is very different. It is much less grandiose, his colours are cooler and weaker than those of his master and his earlier work is almost over-elegant. Slowly all this changes; his portraits become dark, restrained and severe, as they are filled with the tragic mood of the collapsing Swedish empire. He is remembered today as the painter of Karl XII. At Drottningholm he painted an outstanding series of the king and his generals: truthful, individual portraits linked by their sombreness. The National Museum has a full-length portrait of the young Karl XII, boyish and handsome, confidently turned towards the viewer. It is interesting to compare this with the picture at Gripsholm, painted sixteen years later. The pose is the same, the left hand grips the hilt of his sword, but the face in the later painting is withdrawn and hard and prematurely old.

Karl XI knew that his empire was threatened; but while he lived there was peace. 'The Royal Bailiff', as he was known for his economy and administrative ability, managed his country well. He was not often in Stockholm, and preferred the lonely castle of Kungsör where he could hunt, but usually he was travelling around inspecting his new or rebuilt fortresses. The reduction had broken the power of the council and the old nobility, and the power of the crown was absolute. Indeed, Karl XI, in spite of his lack of romance, was the ideal enlightened despot: frugal, pious, just and hard-working. His last important achievement was the reorganization of the army into what was to prove itself one of the finest fighting forces in history. Each county was obliged to maintain a regiment of a certain size, and to provide the soldiers with pay and a cottage or torp. All weapons were standardized, and there were regular manoeuvres. The guard became a school for officers, where everyone began as a private.

In 1697, Karl XI died, to be succeeded by another Karl, only fifteen years old. The dead king had preserved his empire against heavy odds, and the constant bad luck of Sweden that left her to be ruled by minors in times of crisis had struck again. While Karl XI lay in state in Stockholm palace, there suddenly broke out a violent fire; the young king and his grand-mother had to flee, and the royal coffin was only just saved from an unintentional cremation. The whole palace was destroyed, except for the new wing, and even the medieval keep, the famous old tower, the Three Crowns, ominously crashed in ruins. It was to prove an appropriate beginning for the new reign.

However, there was to be a lighter prologue for a couple of years. Every eligible princess in Europe hastened to Stockholm, and the court came alive with balls and masquerades, operas and concerts, for music was one of the new king's loves. The only marriage to result from all this was that of Karl's sister, Hedvig Sofia, to Frederik of Holstein, who was again threatening Denmark with encirclement. Frederik was a wild youth and took his younger cousin Karl with him on his escapades; together they went around breaking windows in Stockholm and cutting the heads off wild dogs.

Politically, Karl XI had left a Council of Regency; but, remembering what had happened to the last regents, there was an understandable reluctance among its members to take on the job. His father had seen to it that Karl was extremely well educated by the great humanist, Lindschöld, and the regents declared that, with such a prince, they were unnecessary; so Karl XII came of age at once.

For Sweden's enemies the great opportunity had come – to destroy a fifteen-year-old boy's empire and divide it between themselves. Russia, Denmark, Prussia, Poland, Saxony, all looked forward to the spoils. Against such odds, his defeat was logically inevitable. Yet against this background, he played an astonishing role.

Karl XII's wars are the epic of the whole Swedish nation. Never during his reign did a Swedish army enter battle against an enemy weaker than itself. It was usually out-numbered two to one, five to one was not uncommon, and the ridiculous ultimate in Carolean odds was reached at Bender where 35 Swedes fought 12,000 Turks. It was a total war, for Sweden offered everything she possessed in blood and treasure. Although the king has to appear as the hero, his people were equal to him, from old men in their seventies like Dahlberg at Riga, to the teenagers with whom Stenbock defended the soil of Sweden itself, or the women who ploughed the fields in villages where the only males were cripples and children, or who, like Christina Piper, administered a province.

The Swedish Empire was never decadent, it was defeated. Modern historians have tended to blame Karl XII for its ruin; but this is wrong. The ruin was already accomplished. The empire was doomed by the facts of history; what Karl did was almost to confound those facts. To blame him for not making peace at the height of his power is foolish, for, had he been the man to compromise then, he would never have won the chance to do so.

The young man at the centre of this drama is a complex character. He had a happy childhood, hunting and shooting with his father, and to his physical health was added a first-class mind. His tutor, Count Lindschöld, who had been born the son of a smith, made his education a pleasure. Karl learnt Latin, Greek, French and German, but his great loves were mathematics, where he would work out astronomical sums in his head, and music. Yet the same youth, on first hearing the whine of bullets in battle, said, 'From now on this shall be my music.' Great music was written for him all the same. The *Marcia Carolus Rex* is as stirring as the great march in *Aïda*, and it is music to which men have fought and died. His logical, mathematical mind made him fanatically honest. He could not tolerate liars; when Augustus the Strong or Peter the Great broke their word to him, he could see only one answer, their total destruction. Similarly, having decided on a course of action, he would hold to it with unwavering obstinacy. Deeply but unostentatiously religious, Karl believed without question in his divine right. He never bothered about the views and opinions of other men; since God had appointed him, that

135

was the only power that was his superior. His personal tastes were spartan. On his first campaign he ceased to wear a wig, and never wore one again, to the horror of fashionable Europe. He was always dressed in a plain blue uniform coat with brass buttons, no marks of rank, and carried his typical long sword. After his first campaign he never touched wine or spirits. He lived exactly like one of his troopers in the middle of his army, instead of in comfortable billets. In the winter, his plain tent would be heated by glowing cannon-balls. Like one of the Jomsborg Vikings, there was never a woman in his life.

To his contemporaries, he was a figure of wonder. Defoe and Voltaire both wrote histories of him, and this slim, handsome young hero fascinated all Europe. Later generations have either loathed or loved him. Frans Bengtsson wrote well that he was a hero, a saint or a madman, depending on one's prejudices; perhaps he was all three.

It took Sweden's enemies a couple of years to get organized, in spite of the restless energy of Patkul, who had appointed himself their co-ordinator. Augustus the Strong of Saxony had bought a diet to elect him king of Poland, and the conquest of Livonia seemed to him an excellent way of justifying his title; so he invested Riga, where the defence was led by the aged governor, Erik Dahlberg, who filled the dull hours by making some beautiful engravings of the siege. Meanwhile, the Danes attacked Holstein. On 14 April 1700 Karl left Stockholm, never to return; and, covered by Admiral Rooke's English fleet, the Swedes landed in Zealand. Copenhagen lay at Karl's mercy, but his English allies insisted on his making peace instead.

Across the Baltic, the tsar, Peter the Great, had laid seige to the key fortress of Narva, which was being gallantly defended by Colonel Henning Horn. Although it was autumn, Karl took his army across the sea, and in November marched to the relief of Narva. The Swedes had food for four days, and the march took seven. They had no tents, but slept on the frosty ground. The Russians had ravaged the countryside and amused themselves with such games as impaling babies along the fences. They had little cause for alarm. There were only 10,537 Swedes, led by a boy, while they were some 80,000 strong. Peter, however, was alarmed. After drinking himself into a stupor, he suddenly ran away, leaving an elderly Belgian mercenary, the Duc de Croy, in command. Narva lay on a river, and the Russians had surrounded it with a strongly fortified crescent. The plan worked out by Karl and his chief of staff, General Rehnsköld, was simplicity itself. The Swedes in two columns, with a snowstorm behind them, attacked the centre of the Russian lines. Then each column wheeled outwards, and drove the Russians between their own fortifications down to the river. It worked perfectly. The Russians collapsed in chaos, and by dusk Peter's army was annihilated.

The news of this victory resounded round Europe. Most statesmen had written the young king off when he sailed against Peter. Now his victory and the odds against which it had been won made him an instant hero, for he had led the attack sword in hand. Karl was not interested. Instead, he went into winter quarters in an old castle of the Teutonic Knights and had snowball fights with his officers. Next spring, reinforcements came from home, and Karl marched down to Riga, where old Dahlberg had resisted every attack.

Karl's army was now ready for action, and we may look at its men. They were a tough breed, these Carolean warriors; several kept diaries, so we known them well. There was Carl Gustav Rehnsköld, field-marshal and second-in-command, a brilliant soldier in his own right; Adam Lewenhaupt, the Latin colonel, a dry intellectual; the gay and popular Magnus Stenbock; Arvid Horn, a Finnish noble so poor he had to enlist as a private; Stuart, Karl's old teacher; Gyllenkrok, the quartermaster-general; Stålhammar, the diarist; the charmer Axel Sparre; and Karl's favourite, young Prince Max of Württemberg, sent to learn about soldiering. The camp was the centre of government. There was Karl's prime minister, Count Carl Piper, a very able parvenu and a comfortable man, who still lasted all the campaign, Hermelin, the Latin secretary, and lastly Karl's valet Hultman. Nor should we forget his horse, Brandklipparen and his dog Pompe. The crack regiment was the Guards, the *Drabanterna*, to which regardless of rank, merit was the only passport.

In the summer of 1701, Karl moved to the offensive. The Saxon army of 28,000 men under Steinau was holding the south bank of the Dvina on the border of Livonia. There were only 18,000 Swedes, but the old engineer Dahlberg had been building pontoons, and he and Karl landed in the first boats under the Saxon guns. The Swedes charged the fortifications, and by seven in the morning the enemy was in flight. The passage of the Dvina laid Poland at Karl's mercy. Karl now decided his policy. With mathematical simplicity and no sense of politics he concluded that Augustus must be punished for his treacherous attack, and there could be no peace in Poland until he was removed from the throne.

It was, however, not until next May, in 1702, that Karl captured Warsaw. By this time Augustus was also beginning to become worried. He had sent his mistress Aurora Königsmarck to Karl to beg for peace; she was a siren famous throughout Europe for her beauty, but Karl had refused to see her. Instead, he had all the whores in the camp assembled, preached at and chased away; poor Aurora had to take the hint.

The Saxons retreated deeper and deeper into Poland. At last Karl caught up with them at Kliszow. He had only some 12,000 Swedes against about 27,000 Saxons and Poles, but attacked at once. Karl himself swept the Poles from the field, while Rehnsköld, surrounded by the vastly stronger Saxon army, waited stubbornly for Karl to relieve him. Soon they together put Steinau's army to flight again. From Kliszow it is only a short march to Crakow. On arrival, Karl bluffed his way into the town by sheer cheek, and Poland's second city was in Swedish hands.

Piper now very reasonably wanted Karl to make peace, but he would have none of it. He was not interested in a couple of provinces; he wanted to see Augustus deposed, and his own candidate, a mild old gentleman called Stanislas Leszczyński, elected king of Poland. He had enough

Polish allies, like the brothers Sapicha or Poniatowski, to form a party.

The following year was spent chasing the unfortunate Steinau all over Poland. He was defeated again at Pultusk, with odds of three to one in his favour. Then the Carolean army had a restful three months, besieging the key fortress of Thorn on the bend of the Vistula. With its eventual fall, Karl's strategic position was complete. At Thorn, Karl's dog Pompe died at the end of his master's bed. A witty officer called Holmström promptly wrote his epitaph on the theme of how many women would have loved to live like Pompe, and men to die like him.

In the Baltic provinces, the situation was not so satisfactory. The governor was an incompetent de la Gardie, and the troops under Schlippenbach were conducting a heroic but hopeless defence against the whole of the Russian army. However, Karl saw that these provinces would easily be his again once the main victory was won.

At last, in January 1704, Arvid Horn at Warsaw used a combination of bribes and threats to get a Polish Diet to depose Augustus. (There were usually at least two diets in Poland at any one time, obviously not in agreement with one another.) Horn had to spend an afternoon drinking with the Bishop of Posen to give him the pot-courage to open the Diet, and Leszczyński was elected king. Meanwhile Karl amused himself by capturing Lemburg with a few dragoons. Up in the north, Peter's progress continued. After gallant but useless defences, first Dorpat and then even Narva fell to him, and the tsar founded his new capital of St Petersburg. Riga was only saved by Lewenhaupt's brilliant victory of Germauerthof against odds of three to one. Nieroth held Warsaw against the Saxons with the same odds.

Finally, Stanislas could hold his coronation. Unfortunately, Augustus had made off with the regalia, so that Karl, after providing him with a kingdom, had to provide his protégé with a crown as well. Now surely was the time to defend his exposed empire against Peter; but Karl did not wish to defeat his enemies, he wished to destroy them.

In 1706 he marched on Saxony. The year opened well. The Saxon army under Schulenberg had attacked Rehnsköld at Fraustadt on the borders of Silesia. Twice as strong as the Swedes, the main body of whom were at the other end of Poland, it should have been an easy victory. Rehnsköld lured his enemy onto open ground, and there his cavalry, attacking across the frozen swamps, annihilated the Saxons. Augustus had no army left.

The Swedish army then marched into Saxony, and Karl established himself in the castle of Alt-Ranstadt. The humiliation of Augustus was absolute. He had no choice but to abdicate the Polish crown, recognize Stanislas, end his alliance with Peter the Great, and return his prisoners. That was all that Karl deigned to ask. Again he was interested not in conquest but in justice. Patkul was handed over, and sent to Stockholm to be broken on the wheel. For the Swedish army it was a marvellous rest, their first taste of civilian life in six years. Discipline remained impeccable, and all Europe flocked to see these heroes. Axel Sparre tried in vain to dance with every girl in Dresden, and even flirted with Aurora Königsmarck.

Politically, too, all Europe looked to Alt-Ranstadt. The War of the Spanish Succession was at its height, and here was the finest army in Europe uncommitted to either side. The diplomats span their plots, and all the time Karl, true to his nature, gave no inkling of his plans. As they talked, Karl quoted Curtius' history, *Memini me Alexandrum nisi mercatorem*. With thoughts of the peace of Westphalia, he ordered the Emperor to return their churches to the Lutherans of Silesia, and was obeyed. Next spring, the Duke of Marlborough arrived in person from England with a letter from Queen Anne. The two great soldiers utterly failed to understand one another, which is not surprising, the one a sublimely self-confident aristocrat, the other an ambitious parvenu.

At last a decision was taken. In August 1707, Europe watched with bated breath as the Swedish army, led by its king, marched eastwards towards Russia. Augustus the Strong had been punished and now it was to be the turn of Peter the Great. Peter was in a panic; his agents promised anything, in vain. Karl was as implacable as abstract justice. With him went 32,136 men to act in an epic and a tragedy. Europe had seen the Swedish army for the last time, and the tradition of Breitenfeld and Lützen was to pass into history.

The strategy of the invasion of Russia has been argued *ad nauseam*. Apparently Karl made the mistake which Napoleon and Hitler were to make after him; but he had no such warning examples. On the contrary, just over a century before, the Swedes had succeeded in occupying Moscow. A Swedish army was as used to the cold as a Russian one. It might have been expected, however, that Karl would have learnt from chasing Augustus round Poland how difficult it is to bring an unwilling enemy to battle. But Sweden was too weak for a war of attrition, and had to stake everything on a victory in the field. That she had been victorious so far was theoretically impossible, and the miracle would have to continue.

The Swedish generals argued as much as the historians. Piper, who knew the exact value of most things, wanted to make a profitable peace. Gyllenkrok wanted a sweep to the north to free the Baltic provinces, now almost entirely in Russian hands. Karl was obstinate; they would march to Moscow. He was twenty-five years old. In June 1708, the Russian army under Scheremetyev and Menshikov had to stand and fight to defend the Dnieper, the last river before Moscow. They had 38,000 men and a position defended by swamps. After short prayers in the midnight rain, the 12,000 Swedes attacked. Karl led them on foot through the water; at the deepest part he had to carry Gyllenkrok, who was too short to wade. For the Russians, Prince Repnin put his own men into total confusion, and they fled almost before the Swedish infantry could get to grips with them. To the south, outnumbered by more than four to one, Rehnsköld fought a brilliant cavalry action, utterly destroying three Russian brigades.

The road was clear, but it was autumn and supplies were running low. So, at Tartarsk, Karl halted like a good general to wait for the supply train and reinforcements which Lewenhaupt was bringing from Riga.

Now fate struck the first of several blows at Karl; and it needed several to finish off such a man. Lewenhaupt's behaviour seems extraordinary. He was a good soldier and he knew that the whole army depended on him. Yet he left Riga late with his 12,000 men and precious supplies, and then marched so slowly that he lagged weeks behind his timetable. At Lesna he was overwhelmed by 30,000 Russians. After half his men were gone, there was nothing for it but to sink the guns in the marsh, burn the supplies and retreat to the south.

Further east, Karl had reluctantly come to the same conclusion. After waiting in vain for Lewenhaupt, he turned south to find winter quarters with Mazeppa, the Cossack leader who had offered his alliance against Peter. There, at last, he was joined by Lewenhaupt. Now fate struck her second blow. The winter of 1708/9 was one of the coldest in recorded history. In that God-fearing Swedish army, it was too cold to hold a Christmas service. In their provisional camp, the sufferings of the Swedes were intense. Food was short and hunger and cold killed thousands. Frostbite was common. One sentry was found frozen to death, mounted on his dead horse. All suffered equally, king, officers and men.

By spring, every other man in the army had perished. Yet, when spring came, Karl laid siege to the fortress of Poltava. After that winter the amazing fact is not that the Swedish army was defeated at Poltava, but that there was any army there to fight at all. Peter meanwhile assembled his force in a fortified camp not far from the besieged town.

Fate's third blow now descended. Karl was shot in the foot in a minor skirmish. Stoically ignoring it for some hours, he then held the wound open himself while a doctor operated. However, with the bad food, gangrene and fever set in and Karl became seriously ill. Command of the army was left to Rehnsköld, with Lewenhaupt as second-in-command. Their dislike for each other was mutual.

Now, at last, Tsar Peter and the Russian army were within range. They had built a strongly fortified camp a few miles north of Poltava, but did not dare to attack the Swedish lines to relieve the town. Karl was determined to bring them to battle, and instead it was the Swedes who attacked. By now the Swedish army was only 20,000 strong, of whom 7,000 had to be left behind to watch Poltava. The Russians, behind their fortifications, were 45,000. Karl was too ill to command on the day of decision; he had to be carried on to the battlefield in a litter on the shoulders of the guards. Rehnsköld formed the Swedes into three columns, Creutz on the left, Lewenhaupt in the centre and Schlippenbach on the right. The attack began in the early morning. Colonel Roos had been sent to storm the redoubt defending the Russian guns, but his force was too weak to break the far stronger enemy. After several hopeless attempts, he was forced back by weight of numbers, and when at last he surrendered, he had 400 men left out of 2,000 men. The rest of the army knew nothing of this desperate struggle. They were waiting for Roos to catch up. After precious hours had been wasted, Rehnsköld went ahead with the attack, ten battalions against fifty-one. The Russian artillery were inflicting heavy losses, and even Karl's litter was shot to pieces. Yet, the Russian line bent, and on the right broke under the attack, until at last sheer mass of the enemy moved forward, swamping the Swedes. In vain did Anders Torsttensson, true to his grandfather, led his cavalry in a suicidal charge on the left. Even an orderly retreat was impossible against the tide of enemy troops. Rehnsköld and Piper were both captured. Lewenhaupt led the remnant of the army back to Poltava.

The dice were cast. Karl had staked everything on one battle, and now, in spite of every heroism, he had lost it. Unconscious with sickness, he followed Lewenhaupt's flight southwards to the borders of Turkey. Then, as the Russians approached, he crossed with a few followers into neutral territory, leaving Lewenhaupt to surrender his remaining troops to Menshikov. The Carolean army had ceased to exist.

The fundamental weakness of the Swedish position was now revealed. Her enemies had come to think of her as far stronger than she was; for all they saw was this apparently invincible army. Once that was destroyed, there was nothing left, for Sweden had not the resources, neither in men nor money, to raise another. Karl was like a brilliant fencer, his back to the wall, keeping a dozen enemies at bay with his sword. Now the blade had broken.

In Turkey, Karl was received as an honoured guest and lodged at Bender. He began to make plans for a new coalition against Russia, with the Swedes coming from Pomerania to link up with the Turks. His ambassador, Poniatowski, a Polish patriot, persuaded the Sultan to attack Russia, and Tsar Peter only escaped total defeat and capture through the cowardice and incompetence of the Turkish commander. Karl himself remained in Turkey for five years, an absence which was grossly irresponsible and can be explained only by his fixation that he must defeat Peter.

He was certainly needed at home. When the news of Poltava reached the West, all Sweden's enemies attacked. The Danes landed in Skåne; the Elector George occupied Bremen-Verden to give Hanover a port; the Russians captured Riga after a suicide defence and invaded Finland; Viborg fell after 400 years. In Sweden itself, there were three bad harvests followed by plague; a twilight of the Gods was setting over the whole nation.

The man of the hour was Count Arvid Horn, a yet greater statesman than he was a general. As chancellor, he undertook the herculean task of saving his country from dissolution. While the old queen, Hedvig Eleonora melted down her silver, and Admiral Wachtmeister commissioned his ships out of his own pocket, Magnus Stenbock in Skåne raised an army of old men and boys for whom he could not even find uniforms. On a February morning in 1710, he attacked the larger Danish army at Hälsingborg, and drove them into the Sound. Horn had managed to get

Sweden's German territories declared neutral, but Karl, angry at his realism, had cancelled this. So Stenbock was sent to Stralsund with 9,000 men in 1712. There he routed a Danish army more than twice the size of his own at Gadebusch; then, threatened by Danes, Russians and Saxons, he was cut off in the fortress of Tönning in Holstein, and forced to surrender to such vastly superior forces, to die as a prisoner. The Russian invasion of Finland went slowly forward, until in 1714 General Armfeldt's levies of boys were defeated at Storkyrka by an enemy three times their size in a battle in which only ten Swedish officers survived.

The state of the nation was desperate. Sweden had not an ally in Europe, and Horn, constantly trying to save something from the wreck, was constantly thwarted by Karl, who would surrender nothing. By 1714, everyone wanted to be in at the death, and Sweden was at war with Russia, Prussia, Saxony, Poland, Hanover-Britain and Denmark/Norway.

Down in Turkey, Karl had outstayed his welcome and diplomatic efforts were made to get him to leave. Among the Turkish soldiers he had become a legend; they called him 'the Iron Head' and regarded him as super-human, even perhaps smitten by Allah. The efforts to get rid of him ended in the fantastic *Calabalik* at Bender. *Calabalik* is Turkish for a wild animal hunt. A Turkish army of 12,000 Janissaries was ordered to arrest the few hundred Swedes. Most of them surrendered, but Karl and thirty-four of his men, including his valet Hultman, fought their way into a stone house from which they defied their enemies. The Turks made repeated efforts to storm it, and there was hand-to-hand fighting in every room. At last the roof was fired, and the defenders fought with their backs against the flames. The whole scene, the struggle in the burning hall, could have been lifted straight from a Viking saga, an epic anachronism from Sweden's distant past. It ended with Karl's capture and removal to another camp.

It was after midnight in November 1714 that the sentries at the gate of Stralsund were asked to admit two couriers. They were naturally reluctant to do so, for Stralsund was threatened, and it was Sweden's only fortress left across the Baltic. When the elder courier reached the governor, he was recognized as the king. Karl had ridden from Turkey to Stralsund in fourteen days, a distance of 1,500 miles. He had travelled disguised, and had even drunk wine to make it more convincing. His staff had all dropped out with exhaustion along the road, and only his companion, the twenty-year-old During, had lasted the course. On arrival, Karl's boots had to be cut from his feet.

The enemy soon attacked, but, led once more by their king, the Swedes fought with berserk courage. With 3,000 men, Karl tried to drive back 20,000, and after a siege of two months, the fortress surrendered as a heap of rubble. Karl himself escaped in a fishing boat.

Next year the allies made their plans. A joint Russian and Prussian army, escorted by a British fleet, was to land in Skåne. From his headquarters at Lund, Karl prepared to defend the province *à l'outrance*. The allies had a superiority of more than three to one; but, faced by the

142

greatest general of the age, leading his desperate people in defence of their own soil, they thought better of it and called the invasion off.

Negotiations had begun for peace. Karl had very unfairly dismissed Horn, and instead Sweden was represented by Baron Görtz. Görtz was a remarkable man; he had come to Sweden as a refugee with his master, Karl's nephew, the orphaned Carl Frederick of Holstein. As Karl's minister, he was brilliant but hated by many Swedish nobles who wished to see Karl removed, and nicknamed 'the Grand Vizier'. He gave the economy some stability by coining the notorious need-money in which copper replaced the silver. As a diplomat, he could juggle a dazzling number of balls in the air at once, but the basis of his policy was to work on the latent enmity between Tsar Peter and King George I of Britian, elector of Hanover.

Lacking a fleet, there was only one front on which Karl could attack, Norway, and in November 1718 the Swedish army was besieging the fortress of Fredrikshald. In the evening of 30 November, Karl and a few of his staff went to inspect the siege-work and the king climbed into an exposed position to get a better view. A couple of minutes later a single shot was heard, and Karl XII was dead. Sweden's time as a great power was over. A French officer in the trench concluded aptly '*Voilà, la pièce est finie; allons souper.*'

Bringing home the dead King Karl XII, by Gustaf Cederström, 1884

The shot at Fredrikshald will always remain a mystery, and it is perhaps as well if it does. It may simply have been a lucky sniper, but from the first there were rumours of murder. Legend claims that it was a silver bullet, cast by a witch; and the wound suggested that it came from the Swedish lines. Both physically and mentally, however, the Swedish nation was exhausted; never again has she sought a role beyond her frontiers.

For Englishmen, Karl's most appropriate epitaph must be Samuel Johnson's verse:

> His fall was destined to a barren strand,
> A petty fortress and a dubious hand;
> He left a name at which the world grew pale,
> To point a moral and adorn a tale.

9. The Eighteenth Century

If there is doubt over Karl's death, it is certain who benefited from it. Karl had never named an heir, and the choice lay between the young duke of Holstein, the son of his elder sister Hedvig Sofia, living in exile in Sweden, and his younger sister herself, Ulrika Eleonora, married to Frederick of Hesse.

Ulrika Eleonora received the news of her brother's death with suspicious speed. Her husband's adjutant, Sicre, was even rumoured to be the assassin, and she promptly arrested Görtz and the other leading Holsteiners. Her nephew Carl Frederick was too young to want to do more than continue the war. Görtz was condemned after a parody of a trial, and executed immediately. It was a contemptible political murder of a man who had done his adopted country great service. Ulrika Eleonora had herself proclaimed queen before the army had returned from Norway, and then was elected by the *Riksdag*. Carl Frederick of Holstein went into exile in Russia.

The first concern of everyone was to bring the war to an end. Britain was already worried by the pretensions of Russia, and sent Lord James Stanhope to negotiate a peace. George I at last got Bremen-Verden, and even paid a million talers for it. Prussia received Stettin and Eastern Pomerania, which gave her the long-coveted control of the mouths of the Oder, and formalized her conquest for a fee of two million talers. Only Russia remained, and the alliance against Sweden was broken. Ulrika and Frederick, however, were becoming worried by the strength of the Holstein party, and the support of Peter the Great could be bought. By the Peace of Nystadt in 1721, Russia received Livonia, Estonia, Ingermanland and Eastern Karelia, including the great fortress of Viborg.

Unable to have Frederick proclaimed her consort, Ulrika Eleonora abdicated to let her husband be elected to the throne. After Karl XII, any king would have seemed mediocre, but Frederick I was bathetic. He was an idle, middle-aged lecher, whose chief interests were hunting bears and young girls. With the years, this old goat acquired a succession of teenage mistresses, and one old Carolean soldier's widow even ordered him out of her home for making a pass at her granddaughter. His sole claim to honour was founding Sweden's senior order of chivalry, the 'Seraphim'.

Understandably, all this left him little time or inclination for politics, and Sweden entered a period of party government known as 'the Age of

Freedom'. From the first, Arvid Horn was elected president of the council by an overwhelming majority, and remained for years the effective ruler of the country. His constitutional principle was aristocratic rule behind a royal figurehead. In the council, the king had a mere two votes. The *Riksdag* was to meet every three years, the head of each noble family attending as a right, as did the bishops, but the representatives of the burghers and the yeomen were elected. Horn's overriding purpose was to give his exhausted country peace and a chance to recover, and this he did with common sense and good husbandry, a fitting climax to a great soldier's career.

Sweden was a much reduced state in every sense. Her Baltic empire was gone, and the Finnish frontier undefendable; she would never again be fit for an offensive war. The loss of the rich, corn-growing province of Livonia drove her back on her own agricultural resources, still farmed as in the Middle Ages. Only in 1757 was the strip system abandoned. In industry, iron began to replace copper as the most important export, mainly to England. Slowly the prisoners-of-war started to return from Russia, young men captured at Poltava to see their now middle-aged wives and almost forgotten homes.

It was inevitable that Horn's cautious and unglamorous government should begin to bore the younger men. He and his supporters were nicknamed 'the Caps', after the nightcaps which, it was said by von Höpken, were all they were fit to wear. Their opponents instead were called 'the Hats', and this party was joined by many of the ex-prisoners seeking for revenge. Their power in the *Riksdag* grew, until the day came when Horn broke with Frederick; his pimp Broman had been given a senior civil service post, and his latest royal mistress was the sixteen-year-old Hedvig Taube, daughter of an old admiral, whose ruinous gaming debts were duly paid. This was too much for the old Carolean, and Horn resigned. The Hat candidate, Carl Gustav Tessin, whose father built Stockholm's palace, was elected to succeed him in 1738.

The Hat party was financed by France, eager to re-establish her old influence. During the years of peace, many young Swedes served in the French army, until, in 1742, a separate regiment of guards was formed called the 'Royal Suèdois'. Such support, and the succession of an infant to the Russian throne, suggested a war of revenge. In 1741, war was declared, and Sweden was entirely the aggressor. However, Lewenhaupt in Finland did nothing, both army and navy were inadequate, and when Elizabeth became empress of Russia by a *coup*, the Russians invaded and occupied Finland. The whole coast of Sweden was harried by the Russian fleet, villages burnt and towns shelled. The Hats' Russian war had been a fiasco.

Luckily for them, the problem of the succession to the senile and childless Frederick had arisen. The peasantry proposed the Danish crown prince, which would have led to the peaceful union of Scandinavia. To avoid this, the Empress Elizabeth supported Adolf Frederick of Holstein-Gottorp, a descendant of Karl IX, and offered, if he were elected, to return most of Finland. Her candidate was approved against violent opposition, and in 1744, at the Peace of Åbo, Russia was content with a thin tranche of Finland, Savolax and the fortress of Nyslott.

In 1751, Frederick died unlamented, and the prince-bishop of Lübeck, Adolf Frederick, became the king. Adolf Frederick was a far better man than his predecessor; civilized and upright, he possessed many of the finest qualities of the Enlightenment. He learnt Swedish and took his responsibilities to his new kingdom seriously. His wife, however, was the more outstanding personality: Louisa Ulrika, sister of Frederick the Great of Prussia, and sharing many of her brother's qualities. The family likeness of the hard, cold face is striking in Roslin's portraits.

Although he owed his throne to Russia, Adolf Frederick was shrewd enough to realize that the Russian policy was to make Sweden a satellite of the Russian empire, so his sympathies at first lay with the Hats and their charming leader, Tessin. The defence of Finland was taken seriously in hand. A fleet of galleys, manned by oarsmen and shallow enough in draught to penetrate the archipelagoes of the Baltic and the Gulf of Finland, was built. This Skerries Fleet was to win great renown under Adolf Frederick's son, Gustav (the future Gustavus III). On land, General Augustin Ehrensvärd began the building of a vast fortress on the islands outside Helsinki. Like an impregnable Gibraltar, it was designed to cut the lines of communication of any Russian invasion.

The Hats, however, had no intention of letting any power revert to the crown, and by 1756 the king, and above all the queen, were ready to attempt a *coup* against the *Riksdag*. The plot was betrayed and ruthlessly crushed by Ehrensvärd. The royalist leader, Count Brahe, was executed, and the royal couple publicly humiliated. Still unbowed, Louisa Ulrika wrote to her brother, 'In these most difficult hours I remind myself that I am the sister of Frederick the Great.' When Adolf Frederick invoked his last constitutional right and refused to sign any Bills, the *Riksdag* had a stamp made with his name.

Next year, flushed with success and well supplied with gold from Paris, the Hats joined the French side in the Seven Years War. Their invasion of Prussia proved as ludicrously incompetent as their earlier invasion of Russia. The war was unpopular at home, and caused such inflation that the Swedish mark dropped by 70 per cent on the Hamburg Bourse. The Hats found themselves a new leader in Axel von Fersen the Elder, who set about ending the whole adventure. Peace was signed at Hamburg in 1762, and, thanks to the intervention of Louisa Ulrika, Sweden's main losses were in prestige.

At the next *Riksdag*, three years later, the Hats were deservedly swept from power to be replaced by Rudbeck and the Caps. The first task was to put the national finances in order. To do this, the use of luxuries like tea and coffee was forbidden, and, more suspiciously, the defence works in Finland were stopped. Their only real claim to fame is the law of 1766 which guarantees the freedom of the press. The public, as usual, disliked deflation, and the Cap government soon fell.

The Age of Freedom, although most of the nation could elect its delegates to the *Riksdag*, was no good advertisement for democracy. Both parties had strong foreign sympathies, the Hats with France, the Caps with England and then Russia. The respective ambassadors of these countries poured out on the *Riksdag* delegates a constant and not very discriminating river of bribes and, when the party they backed was in power, effectively controlled policy. Since Arvid Horn, no politician, although they were often men of great charm and culture, showed any inclination to put his country before himself. The *Riksdag* itself was far too unwieldy to manage any actual administration, and the

Gustav III, by Alexander Roslin

country was effectively ruled by a series of secret committees. The debates in the *Riksdag* frequently deteriorated into scuffles and open brawls; one was cleverly stopped by an imaginative parson who began singing hymns and thereby brought his God-fearing colleagues back to their senses. The king had little part to play in all this; but Louisa Ulrika, with her usual energy, succeeded in creating a court party whose aim was to replace democratic chaos with royal autocracy.

It was, however, left to their son to achieve this. Gustav was the first prince to be born in Sweden since Karl XII, and the crowds celebrating his birth read it as a good omen for the nation. Nor were they to be disappointed. Young Gustav showed a precocious intelligence, which was driven hard by his having some of the most outstanding Swedes of the period as tutors. The only regret was that they were changed along with the government. The first was Carl Gustav Tessin, the 'Admirable Crichton' of Stockholm and an ex-ambassador to Paris. His teaching methods were very advanced, and he wrote the delightful *Letters of an Old Man To a Young Prince*, which are a model both of good prose style and of good sense. Gustav then had to write back. Tessin told him all about the intellectual life of Paris, where the thought of the Age of Reason was being created, and from these years French was his second mother-tongue.

Louisa Ulrika then quarrelled with Tessin, as she quarrelled with most people, and he was replaced with the writer, Olof Dalin, who had founded the first Swedish newspaper. More influential was the next tutor, Carl Frederick Scheffer, another scholarly and francophile aristocrat, who was a great admirer of Locke's philosophy. The greatest influence on the boy was without doubt his mother. She was very proud of her gifted son and encouraged all his studies; yet her temperament was so violent that she often had fits of spitefulness and almost hysterical rage. Perhaps to counter this, Gustav, even as a child, developed particular charm. Tessin wrote that it was impossible ever to be angry with him for long.

His education inevitably prejudiced the crown prince against the excesses of the Age of Freedom, and he was soon helping his father to resist the pretensions of the *Riksdag*. In 1768, he actually read the speech threatening abdication for his father, and did so with a born actor's timing and delivery.

Then, in 1771, he set off for France, ostensibly for his general education, but also to gain French support for the court party. Paris was a revelation. Louis XV lodged him at Marly, and the young prince was lionized by society. He met all the philosophers and artists of the day, and assiduously attended the intellectual salons, where his abilities impressed even that critical audience. He made a personal friend of Madame de Bouffiers. He admitted, however, that he preferred reading to meeting the *philosophes*. The contrast with the narrow-minded and provincial life of Sweden was striking, and Gustav was given a new standard for his homeland. Politically, the journey was promising, and

Choiseul, Louis' chief minister, was sympathetic. Then, one March evening at the Opéra, news was brought to Gustav that his father had died.

The young king who returned to Stockholm was to become one of the greatest of his country's rulers. Furthermore, he is important to European history, for he was certainly the most gifted, and in his real achievements probably the most successful, of those remarkable eighteenth-century monarchs who ruled as enlightened despots. In Sweden he is remembered as *Tjusare kungen*, 'the Charmer King'. He would have appreciated the compliment of Bain, who called his reign 'the Antonine Age of Sweden'.

Gustav was not particularly tall, and his birth had been difficult, leaving him with a limp and a slightly deformed skull, of which he was extremely conscious. In character, he was inflexibly honest, and this no doubt fed his contempt for Sweden's politicians. He was also a very able diplomat, being decisive, charming, inscrutable, and an excellent actor – an ideal set of qualities for that task. The famous charm was entirely genuine, for he was naturally considerate and courteous. He was, all the same, an uncompromising snob, proud of his somewhat diluted Vasa blood and a stickler for etiquette. On the other hand, he had the quality essential in an autocrat of choosing the best men for his staff, regardless of background. In crises, Gustav was at his best, and one recognizes unexpectedly his uncle, Frederick the Great.

Above all, Gustav was proud to be the standard-bearer of the Enlightenment, and, of course, the priests and reactionaries hated him for it. As the years proved to him that there is no final cure for human viciousness, he became not disillusioned but more melancholic. At all events, eighteenth-century Sweden provided plenty of scope for an enthusiastic reformer. Gustav started with abolishing the use of torture, and reducing the merry slaughter of executions for trivial crimes and even ones as grave as infanticide. He set an example by having his own son vaccinated. He permitted the Jews to live in Sweden and worship openly for the first time. Finally, he gave Sweden a cultural life which, apart from a brief spell under Queen Christina, she had never possessed before.

His greeting to the Estates at his first *Riksdag* is a moving speech. 'It is my greatest fortune to be Swedish, and my greatest honour to be the first citizen among a free people.' However, the free people were in some danger. It was not unlikely that Sweden might share the fate of Poland, and men like the Cap general Pechlin were constantly intriguing with Russia. Both Caps and Hats were unpopular, and many young officers belonged to the anti-party club, Svensk Botten. Gustav waited his opportunity.

By the autumn, all was ready. In Finland, J. M. Sprengporten, one of the leaders of Svensk Botten, seized Sveaborg with his regiment, and prepared to cross to Sweden. In Skåne, Colonel Toll won over the garrison of Kristianstad, so that when the local leader of the Caps tried to enter, the officer of the watch refused to admit to knowing anything including his own name. The *coup* would be won or lost in Stockholm. On the morning of 19 August, Gustav spoke to the officers and NCOs of the guard assembled at the palace. He told them that he was determined to restore her old liberties to Sweden, and to make an end of the party rule. The response was enthusiastic, and the king tied a white handkerchief round his arm as a badge. The troops followed his example, and soon the whole of Stockholm was sporting these handkerchiefs. The chancellor, Rudbeck, rushed around the city in a panic, only to be laughed at when he called on the people to arrest the king.

Gustav then delivered one of his finest speeches to the *Riksdag*. In rolling prose, he explained how freedom had degenerated into an intolerable aristocratic despotism; the law would now rule both king and people. The old days of party strife were over, and the very names of Cap and Hat were forbidden. The nobility were taken unawares, and support for the king in the other three Estates was overwhelming. The only hope of the opposition was foreign intervention. For Catherine the Great of Russia, used to seeing Sweden as a satellite, the *coup* was almost a rebellion; but, fortunately, both Russia and Prussia were too busy dividing Poland to act. Gustav even warned Frederick that he would recognize his own blood in his nephew if he attacked him.

The new government was popular inside the country. Abroad, the French were delighted, and Creutz, the Swedish ambassador, could report that Gustav was the romantic hero of Paris. Voltaire even wrote a triumphal ode for his royal admirer.

> Jeune et digne héritier du grand nom de Gustave,
> Sauveur d'un peuple libre, et roi d'un peuple brave.

Ulric Scheffer, the brother of Gustav's old tutor, was made chancellor, and energetically set about overhauling the entire administration. The civil service even caught up with its work. In Finland, the fortifications of Sveaborg were taken up again and completed. At home, Chapman began building the ships of the galley fleet and the men-of-war that gave Sweden a navy again.

Once the revolution was secure, Gustav himself set out on an *Eriksgata*, the traditional journey of the medieval kings round the country, and even went to Finland. Of all Sweden's kings, Gustav is the one who spent most time in Finland, and who was most interested in that country. On his return, he founded a new Order of chivalry, the Vasa Order, which, in keeping with the spirit of the Enlightenment, was awarded not for military exploits but for achievements to the benefit of mankind.

The commission on currency reform was unanimously pessimistic about the chances of redeeming the inflated paper of the Riksbank, except for its most junior member. This obstinate young man, Johan Liljenkranz, was summoned to the king to explain his arguments; Gustav was so impressed that he made him president of the Finance

Council. Liljenkranz successfully stabilized the currency, consolidated the state's debts and got remarkably favourable loan terms out of the Dutch. Liljenkranz was an outstanding economist, who provided his king with the sinews of government without ever straining the nation's resources. Gustav fully appreciated this, and at the next *Riksdag* he summoned Liljenkranz from the back benches to receive the thanks of the Estates beside him. Their only error was the very reasonable decision to make the distilling of schnaps a government monopoly; nothing else could have stirred up so much unpopularity as this infringement of the Swede's ancient right to get drunk as cheaply as possible.

The new queen, Sofia Magdalena, was very different from her husband; shy, pious and introvert. She had been a Danish princess, and it was a purely political marriage arranged by the Caps, directly against the wishes of Louisa Ulrika, who had wanted a Prussian princess. As a result, the queen mother was scrupulously spiteful to her daughter-in-law. The marriage was also a sexual failure. The shyness of the bride and a physical difficulty for the king had led to their living apart, until Gustav asked his friend the equerry Count Munck, whose fiancée was a lady-in-waiting, to reconcile them. Munck gave Gustav some man-to-man advice and left him at a lover's rendezvous with the queen; even then, there was some embarrassment, until Munck returned, hustled his king into the queen's bedroom and locked the door on the pair of them. The results were up to best expectations, and in 1778 their son Gustav Adolf was born. Louisa Ulrika, who had watched the estrangement of the couple with satisfaction, was furious at this success. She wrote to her second son, Duke Karl of Södermanland, that the heir to the throne who had replaced him was illegitimate. When the gossip reached Gustav, he was ill with rage and misery at this betrayal by the person who was closest to him in the world. He wrote to his mother that she had poisoned the happiest day of his life. She replied with the hope that time would open his eyes. This was more than the most loving son could take, and as king he forced the queen mother to publish an official rejection of the rumours. The breach between them, with all its pain, was irreconcilable.

Gustav III surrounded himself with the most civilized and intellectual Rococo court in Europe. Here was his life, and here he made himself the most important single character in Sweden's cultural history. The days were given over to administration, but the evenings, and Gustav seldom went to bed before three in the morning, were filled by plays and operas, by literary readings, studies of antiques, designing of palaces, and even by the king's own writing for the stage. With Versailles as his model, he succeeded in creating a far more civilized court.

Russia remained sullenly hostile to the new régime, and in 1777 Gustav decided to take the bull by the horns, or to visit the Empress Catherine in person. He arrived in St Petersburg under the well-publicized incognito of the count of Gotland, and the pair of royal actors gave a superb display of amateur dramatics. The entertainments were lavish, the cordiality extravagant and the gifts brash, but of serious diplomacy there was none. Gustav returned with a sincere admiration for the empress, but she liked her men tough and was less impressed, although she learnt to respect the Swedish king.

In 1780, Gustav Philip Creutz was recalled from the embassy in Paris to become chancellor. He was the epitome of the best kind of eighteenth-century aristocrat, responsible and sophisticated; and with his experience of the great world, he became one of the king's personal friends. A good poet in his own right, he had made the best of Paris and his time as ambassador had been a great success. He had succeeded in obtaining massive subsidies from the French government for Sweden; but his most tangible relic is the superb Sèvres dinner service which he brought to Gustav, and which was discovered only a few years ago in Stockholm's palace where it had been hidden by some loyal Vasa servants. Almost his last act in Paris was to sign a commercial treaty with Benjamin Franklin, when Sweden became the first neutral to recognize the independent United States of America. Creutz was replaced by Baron Staël von Holstein, whose greatest achievement was to pay his gambling debts by marrying the daughter of the fabulously wealthy Swiss banker Necker, who was later to try to save France from bankruptcy before the Revolution broke out. He saw little of his wife in later years, for Madame de Staël was more interested in politics and literature, and, as one of the first Romantics, had to live up to her principles.

For any well-born young man of the period, the Grand Tour was an essential part of his education. The pressure of events had robbed Gustav III of the opportunity, and only in 1783 did he feel free to travel for his own pleasure. Once again, he used an incognito, this time the Count of Haga. The royal party was made up of a few personal friends, Evert Taube, Axel von Fersen the Younger, Mauritz Armfelt, Hans Essen, Carl Peyron, his secretary Adlerbeth, who kept an entertaining diary, and, in Italy, the sculptor Sergel.

The group left Sweden in the autumn, and reached the valley of the Po by the end of October. In Venice, they took part in the carnival and the masked balls with enthusiasm. In Florence, Gustav spent days with Sergel in the galleries, although Armfelt noted in his diary that he was getting bored with churches. In Rome, Gustav was received by the pope and attended mass in St Peter's. He also met there another of Europe's enlightened despots, the Emperor Joseph II of Austria, also travelling incognito as Count Falkenstein. It is interesting to speculate on what the conversation may have been between the consciously aristocratic Swedish king and the equally consciously popular emperor. The next stop was Naples and the newly discovered ruins of Pompeii.

By the following summer, the tour had reached France, and Gustav could write that he felt he had returned to his fatherland. In Paris, he was received enthusiastically. Louis XVI and Marie Antoinette did their guest all honour; there was a brilliant reception at the Trianon, dinner in the pavilions of the park and a special performance at the theatre of Versailles. One night Gustavus was late for the Opéra, and the audience cheering him forced the cast to start the performance over again. He was specially invited to take part in an ordinary session of the Académie Française.

Politically, too, the visit was a success. The friendship between the two countries was further cemented, and Louis gave Sweden the West Indian island of St Barthelemy, so that Sweden had her only colony and free port in the new world. Only the end was a tragedy, when young Peyron was killed in a duel.

This Grand Tour is the first time that attention is drawn to Gustav Mauritz Armfelt; but of all their contemporaries, his is the name most closely linked to Gustav III's. He is for Swedes the epitome of a royal favourite. The Armfelts were impoverished Finnish nobles, and usually became soldiers. Gustav Mauritz had his full share of their courage, impulsiveness and hot temper. He once pulled a pistol in a quarrel with his father, to which the old man cried, 'Give me the other one, or it will be murder!' He was as much a charmer as his king; gay, light-hearted and irrepressible, and all in all was excellent company. Nor was he just another mess hero, for he was genuinely interested in the theatre, and a good amateur actor with a penchant for playing romantic lovers. Finally, he was strikingly good-looking, tall and strong. Gustav always liked to be surrounded by handsome young men, and his sister-in-law the duchess of Södermanland wrote of his Italian tastes; with a mother like Louisa Ulrika, they are scarcely surprising. Armfelt, although eleven years younger, became the king's closest and most intimate friend, and it is clear that the affection was sincere and two-sided. Gustav encouraged his marriage to the match of the day, the heiress Hedvig de la Gardie.

At home in Sweden, all was not well. Although Gustav's administration had been both just and efficient, there had been a couple of failed harvests. The aristocracy were still determined to win back the power they had held in the Age of Freedom, and the farmers were still bitter about not being allowed to make their own *schnaps*. As a result, the *Riksdag* of 1786 only lasted two months, before it was dismissed in response to the king's unpopularity.

In Finland, too, matters were no better. The country was already divided by Russian conquest, and among the Finnish nobility, as opposed to the people, there were many who wished to back the winning side and join the Russian empire. Their leader was the brother of the Sprengporten who had helped Gustav III in his first *coup d'état*.

In 1788, the opportunity came for Gustav to assert himself. Russia was at war with Turkey, when Sweden attacked her on the grounds of a very suspicious frontier incident. The war was entirely of Gustav's choice; he made a theatrical departure from Stockholm, but matched up unexpectedly well to the real thing. He fought through a winter campaign, eating salt herring with the men, and once used his scarf as a tourniquet for a wounded rower.

The war opened with an indecisive naval battle off Högland in the Gulf of Finland, but on land there was a disaster. No less than a 113 serving officers, among them Armfelt's uncle, and led by Colonel Hästesko, met at Anjala, and there signed a declaration that the war was in breach of the constitution as Sweden had started it, and therefore they refused to obey royal orders. The latent enmity of the aristocracy reinforced by the defeatism carried over from Karl XII's tragic wars had broken into open revolt. Gustav took this crisis bravely, and refused point-blank to negotiate with rebels. It was, however, obviously impossible for the army to advance, but Gustav's position was saved within a few days by the considerate entry of Denmark into the war.

This gave him an excuse to return to Sweden. Here there was far less defeatism and rather much bitterness against the officers who had resigned. First the king went to Dalecarlia, like Gustav Vasa, and raised a regiment of volunteers to be commanded by Mauritz Armfelt. He then reached the undefended Göteborg a day before the invading Danes, and put such heart into the burghers that the enemy withdrew.

Next spring the *Riksdag* met. Tempers ran high; the nobles were mostly Anjala men, while the other three estates were firmly royalist. Gustav made one of his finest speeches, denouncing the men who 'sought in the name of liberty to revive aristocratic tyranny'. Several nobles had their hands on their swords when the king ordered them to leave. For a tense moment, no one moved, then the elder statesman, Axel von Fersen, took Brahe, the premier count, by the arm and said, 'Let us go!' The Estates then passed the Act of Unity and Security which effectively made the king a dictator. The medieval council was abolished and the privileges of the nobility opened to the other estates. The Anjala rebels were arrested, but the humane Gustav allowed only one execution, that of Hästesko.

That summer the war was reduced to some desultory marching. Then, in 1790, the Swedes broke the impasse by attempting to capture the fortress of Viborg from the sea. It was a bold stroke and it failed. Instead of opening the land route into Russia, the Swedish fleet was trapped at the head of the Gulf of Finland by the larger Russian fleet. Catherine's admiral, the Prince of Nassau, had fifty ships-of-the-line to Gustav's thirty-four. Gustav and his flag-captain, Stedinck, had no choice but to fight their way out. What followed is known as the Viborg Gauntlet, and is one of the few feats of the Swedish navy. In the early summer dawn, the first Swedish ships broke the enemy line, and almost the whole fleet fought its way out, taking a savage punishment from the Russian guns. The king himself had to row for it from a crippled ship.

The fleet regrouped in the shelter of the Finnish islands. Then, on the glorious 9 July, Gustav led the Swedish navy to its Trafalgar at Svensksund. The Russians were stronger both in ships and fire-power, and the gunfire was audible in St Petersburg. That was the only Russian satisfaction. Their line was broken by Törning's squadron, and then Hjelmstierna slipped through the islands and caught them in the rear.

Gustav was on board his flagship, *Seraphimerordern*, throughout the action. The cannonade lasted throughout the night, and by dawn the Russians had lost fifty-two ships against Swedish losses of six.

All Europe was surprised, and the Empress Catherine shaken by her defeat. The dilettante intellectual had suddenly turned into a warrior. Soon afterwards, peace was signed at Värälä, restoring the *status quo ante*. Gustav had won prestige by his war, but had lost a lot of money. There was also one very important intangible benefit: Russian interference in Sweden's internal politics was over and the status of satellite conclusively broken.

Meanwhile, greater events were shaking the outside world. Gustavus III, with his romantic royalism, his autocracy and his love of France, was bound to oppose the Revolution, and he threw himself into what was almost a personal duel. Wildly unrealistic plans were drawn up to land Swedish and Russian troops in Normandy or at Ostend; but, luckily, Catherine would not play. Gustav himself went to Aix-la-Chapelle, the capital of the émigrés, to encourage them. His ambassador in Paris was useless, for Madame de Staël was a leading revolutionary. Instead, Gustav used a Swedish soldier in French service, Axel von Fersen.

Axel von Fersen the Younger was the son of the distinguished leader of the Hats. His father sent him to Paris as a junior officer, where, in spite of his reserve, his good looks made him a social success. One old lady wrote, 'Son figure et son air convenaient parfaitement à un heros de roman!' And he was, indeed, to live a romantic story. There was one girl with a dull husband who found him particularly attractive; and that was the pretty young Dauphiness of France, Marie Antoinette. But Fersen, rather than boasting of his conquest, gallantly left Versailles to avoid the temptation of such a scandalous *affaire*. He joined his friend Evert Taube to serve as an ADC to Lafayette with the French troops fighting for the Americans in the War of Independence. When he returned, Marie Antoinette was queen, but Fersen remained her respectful servant as colonel of the Royal Suèdois.

The eighteenth century was heedlessly approaching its grim end. The idealism of the *philosophes* and the elegance of the Trianon were about to disappear in the horrors of the Revolution. When the old favourites, the spongers and the flatterers had abandoned the king and the queen, one foreigner lived up to the code of chivalry for his lady. Fersen saw more of Marie Antoinette in those twilight days at Versailles than ever before. He galloped from Paris with the news of the march of the women, and gave Louis the hours of warning that he wasted.

After the royal family's removal to the Tuileries, Fersen was their constant visitor with news of the outside world and messages, regardless of his personal danger. There was only one serious attempt to save the king and queen of France, and it was entirely the work of this Swede. Fersen had a carriage specially built, arranged with Bouillé for troops to meet the refugees, bribed the guards and planned the escape from the palace. Late in the evening on 20 June 1791, the dauphin and his sister were led disguised to a big carriage outside the Tuileries. Soon Marie Antoinette slipped out to join them, and at last Louis too was free. On the box, dressed as the coachman, Fersen drove them across Paris, through the gate and out into the country. There another officer took over, and Fersen went independently to Mons. The ghastly suspense of the flight is famous, the arrest at Varennes and Choiseul's dragoons who arrived too late.

On the 23rd, Fersen made the brief controlled note in his diary, 'Was informed the king was taken.' Next week, broken by the failure, he joined Gustavus III at Aix. Yet Fersen was to see Marie Antoinette once again. The juggernaut of the revolution had gone far by February 1792 when Fersen and a companion returned to Paris, disguised as couriers. The Terror was beginning, and there could be no more welcome victim than the man who had almost saved the king and queen. Fersen entered the Tuileries disguised and was hidden there in the queen's rooms on the night of the 13th, to leave next day. Outside France, appalled by the indifference even of Vienna, he made hopeless plans for escape and bullied the allied commanders, until the guillotine made his efforts in vain.

It will never be known for certain whether Marie Antoinette became Fersen's mistress. Yet all their letters and Fersen's diary survived into this century in an old castle in Sweden. Some were published by his descendant, Klinkowström; the details of Fersen's loyal service to 'Josephine', which was her code name, and her pathetic last farewell to the dearest and most loved of men. There were many omissions which historians were waiting to fill; but when Klinkowström died, not one letter was to be found. He was a gentleman of the old school, and rather than have the world read a woman's love letters, he had burnt them all.

The violence of the time was restricted neither to France nor to the mob. In Sweden, the nobles sulked after Anjala, shunning the court and building a secret opposition. On 16 March, there was a grand masked ball at the new opera house in Stockholm. Of course, the king would attend, and he dined in his flat at the Opera with Baron Essen. During the meal a letter was delivered that contained an anonymous warning to avoid the ball. Gustavus, however, scorned to appear afraid. He went downstairs, dressed in a black domino and a white mask, but the ribbon of the Order of the Seraphim easily gave him away. In the throng, a group of black dominoes surrounded the king, and suddenly a shot was heard. Gustavus cried out, 'Je suis blessé!' and the murderers fled. Essen's drawn sword had prevented the *coup de grâce*, and, taking command, he had all the doors to the opera locked. Gustavus was helped to a sofa in his room, and among the first to arrive was Armfelt, who had not been at the ball. He was greeted by the king with a jest and asked whether he would have expected to find Gustavus wounded in the back, all the while that the blood was staining the sofa.

In the foyer, Liljensparre, the chief of police, was examining each guest before they could depart. No evidence was found, but the next day the anonymous warning gave away its author, Lilliehorn, and he in turn led to Counts Clas Horn and Adolf Ribbing, and finally to the man who fired the actual shot, Captain Ankarström. Their motives were various. Horn and Ribbing were aristocrats who bitterly resented Gustavus' abolition of the political power of their order; they were egged on by a veteran plotter of the Age of Freedom, General Pechlin. Ankarström was a more complex character. He was an ardent disciple of Jean-Jacques Rousseau, and an admirer of the Revolution. He had also conceived a pathological hatred of Gustav as a man.

At first the wound was not regarded as fatal, and the king received all the world in his bedroom at the palace. Typically, he refused to be told the names of his assassins. Soon, however, blood-poisoning set in. It is a slow and painful death, but Gustav never showed any sign of suffering, and only when the agony became too great did he ask to be alone. At last the day came when the doctor told him that there were only six hours left. Gustav drew up a regency, with Armfelt as governor of Stockholm and Taube as foreign minister. His last hours were spent talking with his closest friends. It was a brave and dignified death.

Such is the factual background to Verdi's opera, *Un Ballo in Maschera*, Gustavus was seen as a martyr by his people, and the nobility were openly blamed for his murder. The aristocratic opposition had finally won its duel with the king. But Anjala and the assassination left the Swedish aristocracy in a position of popular contempt.

Gustav III's son, Gustav IV Adolf, was aged thirteen when he became king. His father's will was confused, and Duke Karl as the regent soon edged out all able Gustavians like Armfelt, Taube and Toll from positions of power. No attempt was made to punish any of the conspirators, except Ankarström, who, as the actual murderer, had to die. One cannot escape the impression that Duke Karl was not entirely ignorant of the plot.

The new regent was a pathetic contrast to his brilliant brother. Intellectually, he represented the soft underside of the Enlightenment. Uninterested in art or science, he was a dabbler in the occult and a leading freemason, and had already run up large debts to back various pseudo-mystical con men. His great ambition was to be king, but he was quite unable to use power himself. It was obvious that such a man and the other Gustavians would not have much in common. Instead, Duke Karl took as his minister Baron G. A. Reuterholm, and so great was his influence that he was soon the effective ruler of the country. Reuterholm was another freemason, and, indeed, a religious maniac who had found it expedient to leave the country a few years before. He too was a follower of Rousseau and an admirer of the French Revolution, and soon introduced such revolutionary ideas as abolishing the freedom of the press and starting a secret police. When the Swedish Academy failed to elect him a member, he suspended it.

Armfelt had been made ambassador to Naples to get him out of the way. However, he was genuinely fond of his royal friend's son and hoped to save him from this upbringing. Some indiscreet letters were written, and from them Reuterholm was able to concoct a plot. Armfelt himself took refuge in Russia; and Reuterholm was only able to take out his spite on a woman, Armfelt's mistress, the Countess Magdalena Rüdensköld, who was put in the stocks as a whore and imprisoned in the house of correction.

The new régime reversed Gustav III's foreign policy and signed a treaty with the French Republic. Reuterholm then tried to be reconciled with Russia by proposing the marriage of Gustav Adolf to a Russian princess; but on the visit to St Petersburg, the empress made a complete fool of him and broke the engagement off, in spite of the fact that there was real affection between the two young people.

In 1796, Gustav Adolf came of age, and his first acts were to dismiss Reuterholm and to send his uncle, Duke Karl, to live on his estates. The new king was a strange, sad figure. As a royal only child, he had grown up to be very lonely and suffered from severe fits of melancholy, which became more intense as he grew older. He had a boundless admiration for his father, but they had little in common. As a man, Gustav Adolf was obstinate, simple, religious, hard-working, extremely conscientious and rather stupid; as a king, he was respected more than loved. In 1797, he married the beautiful princess, Frederika of Baden, who bore him three children.

The economy was in a parlous state after the Finnish War. The king himself set an example of frugal living, even having his boots resoled, and he refused to pay his uncle's debts. However, more was needed to support the currency, and the town of Wismar in Germany was pawned for one and a half million talers. Gustav Adolf was interested in his German territories and was responsible for freeing the serfs in Swedish Pomerania. His father's wish for a school for Swedish military cadets was also fulfilled, and the palace of Karlberg on the outskirts of Stockholm was bought in 1792 to be the Swedish Sandhurst. The most important event for the economy was the *Enskifte*, which meant the final end of the medieval system of farming. The holdings of land were consolidated, and the farms moved out of the villages into the countryside, with an enormous increase in productivity. The leading advocate of this reform was Rutger Maclean of Svaneholm in Skåne, where it was carried through in 1803, and four years later this was extended to the rest of the country.

Throughout the rest of Europe, France was waging war, and although Sweden took no part, many of her merchantmen had been captured as prizes by English privateers. It was difficult to get other countries to share the British view that, in war-time, the oceans of the world are British territory, and Sweden, Russia, Prussia and Denmark joined together to form the League of Nordic Neutrality. As a response, Sir Hyde Parker's fleet was sent to the Baltic in 1801. Nelson, the second-in-command, destroyed the Danish fleet at Copenhagen, watched impotently by Gustav·Adolf from across the Sound. The British fleet then sailed for the Swedish naval base of Karlskrona, but before it arrived, the League had collapsed with the murder of the tsar, Paul I.

After the Treaty of Amiens, Gustav Adolf set off for Germany, and was absent for over a year. While he was staying with his wife's family in Baden, the duke of Enghein was abducted and executed by Napoleon. Gustav Adolf was particularly horrified by this murder, and his hatred of Napoleon grew to be fanatical. In his obstinate brain, he saw himself as the Karl XII who would rid Europe of the Corsican tyrant. In 1805, Sweden declared war on France, and so joined Britain and Russia, with the essential help of Canning's subsidies. Sweden's strategic importance lay in the fact that she was the only serious gap in the Continental System and half her exports of iron went to England. Her military part was, in fact, most inglorious. There was some vague marching in Northern Germany, and the French marshal, Bernadotte, captured some Swedish officers at Lübeck. Napoleon's victory at Austerlitz broke the coalition in 1807, and Pomerania and Stralsund soon fell. When Russia and France made peace at Tilsit, Sweden was left as Britain's only ally in Europe, loyal but ineffective.

Her position was desperate when, in 1808, the Russians invaded Finland. In Denmark, Bernadotte's army was only kept out by the British navy, watched by the king and the old Gustavian, General Toll, at his headquarters at Bäckaskog castle. Britain's other gesture of support was to send Sir John Moore with an army of 11,000 to Gothenborg, but Gustav Adolf forbade him to land his men and he soon sailed away to meet his end in Spain.

In Finland, the Swedish field-marshal, Klingspor, simply retreated northwards in face of the stronger Russian forces, in spite of acts of useless heroism from men like Döbeln and Adlerkreutz. Strategically, all was far from lost; for the fortress of Sveaborg outside Helsinki posed a constant threat to cut the Russian invaders off from their bases. Then, with 5,000 men and all its provisions, unassaulted, faced by a weaker enemy, Sveaborg surrendered after a two-month seige. The motives of its commander, Admiral Cronstedt, are still a mystery. He may well have been bribed by the Russians; but it is equally possible that he was a victim of the general defeatism that had been spreading for years among Sweden's officers. To the men, and above all to the ordinary Finns, it was treachery.

Defeat only made Gustav Adolf more obstinate in his hopeless war. In 1809, the pardonable exasperation erupted, and Colonel Adlersparre marched on Stockholm from Värmland to make peace. In the capital others acted, and on the morning of 13 March General Adlercreutz arrested the king in the palace. In a dramatic scene, his sword was taken away from him. Then Gustav Adolf gave his captors the slip through a secret spiral staircase, only to be held again in the great courtyard and dragged back to his rooms. The conspirators then imprisoned him at

Gripsholm, where, years before, the unhappy Erik XIV had been incarcerated.

A *Riksdag* was summoned to work under the slogan, 'First the constitution, then the king.' The Swedish constitution of 1809 is the oldest written constitution still in force in Europe. It established a liberal monarchy, responsible to the freely elected *Riksdag*, with, as in Britain, parliament holding the purse-strings. Next the Peace of Fredrikshamn was signed with Russia, leaving the enemy in possession of all her conquests, Finland, north-eastern Sweden and the Åland Isles.

Gustav Adolf was a broken man and he abdicated his throne gladly. He lived on for another twenty-eight years, divorced from his wife, wandering restlessly and pathetically across Europe, first as the count of Gottorp, then merely as Colonel Gustavson. Duke Karl was elected king, and took the title of Karl XIII; but he was clearly only a childless caretaker. The nobility's hatred for the Gustavs appeared at its most contemptible when the rights of the young Prince Gustav were thrown aside. Instead, the Danish prince, Christian August, was elected as Karl's heir. His fate was to be promptly killed in a riding accident. There were rumours of poison, and at his funeral the Stockholm mob tore the earl marshal, Axel von Fersen, from his carriage and beat him to death in the street in front of troops who refused to intervene. It was the anniversary of the flight to Varennes. The eighteenth century was indeed over.

10. Baroque and Rococo

In the very heart of Stockholm, on the shore of the island that is the old town, stands one of the most beautiful buildings in Europe. The royal palace is a masterpiece of proportion in architecture, and perhaps the only royal city residence that can rival it is the Hradčany Castle in Prague. The design is simplicity itself; a square block with a central courtyard whose north and south façades are extended in both directions by lower wings. But the result has the perfection of a mathematical law.

The fire that destroyed the old castle at the beginning of Karl XII's reign left Nicodemus Tessin the Younger with a clear site. All that remained was the north front he himself had built, and this formed the basis for the rest of the palace. The mood is serious, almost austere, as suited those epic years. There is no decoration, no central pediment, the regular line of the windows crosses the rust-coloured plaster like soldiers on parade. Of the courtyard, one can but say that it shows that the Louvre is too big, the Palazzo Farnese too small.

The palace had three functions to fulfil: ceremonial, residential and

The Royal Palace at Stockholm

administrative. The south front bears its pomp well; at the centre, applied to the wall, is a triumphal arch six columns wide, dedicated to the military glories of Karl XII and rising the full height of the façade. On passing through the central door, one enters a superb hall, equally reaching to the roof, its vault and walls covered by the panoplies of Mars; on either side, double Baroque stairs lead up to the Rikssalen, the Throne Room, and to the chapel, which occupy the rest of this front. The Throne Room is essentially Baroque, too, with its fluted Corinthian columns, but, on the gallery level, the next architect, Hårleman, has put Rococo statues of the mythological virtues. The chapel is purer in style; the high altar is an exuberant group of stucco by the Frenchman, L'Archévêque, worthy of Bernini, and the whole room has the splendour of the seventeenth century. The royal apartments are in the east front and look across a garden flanked by the wings down to the river. In the courtyard, this is the most decorated side and looks like a Roman palace with its rusticated pillars and its caryatids. Opposite, to the west, was housed the civil service, and their offices spread into the out-buildings that form a separate semicircular courtyard.

The site of the palace is also striking, for it occupies a corner of the island and all the state rooms look out over the water. Seen from the other shore, its horizontals match the expanse of the river. Originally, Tessin had intended a mall across the island where the Parliament now is, to Gustav Adolf's Square, with a church to close the vista; but all that now recalls the concept is the façade of the crown prince's palace. On the other side, towards the town, Tessin planned great houses for the nobles to match the splendour of the palace. He set an example with his own house, which is now the residence of the governor of Stockholm. Its plain Roman façade respectfully faces the south front of the palace, but inside it is an architect's playground. Tessin employed all his favourite craftsmen to decorate its pleasant rooms. The site is an awkward wedge: on the ground floor, a hall of pillars leads through to a minute garden that is a dramatic exercise in false perspective, ending in an architectural vista. Here Nicodemus's son, Count Carl Gustav Tessin, who took over and completed the work on the royal palace, held court.

He was one of many remarkable men who flourished in the Age of Freedom. It was as if all the energy which their fathers had expended in the wars of Karl XII had been bottled up by peace and needed to be released elsewhere. Sweden's intellectual life has never been so active as during the first half of the eighteenth century, and two names in it are world famous: Swedenborg and Linneaus.

Emanuel Swedenborg came from a religious family. His father, Jesper Svedberg, was a bluff and rather intolerant cleric who became bishop of Skara and wrote several hymns which are still sung in church today. The family was later ennobled as Swedenborg. Emanuel, although he spoke with angels even as a child, had a practical start in life, studying at Uppsala and then at London and Oxford. He made his career at the

College of Mines, and also had to work as a military engineer in the fateful Norwegian campaign. At Lund, he met Karl XII, and noted in his diary his admiration for the king's mathematical talents.

With the return of peace, Swedenborg continued his practical work. His European scientific reputation was made with the *Opera philosophica et mineralia*, in which he identified that Sweden had once lain beneath the ocean, although he assumed this to have been a consequence of the Flood. He also published useful work on anatomy and physics. Although he refused to be either Hat or Cap, Swedenborg spoke often and well as a peer in the *Riksdag* debates. This was a man of the world, who was able to charm even those who came to scoff. We can see him in Per Krafft's portrait at Gripsholm, with his very long face, high forehead and square jaw.

Then, at the age of about fifty-seven, Swedenborg had a revelation as drastic as Pascal's. It is not fair for a rational man to write about Swedenborg. He is undoubtedly one of the religious geniuses of Europe; yet he claimed that his first important vision came after a good dinner, when God appeared in person and warned him not to eat so much. That seems to be really making things too easy for the behaviourists!

Swedenborg thereafter saw himself sent by God to proclaim a new church, the fifth in a series, to replace Christianity, which mankind had outgrown. Throughout his work there is a confusing contrast between a reasonable and ingenious theology and the mystical and at times ludicrous descriptions of the next world. The human will is central to Swedenborg's thought, in which he was to be followed by Kant and Schopenhauer, and heaven and hell are the results of deliberate choice. His views on adultery and sex in general are remarkably broad-minded. It is, however, not for this that Swedenborg is most remembered. No man can ever have explored heaven and hell in quite such detail. Indeed, one suspects that these voyages are the product of those dark, endless nights of the long Swedish winter. Heaven is a most hieratical society, where the angels, who are in fact all men who have died, wear special uniforms and live in grace-and-favour houses. Indeed, the next world is a very close reflection of this one. In the celestial London, where most Englishmen go, the good live near the Royal Exchange, the intelligentsia in Islington and the not-so-good down by Wapping, which seems fair enough! A whole series of books give this revelation to the world, the fundamental one being the *Arcana coelestia*.

Undoubtedly Swedenborg had strange powers. He once frightened a Gothenborg dinner party by accurately describing a fire raging simultaneously in Stockholm. His contemporaries did not quite know what to make of him. When he told C. G. Tessin that he would be a councillor in heaven, he got the sensible reply that Tessin had had enough of that on earth. Swedenborg's last years were spent in London, for he was very fond of England, and there he died in 1772.

The split in the eighteenth-century character between the mystical and the enlightened is neatly personalized by Swedenborg and Linnaeus. Linnaeus, or Carl von Linné, as he became, is one of the greatest scientists of history. He is the founder of systematic botany, and it is for this that he is best remembered, but his work also embraced animals, fishes, even minerals. His influence on Swedish life is still strong today. Dag Hammarskjöld took him as the theme of his presidential address to the Swedish Academy. Every summer, thousands of Swedish school-children set out at weekends to pick the flowers of the countryside, and take them home to be pressed and mounted for the coming lessons. Botany is for the Swedes part of a general education, not a specialist subject.

Linnaeus had a remarkably happy life. He was born of a family of Småland yeomen. His father was the rector of Stenbrohult, where his little turf-roofed rectory still stands, near the idyllically beautiful lake Mökeln. He was a devout and gentle man whose great joy was his garden.

From this home in the depths of the country, Linnaeus went to Lund and then Uppsala to read medicine. He had very little money and had to put paper soles inside his worn-out shoes. Already his great love was

Linnaeus, by Alexander Roslin

botany, and one day the dean of Uppsala, Olof Celsius, picked him up in the university garden, and lodged the poor student in his home. In 1732, Linnaeus got himself a scholarship to visit Lapland, then a wild and unknown country. The purpose of the journey was scientific and practical, and Linnaeus' account describes the plants and animals and the life of the Lapps, but the young man who rode out of Uppsala with a song on his lips was also struck by the beauty of the fells and rivers. The Lapland journey is the most readable of scientific reports. It was an immediate success, both for its novelty and its usefulness. The governor of Dalecarlia invited Linnaeus to cover his province too, and it was at Christmas in Falun, where the great copper mines are, that Linnaeus met his future wife, Sara Lisa Moraea, a rich doctor's daughter. He courted her in his Lapp costume, which no one had seen before.

In 1735, Linnaeus had to go to Holland to take his final degree. His reputation had preceded him, and there he found a patron to publish his *Systema naturae*. This work is the basis of the Linnaean system, which classifies all plants on the basis of gender, dividing them into twenty-four classes, monandria, diandria and so on, depending on the number of stamens. Each plant then has a triple Latin name. It is the first attempt at a rational catalogue of botany, and it was also new in that it was based on observation, not on theory.

In Holland, Linnaeus met George Clifford, a director of the East India Company, whose remarkable garden at Hartekamp was full of exotic specimens which Linnaeus described. Clifford sent him to London to meet his friends, who included Sir Hans Sloane and Robert Boyle. The Linnean Society still has the envelope with the address, 'Lodging at the Swedish Minister in Princes Square', in case Linnaeus, who spoke no English, got lost. The charming story that Linnaeus first saw gorse flowering in England and thanked God on his knees for the joy of the sight, is unfortunately probably only a legend.

Back in Stockholm, Linnaeus set up as a doctor, and soon had a flourishing practice curing young men about town of the clap. He found a generous friend and patron in C. G. Tessin, and even lodged in his palace, earning the nickname 'the Hats' doctor'. Soon Tessin obtained for him the chair of medicine and botany at Uppsala, which he held for the rest of his life. Linnaeus was a born teacher; he was loved by his students, and many of the poor ones ate free at his table. All summer long he would as a don march out at the head of his class to collect flowers. They would all picnic in the fields, and the day would end on the return to Uppsala with a triple shout of, 'Vivat Linnaeus!' Students came from all over Europe, and even the New World sent him Adam Kuhn, later a professor at Philadelphia.

The *Riksdag* commissioned other journeys to Skåne, Öland, Gotland and West Gothland, and Linnaeus described each province and recommended improved farming techniques and different crops in books that are part of Swedish literature. Queen Louisa Ulrika was captivated by his work, and Linnaeus was raised to the nobility as von Linné. He was elected a foreign member of the Royal Society in London, and of most other learned academies, from Philadelphia to St Petersburg.

Many stories are told of his kindness and modesty. In the wild forests of Sweden, there grows a rare plant that creeps among the grass and which has little pink, bell-like flowers; and finding it was nameless, Linnaeus took it for his emblem and christened it *Linnaea borealis*. It became the crest on his coat of arms, and in all his portraits he holds a sprig of it. His sense of wonder before nature never palled, 'the day without night of the Lapland summer and the night without day of the Falun mines'; but the pastoral ideal darkens with the years into a strange and introspective notebook, the *Nemesis divina*. He lies buried in Uppsala cathedral beneath a medallion by Sergel to the prince of botanists.

London has particular links with Linnaeus; for when he died his widow sold his entire collection of plants, insects and even fishes, together with his whole library, to Sir James Smith. It was all sent to England, narrowly escaping, so the story goes, the frigate Gustav III dispatched in pursuit to bring it back. The collection and the library now belong to the Linnean Society of London, which has its seat in Burlington House. The pressed flowers are perfectly preserved, and one can try to decipher the untidy handwriting in the manuscripts of his books.

Sweden has other relics; there is Krafft's portrait at the Academy of Science, with its twinkling, happy eyes; Roslin's at Gripsholm of the serious old man. At Uppsala, the Linné Garden has been restored as it was originally; the beds are laid out according to the Linnaean system, and, at the far end, is the elegant orangery built by his friend Hårleman. At the near-by professor's lodgings are more treasures: the magnificent silver dish that used to be filled with the wild strawberries Linnaeus ate as a cure for gout, and a tea service made in China and painted with the linnaea. There, too, is the famous portrait of Linnaeus in Lapland dress.

The pilgrimage which every admirer of Linnaeus and every lover of flowers must make is to Hammarby, the little manor house which Linnaeus bought himself about six miles from Uppsala. It is a numinous place. Linnaeus' heirs kept Hammarby with great piety for over a hundred years; little was allowed to change. Even today, when it has become a museum, it lacks the deadness of an institution and radiates peace and simplicity. Facing the rich open fields of the Uppsala plain, it stands, a typical Swedish farmhouse with its two-storeyed wooden living quarters and, in front of it, a garden with a low stable on either side enclosing the square. The well-stocked garden is full of flowers which are descendants of the very ones Linnaeus himself planted. Behind the house rises an outcrop of granite, covered in pines and firs; at the summit is the little one-room pavilion that Linnaeus had built to contain his collections in a place safe from fire. Inside, the house has the same charm as the outside. It is simple, homely and welcoming. It is easy to imagine the great botanist sitting there with his family and his favourite students about him. The drawing room, although it has little furniture and only bare pine floors, is a most comfortable room, for its big windows seem to bring the garden into the house. Upstairs, in Linnaeus' study, is the master's writing desk and hard chair. His bedroom is papered with the plates of a botanical work, and also has a picture of the monkey with which Queen Louisa Ulrika presented him.

There was another Uppsala professor in these years who gave something to all the world. Anders Celsius occupied the chair of astronomy, and was one of Linnaeus' earliest friends. The Celsius family were well-known in the clerical and intellectual world. Anders did much original work on the Northern Lights and the returns of comets, but what he will always be remembered for is the invention of the logical thermometer system, where water freezes at zero and boils at 100 degrees, and many countries still refer to this measurement as Celsius rather than calling it centigrade.

So far all this intellectual energy has come from an academic and bourgeois background; the court had contributed nothing, nor was it likely to with a king such as Frederick I. In the politics of the Age of Freedom, however, the spirit of eighteenth-century utilitarianism was strong; it had inspired Linnaeus' journeys, and its theories were spread by Olof Dalin's newspaper, the *Swedish Argus*, modelled on the English *Spectator*. In 1739, the Academy of Sciences (Vetenskapsakademien) was founded, with Linnaeus as its first president, counting among its members Count Anders von Höpken, one of the leading hats, and the great industrialist Alstrom.

As manufacturing expanded, the *bruk* became the centre of industry. The *bruk* is a unique Swedish institution, by no means extinct even today, where a single factory creates a whole community, where the owner living in the manor is the manager as well, and is usually sited far away in the forests. One of the oldest *bruks* belonged to the Dutch industrialist Louis de Geer at Lövsta in Uppland; and although his original home was burnt by the Russians in 1719, it was rebuilt at once. The main street with its homes for the workmen along either side has not been altered since the eighteenth century; and on the east side splendid iron gates made in the factory lead to the plain but grand manor of the 'patron'. The church too is an integral part of the self-contained complex, and still possesses an outstanding contemporary organ. Every building is painted in a warm yellow. Down in Småland the Swedish glass industry has also been built up from the *bruks*, which often started as iron works. Kosta is the oldest, founded in 1742 by Koskull and Stael von Hostein (hence Ko-Sta, soon to be followed by Orrefors, where the old smithies survive, and Boda.

When Adolf Frederick and Louisa Ulrika became king and queen, matters changed. Adolf Frederick was a civilized man, and Louisa Ulrika had the drive and intelligence of her brother Frederick the Great. She had known Voltaire at Potsdam and encouraged the traditional influence of France on Swedish life. French became the second language of the educated classes, and Swedish itself absorbed a host of French words, usually ones to describe the arts and graces of life.

Louisa Ulrika was an unashamed intellectual, interested in art, music and, above all, drama. With the support of Dalin, she founded her own academy in 1753, of Letters, History and Antiquities (Vitterhets-akademien). At Drottningholm, the queen collected an extremely valuable library, which is still undisturbed in the beautiful room which J. E. Rehn designed for it. Louisa Ulrika's great passion was the theatre, and she built one at Drottningholm as well as at Ulriksdal. French actors provided Stockholm with its first resident company.

These years also saw the first Swedish composer of stature, J. H. Roman. As a violin prodigy, he had been sent to study in London by Karl XII, who was no mean musician himself. He produced a stream of very attractive chamber-music and small symphonies, but his best-known piece is the *Drottningholm Music,* written for the wedding of Adolf Frederik and Louisa Ulrika.

The literary world centred on the salon of Madame Nordenflycht, who played hostess to the political rivals of the queen. She herself wrote some pleasant if not very good lyrics. The golden youth of the salon was Count G. F. Gyllenborg, who belonged to one of the leading Hat families; but the better poet was Count Gustav Philip Creutz, later to become ambassador to Paris and first minister of Gustav III. He wrote a delightful Rococo pastoral about Atis and Camilla in a Swedish which has the elegance and lightness of French.

Louisa Ulrika's theatre at Drottningholm has a romantic history. It was built by Adelkrantz in 1766, and while the queen and her son lived, it echoed almost nightly to the lastest operas and to French and Swedish plays. When the Bernadottes came it was literally forgotten, and for over a century the dust grew thicker. Then, in 1921, Professor Agne Beijer went to look at the old theatre. Nothing had been touched; the velvet was frayed and the ropes broken, but otherwise here was a perfect eighteenth-century theatre. It was soon reopened, and every summer there is a season of opera, always such operas as might have been played there in its hey-day, often by Gluck, who was Gustav's favourite composer. Both the singers and the orchestra wear powdered wigs and Rococo clothes. The golden light mimics candles well, and it is easy to forget the last two hundred years. If only in today's democratic Sweden anyone could dare to wear a dinner jacket in public, Drottningholm would be a yet more beautiful Glyndebourne.

The theatre is striking in its simplicity, both within and without. Adelkrantz's design fuses the stage and the auditorium together; the same discreet pilasters surround the whole and the chandeliers catch the plainness of the traditional white and gold. There are thirty-five sets that have survived, with ingenious bits of mechanism, like the enormous screw used to give an impression of distant waves, or the cannon balls rolled about to make thunder. Along the left side of the theatre, Gustav III got Desprez to build him a foyer, whose big windows look out over

Eighteenth-century set in position on the stage at Drottningholm Theatre

his newly made English park. It is a beautiful room, entirely classical and plain to the point of austerity, while from the balustrade surrounded dome of the ceiling, hang five superb chandeliers.

In the park, some way from the main palace, stands the Chinese Pavilion. It was originally built by Adolf Frederik as a birthday present for his wife, and again the architect was Adelkrantz, assisted by J. E. Rehn. The pavilion is a delightful *chinoiserie* fantasy, born just as the fashion for things Oriental had begun to sweep across Europe. It is no more than a summer-house, a central block with one big conversation room and curved wings on either side. All that is Chinese about it is the decoration; the outside is all in red and white, with undulating roofs and flames along the ridges. Inside, Chinese motifs have been employed wherever possible, with a charmingly naïve European effect; much of the porcelain, however, is genuinely oriental. Upstairs is an intimate library with its original books. In the north-west wing is 'La Confidence', a private dining room where the royal family could be free of any servants; the table sinks on a lift into the cellar to be laid and served.

The other great architect of the period was Carl Hårleman. Apart from taking over the Royal Palace at Stockholm from Tessin when he was too busy with politics, his work is mostly private. Down in Skåne he built a home for Baron Hans Ramel at Övedskloster which is an architectural gem. That connoisseur Gustav III, when he saw it for the first time, said enviously, 'C'est trop royal pour un particulier!' (It is too royal for a private citizen!) From the road the house is protected by a vast *cour d'honneur*, walled in with no less than two pavilions on either side. All this is in white, but the decorations on the main house are in the local red sandstone, ideal for such a Rococo scheme. On the garden front, and the formal garden is perfectly kept, the ground drops away and the house stands on a heavily rusticated basement. Inside, the family have kept the original furniture, and, among other treasures, a portrait of Creutz by Per Krafft, and a bust of Ramel by Sergel.

Hårleman also built a country home for C. G. Tessin at Åkerö. The position on an island in the lake is idyllic. What is original is the placing of the living rooms on the ground floor so that the house, only two storeys high, has far better proportions. The drawing room is entirely painted in *trompe l'oeil* convincing beyond its Doric columns stretch false parks and gardens. There is also an elegant *chinoiserie* sitting room.

One practical invention deserves to be mentioned here, and that is Cronstadt's tiled stove with its serpentine flue. It was a most efficient form of heating and made Swedish homes the warmest in Europe, something which they are still today. The china factory at Marieberg specialized in these stoves, making them like columns or like temples, so that they became a major item of furniture in the room.

The second half of the eighteenth century proved to be intellectually yet more important for Sweden – indeed, her Antonine Age when this far-off country was the epitome of the period. At the centre of this cultural blossoming was 'the Charmer King' himself.

Gustav III's greatest love was the theatre. Even as a small child he learnt whole tirades from French plays, and was found by his tutor, dressed in a sheet, declaiming them in his room. His favourite roles were the heroines, a sign of the homosexuality fostered in a sensitive child by a domineering mother, and even in later life he retained a penchant for pages and young guardsmen. As a grown man, however, he always wished to play the hero. The need to deceive the alternating nonchalance and affection of his mother trained his actor's talents, till one of his exasperated contemporaries called him 'Ce grand peut-être'.

As we have already remarked, since Gustav's spiritual home was France, its model was Versailles, but a far more human version. There were constant ceremonies and balls, and even fabulous medieval tournaments with jousting and troubadors. 'La Prise de la Roche Galtare', held at Drottningholm in 1779, is an early hint of Romanticism. The days were given over to administration, but the evenings were filled far into the night by plays and opera, literary readings, studies of antiques, designing of palaces. Creutz would send his king each volume of the French *Encyclopédie* as it was published. Nor was this a man's court, for the fair sex were led by the three graces, Louisa Sparre and the sisters Ulla and Augusta von Fersen. In a mood of patriotism and economy, Gustav introduced a national Swedish dress which was often worn. Marie Antoinette even asked to see Axel Fersen in it at Verailles, with its long cloak and bright colours.

In 1786, Gustav founded the Swedish Academy, on the model of the French, and it takes precedence over the two older academies, with its apt motto *Snille och Smak* ('Talent and Taste'). The original members are an interesting mixture of nobles including Axel von Fersen the Elder, and Armfelt, aristocratic poets like G. F. Gyllenborg and J. G. Oxenstierna, and writers like Kellgren and Leopold. Its first tasks were to produce a Swedish dictionary and grammar. Gustav himself successfully entered an anonymous poem on Torstensson for its first competition.

Another of Gustav's ambitions, only fulfilled in the next century, was for a National Museum. He learnt to be an art lover from his mother and from his tutor Tessin, both great collectors. His favourite painter was Rembrandt, of whose work he bought several examples, as well pictures by contemporaries like Boucher and Fragonard, now in the museum at Stockholm. Happily, Gustav's collection of antiquities is intact and beautifully displayed in the royal palace at Stockholm, whose arcades frame the statues. Its pride is a superb Hellenistic work from Hadrian's villa at Tivoli, a languid sleeping Endymion. There is also a fine set of Roman copies of Apollo and the nine muses.

Swedish drama lacked both plays and theatres, a state of affairs which Gustav energetically set about putting right. He summoned Adelkrantz, the architect of Drottningholm's theatre, to build an opera house for Stockholm. Erected on the site of the present one, it was a masterpiece designed to mirror the crown prince's palace across the square. Adelkrantz himself was a keen musician and it must have been one of the few opera houses ever to have been built by a professional. Sadly, the municipal vandals of the nineteenth century tore it down to replace it with something quite exceptionally ugly. Its first director was Carl Reinhold von Fersen, who was succeeded by Armfelt.

In one of the massive round towers of the renaissance castle at Gripsholm there was a disused chapel, and here Gustav got Erik Palmstedt to build him a delightful little theatre. After walking down grim stone corridors, one stumbles suddenly on this room, glittering in white and gold. Statues of Thalia and Melpomene by Sergel flank the stage, and the auditorium is designed as a classical amphitheatre, at the back of which a lovely crescent of massive Ionic pillars screens the boxes.

The absence of plays was a yet more severe problem, so Gustav set about writing them himself. In fact, he did much of the producer's work as well, designing the sets and choosing the music. However, Gustav was not a natural poet, and he also had a kingdom to administer, so he would write the complete text of the play with the details of all the action, either in Swedish or more usually in French, and then would get a poet to produce a version in Swedish verse. Gustav's best collaborator was Kellgren, who unfortunately disliked the job and was succeeded by Leopold. In fact, Gustav is one of the better playwrights in Swedish literature. He had a very keen dramatic sense and his plays always act extremely well, often being revived even today. As literature, they recall the bourgeois drama which Lessing was writing in Germany at the same time, but Gustav is more romantic in his love of local colour. His favourite historical character and his ideal king was Gustavus Adolphus; in fact, no less than three of Gustav's plays are set in his reign, when the king appears as the *deus ex machina* who preserves the right. Gustav shamelessly mixed comedy, tragedy and masque, and his plays really belong to the genre which became popular in the next century, the drama. Surprisingly, he is at his best when writing humorous or folksy scenes.

His first play, *Thetis and Pêlée*, was written to inaugurate the national theatre in 1773, but owed its wild success more to its author than its merits. There follows a lull of almost ten years, until Armfelt and his fiancée played the hero and heroine in *The Nobleness of Gustavus Adolphus*. The plot is drawn from the religious vendettas of the time of Karl IX, and Gustavus Adolphus, bringing the two lovers together, is shown as the great reconciler of the nation. The verse was written by Gyllenborg. The king himself is the hero in *Ebba Brahe*, a story of duty conquering love. It was enormously popular for its patriotic speeches and was later turned into an opera. Gustav's best play is probably *Helmfelt*. The plot is openly bourgeois, set again in the Thirty Years War, telling of a prodigal son who rises to become a general, and the governor of the province where his ruined merchant father has withdrawn to die in poverty. *Helmfelt* has the most appealingly realistic scenes of ordinary life, where the farmers and old soldiers and Helmfelt himself come alive far more than the grander heroes of the other plays.

The royal author did not ignore the other heroic events of his country's history. His love of the medieval came out in *Birger Jarl*, which is more of a pageant than a play. The most popular of all his works is without doubt *Gustav Vasa*, a splendid opera with some of Kellgren's best verse and Naumann's simple and warm music. The theme was bound to appeal to Gustav, who was so proud of his (weak) Vasa blood. The plot is almost Shakespearian in its ghosts, crowds, murders and battles. The première in 1786 was an outstanding and well-deserved success.

There was a tradition of aristocratic men of letters, such as Creutz, Gyllenborg and Oxenstierna, the latter best remembered for his pastoral idyll, *The Harvest*; but Gustav deliberately sought to raise the social status of writers in his circle. Kellgren is a poet in the classical eighteenth-century tradition. Born in Finland of poor clerical parents, he studied in Åbo and was introduced to the king by his fellow countryman, Armfelt. Gustav, who was always on the lookout for someone to write his plays for him, got Kellgren the job of tutor to the children of Louisa Sparre, one of the 'three graces'. He had already translated Horace and Propertius, but he made his name with the poem *My Laughter*, the thesis of which is that humour is the quality that raises man above the animals. This belief in the Enlightenment was fiercely held. As a journalist,

Kellgren attacked both the narrow-minded Lutherans and the mysta-gogic Swedenborg; more sadly, his uncompromising stand on freedom forced him to break with the king over politics. Before this, the two had collaborated in a series of successful plays. Already a royal librarian, Kellgren was appointed to the academy and was drawn by lot as its first president. There is a neatness in his life which ended in a bitter quarrel with nascent romanticism in the person of the young poet Thorild. After reading Kellgren's satire, 'You're not a genius, just because you're mad', one feels the elder generation won.

After politics had divided him from Kellgren, Gustav found a new collaborator in C.G. af Leopold, a disciple of Kellgren. Leopold had already attracted attention as a student at Uppsala, and later held various posts in the royal household; but, more important, he became Gustav's only real personal friend among the writers of the time. Witty and entertaining, he was always welcome in the king's study and was even summoned to Finland to help Gustav forget the burdens of war. *Helmfelt* is in its final version the work of Leopold.

The last Gustavian poet is Thorild, who really belongs to the period of Reuterholm and Karl XIII. His celebrated conflict with Kellgren heralds the end of the Gustavian era. However, he first attracted the king's attention with a savagely witty defence of his thesis, as a rather arrogant and self-righteous student at Uppsala, and this in spite of Thorild's being an anti-royalist, who enthusiastically welcomed the French Revolution. As a man, he was neurotically self-centred, but much of his poetry has the sheer verbal and rhythmic beauty of the great Romantics.

More than these, Gustav's reign boasts the only Swede, apart from Strindberg, who belongs to universal literature. Carl Michael Bellman is one of the world's few great lyric poets, and it is tragic that these superb poems, utterly untranslatable without a reincarnation, should be locked in an obscure language. He is also the only really great poet of the Rococo anywhere in Europe, and no one else has caught the mood of the late eighteenth century so well: the smile of reason and the awareness of life's sorrows.

Bellman was born in 1740 into a prosperous, bourgeois family. His father was a civil servant and his grandfather a professor at Uppsala. He had a gentleman's education, and friends from his youth included the noble poet Oxenstierna; even then Bellman was always ready with an impromptu poem. Yet, so far as earning his living was concerned, Bellman was hopeless. His father got him into the Bank of Sweden, but that job did not last long; the bank archives still have his *viva*, in which he admits he cannot do maths. Instead, the young man spent his time drinking in the pubs of Stockholm, or going as a welcome guest to any party. It was a common sight to see him arrive, tall, fair-haired and good-looking, and sit down pensively in a corner with his cithern on the table; then suddenly, after a few drinks, he would leap up and sing one of his poems to his own accompaniment on the cithern. It was a merry and bohemian circle, which included most of Sweden's intellectuals,

Sergel, Kellgren, painters like Hilleström and Martin; and then Bellman married a girl who proved, for him, the ideal wife. Inevitably, he came to Gustav's attention. The king got little to show for attempts to make Bellman write plays, but the poet acted willingly in them as an improvising jongleur. However, Gustav fully appreciated his genius and Bellman had a standing invitation to the king's private soirées at the palace on most Wednesdays. Meanwhile, Bellman's finances had not surprisingly broken down, and, living in a jungle of debts, he did regular spells in the debtors' prison until some patron bailed him out; he even applied for a pension on the grounds that his drinking songs had put up the turnover of the royal distilleries. Finally, Gustav took him in hand and provided a sinecure at the National Lottery. In return, Bellman became an enthusiastic royalist and did not long survive his king, dying in 1795.

Most of Bellman's poems were written for some occasion, impromptus casually thrown off. The most famous of these is 'Gustav's Toast', written in 1772. At the royalist *coup d'état*, Admiral Tersmeden, who had won the fleet for the king, entered the wardroom of his flagship to find Bellman improvising the poem to a delighted audience of officers, and next day, when Gustav rode out among the people, it was being sung in the streets to greet him. Later on, in his mock-heroic style, Bellman celebrated the battle of Högland and Gustav's return from Finland. Far greater as poetry are his elegies, deeply moving in their simplicity, for his mother or for their old maid; or his frighteningly beautiful cradle song for his son Karl, in which he bids the child sleep on before he wakes to all life's sorrows.

There are two sets of poems on which Bellman has tried to impose an order and a theme as Baudelaire did in *Les Fleurs du mal* and Horace in the *Odes*. Fredman's *Epistles* are a deliberate parody of St Paul's. In them, St Fredman expounds his philosophy of schnapps and sex so long as we are alive, but does it with a panache and wit that removes all vulgarity. The *Epistles* include a series of brilliant songs which retell well-known biblical stories with the most hilarious anachronisms from contemporary Sweden. Every Swedish child can sing about old gaffer Noah, who climbed out of the ark to replant the world with vines. It expresses the total disrespect which the man of Enlightenment, such as Voltaire himself, felt for the Christian Church.

Other poems are grouped together as the proceedings of the Noble Order of the Knights of Bacchus. Membership was restricted to those who had been found drunk in the gutter at least twice. The chapter would meet in the pub for the investiture of new knights taking their oaths to Bacchus and Freya, or for the obsequies of departed brothers, like the distiller Lundholm. By tradition, the seat of the order was an inn in the old town of Stockholm called Gyllene Freden, 'the Golden Peace', and Bellman's local still survives as a restaurant whose vaulted cellars continue to ring with his drinking songs.

The two essential themes of lyric poetry are death and love, and

POËTEN BELLMAN

Carl Michael Bellman, by P. Krafft

Bellman handles them with a unique originality. His two deities are Bacchus, the Roman god of wine, and Freya, the old Norse goddess of fertility; but Bacchus is the bringer not of joy but of oblivion for human misery, and Freya is only a tart in a pub. No one else, even in the Rococo, has achieved quite the same frivolous use of the vocabulary of mythology as did Bellman. This is realism without obscenity, as in the poem of the drunk who curses the day his parents went to bed to conceive him, and it is apt that Bellman should have written a poem on Hogarth's 'Midnight Conversation'. Yet he also had a real sense for nature, in particular for the archipelago of Stockholm, where the barmaid Ulla Winblad is rowed out to picnic in a poem whose words lap like waves against a boat.

Finally, there is probably no other lyric poet in whose work the underlying music is so essential. All Bellman's poems were written to be sung, usually by the author himself, and to hear them without their music is a major loss. In his music, Bellman did little more than adapt tunes from other composers, often from Mozart, for whom he wrote a sad elegy, and they remained simple so that he could play them on his cithern, which is now in the proud possession of the Swedish Academy.

It is ironical that the greatest writer of the Gustavian age should never have been taken seriously in his own time; but he lives in the modern world in a way that few other poets do.

Bellman's great friend Sergel is also an artist of more than local importance, and he can rank as a neo-classical sculptor with Thorvaldsen and Canova. His first work was Rococo, like his medallion bust of Linnaeus; but then, in 1767, he moved to Rome, where he stayed for the next eleven years, and was captivated by the antique, by the nymphs, fauns and bacchants that were daily being dug up. When Gustav made his Italian journey, Sergel joined the royal party, and it was he who advised the king to buy the newly found Endymion. The king's taste changed as Sergel's had done, and when they returned to Sweden, the sculptor received many royal commissions in his new style.

Two of Sergel's best works are in the National Museum. The first is 'The Faun', a handsome youth lying there caught in the moment that waking up he stretches himself. It is saved from any classical coldness by the sensuality of the movement. The other is the 'Vénus aux Belles Fesses', for which Ulla von Fersen was the model, a free copy of a Hellenistic Venus in Naples. On Skeppsbron, in front of the Royal Palace in Stockholm, stands Sergel's splendid statue of Gustav III. The king is frozen at the moment when he steps ashore after the Finnish war; the pose is copied from the Apollo Belvedere, but Sergel's work has far more rhythm of movement than his original, as the king's cloak falls like a curtain from his outstretched arm. Again clearly in the Roman tradition are Sergel's portrait medallions, of Gustav, Bellman, Kellgren, Armfelt, almost every distinguished Swede of the age. They are superb, and one understands why Armfelt hung casts of them in his Temple of Memory when all was over.

Sergel was a complete bohemian, and he made some dazzling impressionistic sketches of his home, where he lived with his barmaid mistress, Anna Rella. In one, Bellman is on his knees before her. The poet wrote a special play for Sergel's birthday in 1787, in which he is greeted by Silenus, played by the painter C. G. Pilo, who is too drunk to remember his name and reels through a list of great artists until at last he comes to Sergel.

There was no Swedish painter to compare in stature with Bellman and Sergel. Perhaps the best was Roslin, who lived almost the whole of his working life in France, where he was one of the most fashionable portraitists. His outstanding skill lay in the painting of materials, and the silk, satin and lace in his sumptuous pictures seems to shimmer so that one could touch it. At Gripsholm, there is the very fine full-length portrait of Gustav III, and he also, of course, painted Linnaeus and Adelkrantz. Another member of the Swedish colony in Paris painted the lovely night-piece of the party given for Gustav at the Trianon.

Most Swedish country houses have a portrait by C. G. Pilo; but his masterpiece is the 'Coronation of Gustav' in the National Museum. It is large and uncompleted. The whole composition circles round the king, seated at the moment when the archbishop and the earl marshal place the crown upon his head; the light centres on them while, in the shade, are massed the portraits of all the other important people present.

Per Krafft will always be remembered for his portrait of Bellman at Gripsholm. The poet is holding his cithern and is looking down at the strings, obviously about to start playing. He is wearing Gustav's national dress, but has taken his jacket off, so that the bright red waistcoat contrasts with the white lace of his shirt. The face is thoughtful and slightly soft. Lorenz Pasch is another portraitist of talent. Few pictures can so vividly catch the mood of the eighteenth century as one by him of two dancing children in the National Museum.

In Hilleström, Sweden had her best *genre* painter. His pictures record the happy lives of the prosperous citizens of Stockholm. Similar in his subjects, but with a far warmer feeling for nature, for light and shadow, clouds and woods, is Elias Martin. He spent twelve years in England at the height of Gainsborough's success. Back home, his views of Stockholm made him famous; and one in particular, where a girl gets into a boat near Skeppsbron to go on a picnic, could be Ulla Winblad's 'Embarcation pour Cythère'. He also painted a fine portrait of Bellman as a sad and thoughtful older man.

The Gustavian age achieved surprisingly little in architecture, mainly for want of money. In Stockholm, Palmstedt built the Stock Exchange, a fine Palladian building which, by an attractive tradition, is also used by the Swedish Academy. Near-by Carlberg gave the Great Church an eighteenth-century exterior to match the palace.

Gothenburg is really Sweden's only city to reflect this age, and this is the work of Carlberg, who gave the streets of rich merchant houses their unity and harmony, now sadly broken by later buildings. He also rebuilt

Dancing children, by Lorenz Pasch

the cathedral in the austere classical style after it had been destroyed by fire. There, too, is the office and warehouse which Hårleman built for the Swedish East India Company: imposing and heavily rusticated, it mirrors itself in the waters of its quay.

Out in the country, J. E. Rehn built one of the finest Gustavian homes at Gimö in Uppland. It was originally the centre of a prosperous *bruk*, and now belongs to the conservative party. A great courtyard precedes the beautifully proportioned but plain mansion, decorated only by its

179

central pediment; the luxury is saved for the elegant interiors. On the shores of lake Vättern is another delightful Gustavian relic. The eighteenth century was the age of the spa, and Sweden's first sulphur springs were found at Medevi. The pump-room, with its façade of simple and elegant pilasters, lies in the park, and around it are the little pavilions built by various noble families who came to drink the waters and which still carry their names. Many of the interiors are complete with the original furniture, whose straight lines and pearl-greys are the mark of the Gustavian style.

In the park at Haga, in the suburbs of Stockholm, stands one of the most beautiful buildings of the eighteenth century. It is the only building that Gustav managed to see completed, and it is appropriate that it should be a masterpiece. This pavilion at Haga is only part of a far more grandiose plan for a vast palace whose foundations are still to be seen under the trees to the north. In the park are a little temple to Echo and tents of copper. The exterior recalls the Petit Trianon at Versailles, although the central block fits better to the park, thanks to the addition of two low wings. The architect was Tempelman, who built the Doric botanicum at Uppsala. However, the interior at Haga far surpasses its model. Haga was born after Gustav's Italian journey and his taste had changed completely from the Rococo to the Classical; so he entrusted the decoration to an artist just back from Rome, Louis Masreliez. The big drawing room in the centre is inspired by recent finds at Pompeii and Nero's Golden House. The panels on the walls are painted with garlands and classical figures on a white background, while the furniture, which is made for the room, echoes them. The same theme is used in the mirror room beyond it. This superb room occupies the whole southern wing, and at the end, instead of mirrors, there is a whole wall of glass, broken only by the marble pillars, so that the park seems to merge with the house. Other delightful interiors are the king's bedroom, and the library, which now has even its original books restored to it.

Haga was only completed the same year as the king was murdered. That shot also destroyed the greatest age in Sweden's intellectual history, for without their patron there were no more arts or letters. Not only the old Gustavians but many younger men as well looked back nostalgically to it, and years later they applauded Sergel's speech when his bust of the king was at last installed: 'May a thousand devils take me, but Gustav III was a ray of the Eternal Light!'

11. Sweden in the Modern Age

The history of nineteenth-century Sweden is dull and cosy, telling of an obscure little nation trying to live a Victorian idyll. After strutting for centuries on the stage of Europe, Sweden became a backwater of the German region, a nation of Biedermeyers. This was also a century of economic failure, when Swedish iron lost its markets to Lorraine, and the land its people to America, to earn the nickname 'Pauper Sweden'.

The death of the Danish prince had once again left the now practically senile Karl XIII without an heir. These were the years when Napoleon dominated the continent of Europe, and was busy installing French kings on the thrones he had emptied, so the French emperor was the logical man for anyone with a spare throne to turn to.

Instead, something very strange happened. A young Swedish lieutenant called Mörner approached Marshal Bernadotte in Paris, where he was in temporary disgrace, and invited him to become crown prince of Sweden. His only previous contact with Sweden had come when he captured a number of Swedish officers in Lübeck a few years before, and, with typical charm, had then set them free. He had also made himself a reputation as an administrator when he was Napoleon's governor of the Hanseatic cities. Above all, he was a brilliant soldier who might recapture Finland, and a very rich man, who might save the bankrupt state.

Jean-Baptiste Bernadotte was a remarkable personality by any standards. Tall and very handsome with a black mane of hair, he was as fine a diplomat as he was a soldier; a Gascon from Pau, he lived up to the d'Artagnan legend. At the French Revolution, he had been a sergeant-major who wholeheartedly joined the republican cause, and he was closely linked with the Jacobins and with Madame de Staël, who called him 'the true hero of the age'. As a professional soldier, he was soon commanding a division on the Rhine. With his republican principles, Bernadotte was a clear threat to Napoleonic ambition, and there was a long duel of intrigue between the two. At one point, Napoleon thought that he had got Bernadotte safely exiled to Greece, when the other slipped back to command the Army of Italy, the very post Napoleon had just left. At Napoleon's *coup d'état* to become First Consul, Bernadotte tried to stop him, and had to hide in the forest with his wife Desirée disguised as a boy. Years before, Napoleon's brother Joseph had been in love with Desirée, who had turned him down. When Napoleon became emperor, Bernadotte tactfully supported him, and the price of his loyalty was to be made a marshal and to receive the immensely rich princedom of Ponte Corvo. Even so, there was never any warmth between the two men. When Bernadotte was offered the chance to make his own fortune in Sweden, he seized it; and in the long run, the Bernadottes are the only Napoleonic dynasty to have survived.

In the autumn of 1810, Bernadotte landed in his new country at Hälsingborg. For a fox who had survived the French Revolution, it was easy to sit on the fence till the winning side became obvious. Two years later, Napoleon seized Pomerania to plug a leak in the Continental System, and Bernadotte threw in his lot with Britain and Russia. He was appointed commander of the allied Northern Army, and fought at Leipzig, the first time that Napoleon was ever defeated. His Swedish troops played a most undistinguished part. Having had to pay personally for their uniforms and their muskets, Bernadotte kept them firmly in the background.

The new crown prince brought a fresh mind to Sweden's problems. He saw clearly that Finland was lost for ever, and that it was foolish for Sweden to have Russia as an enemy. On the other hand, the weakness of Denmark offered the chance of compensation to the West in the shape of Norway. After a brief campaign, peace was signed at Kiel in 1814, and Denmark agreed to exchange Norway for Swedish Pomerania and a cash payment. The Norwegians had no say in the matter. The two countries were united only by the person of the monarch; although Sweden was the senior partner, Norway kept her own government, the Storting, and the two kingdoms were theoretically equal. Having successfully reorientated the ambitions of his people, Karl XIV Johan, as one must now call Bernadotte, set about their finances. He sold his princedom of Ponte Corva and used the money to restore the Exchequer, a debt still unpaid to the Bernadottes.

As a ruler, the ex-Jacobin proved an arch-conservative. All his reign, which began officially when Karl XIII died unnoticed in 1818, Karl Johan was frightened of a Gustavian restoration, and he soon joined Metternich's Holy Alliance, both as a mark of respectability and to preserve the *status quo*. This fitted well with his pro-Russian policy. In theory, the king's power was strictly limited by the constitution of 1809, which had been based on that of England, but a man like Karl Johan was not to be bothered by constitutions. He ruled as an autocrat, and, indeed, never even bothered to learn Swedish. His mouthpiece was Count Magnus Brahe, the adjutant-general who also became a close personal friend.

The years of peace brought a gradual recovery of prosperity. It became possible to call in all the inflated notes floating about and to re-establish the silver standard. Trade recovered from the blows of the Napoleonic Wars; but Sweden found that many of her traditional markets for iron and timber had been lost. A great benefit to Sweden came in 1832 when the Göta Canal was opened. It was the creation of the engineer Baltzar von Platen, in face of constant difficulties of money and terrain. The canal runs from Gothenburg up the Göta river to lake Vänern; ships then cross the wide lake, and the next section of the canal brings them to lake Vättern; finally, the last section takes them across East Gothland out into the Baltic at Norrköping. It is still possible to take a tourist boat along the whole route, and in the summer it is one of the most beautiful journeys, past the rocks and islands through the fields and forests.

There were other lasting works. In 1822, Stockholm received a medical university, the Caroline Institute, which now has a world-famous reputation. It was preceded in 1813 by the KGCI (Royal Gymnastic Institute) founded by the fencing master Per Henrik Ling. Ling's ideal was to train and perfect the human body, and his college gave the first scientific approach to physical education in the world, so he laid the foundation of Swedish supremacy in that field of medicine as well as her more general tradition of athletics.

After the cultural interregnum imposed by Karl XIII and Reuterholm, the intellectual life of the nation began to revive as well. A new spirit was abroad in the North of Europe, fed by the historical awareness of the Romantics, which stressed the cultural, linguistic and even the political unity of the Danes, Norwegians and Swedes. This 'Scandi-navianism' was by no means confined to the arts, but became an important force in foreign affairs and is still very powerful even today. There was the Gothic Club, one of the few times that adjective has been legitimately used, whose most famous members were Ling, Tegnér and Geijer.

Esaias Tegnér is Sweden's greatest romantic poet, though his life is a model of bourgeois respectability. Born the son of a poor priest, he had the good fortune to become the tutor of the children of a wealthy and enlightened *bruk*-owner called Myrmann. He went on to the University of Lund with his charges, and after getting his degree, married his patron's daughter. He became professor of Greek at Lund, and then bishop of Växjö, where he died, his last years sadly clouded by periods of manic depression.

Tegnér first made his mark by winning the academy's prize with *Svea*, a stirring patriotic poem of defiance to Russia, although he had already written several delightful lyric verses. As a liberal, he was a consistent opponent of Bernadotte and his autocracy, although his views inevitably moved to the right in his later years. As part of Karl Johan's pro-Russian policy, the centenary of Karl XII's death was officially ignored. Tegnér, however, published one of his finest poems in praise of the hero-king. Phrases from it, such as 'Muscovites out of my way!' or 'One man stood to ten', have entered the Swedish language. In spite of this, he was elected to Oxenstierna's chair in the academy and at its fiftieth anniver-sary read a superb poem to the praise of Gustav III and the great poets of his circle, ending with the wise question, 'Where would we stand, if they had never lived?'

Frithiofs Saga is one of the few successful epics of modern literature. Tegnér had taken an old Icelandic plot, and changed it to make the hero a romantic seeker after the ideal. But the original Viking story prevents the work from ever becoming bloodless. As an enthusiastic Scandinavian, Tegnér revived the traditional alliterative Norse metres, and proved how well suited they are to the modern language also.

Erik Gustaf Geijer had almost as quiet a life as Tegnér. He was professor of history at Uppsala, but never became a bishop like most of his colleagues at that period, having faced a blasphemy charge as a student based on some obscure theological point. He wrote a history of the Swedish people which has made his reputation as a scholar. Like Tegnér, Geijer looked back to the days of the Vikings, and several of his finest poems are set in that period and were first published in *Iduna*, the Gothic Club's newspaper. Geijer was not merely a poet but also a composer, and he set many of his verses to music. Probably the best known are his two marches to the memories of Gustavus Adolphus and Karl XII.

As a member of the clerical estate at the *Riksdag*, Geijer had begun his political career as a conservative; but his historical studies convinced him that freedom was the most important asset in any community, and in 1840, after a famous apostasy, he joined the Liberal party. He sat as a Liberal in the commission for reforming the constitution, and devoted the rest of his life to fighting manfully for progress.

These were also the years of Sweden's only internationally known composer, Franz Berwald. He came from a long line of musicians, and began life as a violinist at the royal orchestra, but he soon moved to Berlin and lived for many years in Germany. His music is supremely romantic, and at its best in his three symphonies, although he also composed cantatas and operas on such inevitable Swedish themes as Gustavus Adolphus and Gustav Vasa. One of his most attractive works, with its liberal use of folk melodies, is the opera *Country Wedding in Sweden*. This made a sensational première in Vienna with Jenny Lind as the soprano.

The name of Jenny Lind has now survived for a century in the ephemeral world of the stage. The daughter of a craftsman, she began in the theatre aged ten, and by seventeen was singing at the opera. She went to Paris to improve her singing when she was twenty. There she was discovered by Meyerbeer, who gave her a role in the *Camp in Schleswig*, his latest opera, at its première in Berlin. From that moment her reputation was established. Her triumphs came in every capital in Europe, and she even went to North America, where she married the German composer, Otto Goldschmidt. The later part of her life she lived in London, the city where her popularity was greatest, and there she died, leaving much of her not inconsiderable fortune to provide scholarships in Sweden for singers.

In the other arts, the first half of the nineteenth century produced little that was outstanding. There were no great architects at work; but many men whose names are now forgotten filled the little towns of Sweden with their charming private houses in Empire or what we might call Regency style: modest wooden buildings, but well-proportioned and painted in clear pastel colours which stand out brightly against both the snow and the kind light of the Northern summer.

One of the most attractive homes, and one that merits a visit, is Stjernsunds House to the south of Stockholm. It now belongs to the Royal Academy of History and Antiquities. The house lies beautifully set on a spur that thrusts out into the very northern end of lake Vättern, surrounded by water on three sides. The façades are absolutely plain, except for the southern one, which is broken by a central portico of four tall Doric columns. The interior is typically Swedish, the dining room with its delightful friezes a classical gem, the other rooms more intimate and cosy in the style of the Swedes 'old home'.

Visitors to the palace see another famous room of the period, 'The White Sea'. It is, in fact, a combination of two rooms created during Nyström's restoration. It is a cool, monumental room dominated by Gérard's portrait of Karl Johan's queen, Desirée, in a truly Roman style.

Among the large production of second-rate romantic landscapes, the best belong to Fahlkranz. He is an obstinately Nordic painter, indeed, he never used his scholarship to Rome, and his lyrical pictures of Gripsholm, for instance, evoke marvellously the soft but clear light of the far north. For a really extravagant use of the wild and dramatic landscapes of the Scandinavian mountains and forests, one must enjoy his younger follower, Magnus Larsson. The best portrait painter of the time made his career, oddly enough, in England, including a very productive trip to India, and many old homes have unjustly forgotten portraits by Egon Lundgren.

Of course, the nineteenth century loved pictures of historical events, and many of them have passed into folk-consciousness. Such include Höckert's best work, 'The Fire in the Old Palace of Stockholm, 1697', where, fleeing down a smoke-filled stairway, the old queen, Hedvig Eleonora, leans upon the shoulder of the slim, boyish Karl XII. Later in the century, Gustav Cederström painted an equally famous picture of the end of Karl's career, now in Gothenburg, showing his corpse being carried back from Norway. Past an overhanging cliff marches a ragged regiment with its tattered banners, the colonel with his typical long sword unsheathed, behind him the litter with the dead king. The path is white with the thick snow, and watching them pass, bare-headed, stands an old hunter.

One of the leading Scandinavians was the sculptor Fogelberg, another member of the Gothic Club. The National Museum has his masterpieces, the three enormous statues of Odin, Thor and Balder. In spite of their classical influences, these majestic figures have caught something of the wildness and magic of the old Norse gods. Every visitor to Stockholm knows the Kungsträdgården behind the Opera. It is planned around two works by Molin; the first is the great fountain where the pixies play beneath the bowl; and the second is the statue of Karl XII pointing defiantly eastwards towards Russia.

For the rest of his reign, Karl Johan sought only to preserve the *status quo*. Not until after his death in 1844 did Sweden begin to move again. His son and heir, Oscar I, was a liberal who looked westwards to Victorian Britain rather than to Russia. New and more humane poor laws were introduced, as were compulsory primary schools. The first railway was built in 1856; but it was only in the 1870s that the construction of a railway network really got under way, partly financed by the state. The three great Swedish banks were all founded in the capital-hungry 1850s. With the opening up of distant and sparsely inhabited Norrland, the timber industry exploded into growth, while the Bessemer process for making steel once again made Sweden competitive on the world markets.

Now that it was receiving royal sympathy, Scandinavianism for the first time began to have political influence. The Danish provinces of Schleswig-Holstein were a running sore in Northern Europe. Holstein was wholly German-speaking, while the population of Schleswig was mixed. In the revolutions of 1848, there was an uprising by the people of Holstein who wished to join the nascent German empire. They received prompt support from Prussia, whose troops soon occupied Jutland. It looked as if Denmark might disappear, and a Swedish army was sent to help to defend the Danish islands. British pressure, however, forced the Prussians to withdraw.

A corollary to a Scandinavian policy was opposition to Russia, and when the Crimean War broke out in 1854, it seemed to Oscar the ideal opportunity for Sweden to get back Finland with the help of Britain and France. However, Sweden edged cautiously towards action and the party was over too soon. Peace came partly as a result of the Russian fear of having to fight on two fronts, in the Baltic as well as the Crimea. These events gave a great boost to the Scandinavian cause, and there was even talk of a political union, which faded away with the death of King Oscar in 1859.

His son, Karl XV, was by nature more conservative. Very handsome and a *bon viveur*, his main interests were women and hunting. Karl was a personal friend of Frederik VII of Denmark, who shared his taste for good living, and he made Denmark extravagant promises of support, which his council at home, frightened of foreign involvement, then refused to ratify. When Prussia attacked Denmark in 1864, Sweden left her to her fate and she was soon stripped of the two contested provinces. Ibsen's play *Brand* deals with the betrayal of Scandinavianism.

The most important event of Karl XV's reign was the reform of the *Riksdag*. This was chiefly the work of a great lawyer, Louis de Geer, who had emerged as the effective prime minister inside the royal council. He took as his model the British system of an upper and a lower house, but made them both elective, the franchise for the upper house having a much stricter property qualification. After long and heated debates, the reforms were even carried by the nobility, and so disappeared the last trace of a medieval constitution in Europe, with its four Estates of nobles, clergy, burghers and peasants. It is worth quoting the dignified words of the last speaker of the noble Estate, 'Laws change, rights die, but one's duty to one's country survives, and that is all that concerns a true gentleman.'

Perversely, the first new *Riksdag*, elected in 1866, returned a conservative, agrarian majority, and the further progress and reforms that de Geer intended were abruptly slowed down. No amount of reforms, however, could have solved the absolute revolution that Sweden was going through, which was none the less far-reaching for not being violent.

These were years of upheaval for the Swedish people. The population increased rapidly all through the nineteenth century, but the slow economic progress meant that the lot of many was a grinding poverty. It was made worse by an agricultural crisis, and two years of famine in 1867 and 1868. The only escape lead to the New World, and there was a flood of settlers to America. Between 1860 and 1910, over one million Swedes emigrated from a country whose population in 1860 was only four million. They settled in the Mid-West, in Kansas, Minnesota and Nebraska, in a landscape that was not dissimilar to their homeland, and there they concentrated on agriculture, taming the virgin forest and opening up the prairies. During the Civil War, the Swedes were staunchly Unionist against the wealthy South, and even provided Lincoln with a general, Vegesack. A striking fact about the Swedish emigrants is the speed and ease with which they have been assimilated into America, unlike, say, the Italians, although, of course, they were all by definition WASPS (White Anglo-Saxon Protestants). Many of their descendants have become famous, like Charles Lindbergh.

A modern novelist, Vilhem Moberg, has written a remarkable set of novels called *The Emigrants*, which traces the saga of those days when the Swedish forests were sown with abandoned homesteads. The last link with their old country was, by tradition, a posy of meadow flowers pressed between the pages of the Family Bible.

Many bands of emigrants belonged to tight-knit chapel sects. The Swedes have a passion for left-wing religion, which is still surprisingly strong, even against the atheism predominant today. Methodism, Baptism, evangelism,, and many strange home-grown variants won strong followings. Linked to them is the flourishing temperance movement, very necessary in a country whose climate encourages the excessive drinking of spirits.

When Karl XV died in 1872, he was succeeded by his brother, Oscar II. Strikingly good-looking and well aware of it, he indulged his love of the theatrical by being crowned twice, not merely as king of Sweden at Stockholm, but also as king of Norway at Trondheim. Like many of the Bernadottes, he was an intellectual, a poet in his own right, while his other brother Gustav, nicknamed 'the Troubadour Prince', composed several student songs which are still sung today. In politics, Oscar was a paternalist conservative, but he was shrewd enough not to set himself against the current of the times. His reign saw a flowering of Sweden's artistic life.

The link between the literary generations is Victor Rydberg. As a student, he had lodged with Tegnér at the bishopric in Växjö, but in his admiration for Germany he was in tune with Oscar II. By profession a journalist, he worked on Gothenburg's newspaper, and later sat for the city in the *Riksdag*, where he supported the agrarians. Nowadays Rydberg is known for one novel, *The Last Athenian*, a moving plea for religious tolerance at the time of Julian the Apostate, but his interests covered both classical and Norse mythology and Christian history.

The Romantic tradition in Sweden lasted right through the century. One of its last and best writers is Verner von Heidenstam, an admirer of Nietzsche, and his work is a reaction against the Realists, for he is concerned with human character. In his series of outstanding novels, *The Tree of the Folkungs*, he has created in the founder of the family a true anti-hero, while in *The Caroleans* he presents that great enigma of Swedish history, Karl XII, without any moral judgement, but purely as a tragic figure. Bad health obliged Heidenstam to live in Switzerland, and like all expatriates, he became intensely patriotic, with a genuine love for the beautiful northern countryside. There he met Strindberg, and took on the difficult task of befriending him. Any tourist in East Gothland should visit Övralid, the home Heidenstam made for himself, overlooking lake Vättern in a superb panorama. There he wrote his song 'Sweden', which was then set to music by Stenhammar and is often used as a national anthem.

Many foreigners may have come across Selma Lagerlöf as the authoress of *Nils Holgerson's Wonderful Journey*, the story of a boy who is bewitched by a gnome till he is only inches tall and then befriended by a flock of wild geese, travelling with them the length and breadth of Sweden. She wrote several books apart from this children's classic. Usually they deal with the wild and beautiful countryside of her home province, Värmland, its deep forests and desolate fells, and with the inhabitants marked by this land. Such a novel is *Gösta Berlings Saga* in which the Gothic horror of its Calvinist morality is redeemed by the beauty of nature. Her home there, Mårbacka, is now a museum.

Towering above them as artists is August Strindberg, probably Sweden's only internationally famous writer. He is the most exasperating kind of genius, with every kind of complex, constantly quarrelling with all his friends and on the brink of madness, and yet producing a constant flow of brilliant books and plays.

Strindberg was born in 1849, the illegitimate son of a small-time shipping agent and a waitress who became his housekeeper. There were, in all, twelve children, and after a while the parents got round to getting married. The reason for the delay was probably the social gap, for the father was a very lonely but well-educated man, while the mother was aggressively proletarian. August's resentment at his implied social inferiority all comes out in his autobiography, *The Son of a Servant*. The father's finances were bad and the family was often in real poverty.

August went up to Uppsala, where he studied aimlessly, wanting to be first a priest, then a doctor and then an actor, but made several friends among the young liberal students. The most striking quality of the young intellectual of these years was his remarkable good looks. Then, in 1875, he met and fell wildly in love with Siri von Essen, who abandoned her soldier husband and eloped with him to Paris. Thus began a marriage of sixteen years of hell. The two were supremely ill-matched; Siri was an ambitious, aristocratic bohemian, and August was seeking in his wife the bourgeois security which he had always lacked at home. In 1893, he remarried, after the divorce, an Austrian journalist, Frida von Uhl, but this lasted little more than a year. Strindberg's last marriage to Harriet Bosse in 1901 did not last even a year. After this he isolated himself in a flat in Stockholm, without a bell or knocker, writing on his own till he died of cancer in 1912.

Throughout his life and his work Strindberg was obsessed by his sexual problems. He is often impossibly self-righteous, although he treated his wives atrociously (in their Swiss hotel, Siri von Essen was obliged to eat at a separate table where he could watch her). By his nature, Strindberg was desperately dependent on women, yet hated to be tied and saw marriage as a kind of prostitution. He reserved his particular hatred for emancipated women, although this was the type he always fell for.

In the *Giftas* novels (known in translation as *Married*), his great battle in the sex-war, Strindberg's ideal is the old-fashioned, obedient, domesticated wife, her husband's chattel. *Married,* however, made more religious than sexual news, and made the author internationally famous, for in it Strindberg exposes the fraud of the priest's selling the blood of a popular agitator for 65 pence a bottle. In 1884, he was accused of blasphemy, but after a sensational trial was acquitted.

Such was the man's life. His work is the same kaleidoscope of themes, beginning with pure realism and working through to his later mystical romanticism. His books taken together form a kind of psychological autobiography.

To the outside world, Strindberg is best known for his plays, as one of the finest European writers of realistic drama. *Miss Julie* is an often-revived classic. In its story of a love–hate struggle between the daughter of the house and the valet, one can never be sure who has seduced whom. In her lust to dominate, Julie is like the wife in *The Father*, who drives her husband mad with doubts about the legitimacy of his son. *The Dance of Death* deals simply with a married couple torturing one another. Less well known, because of their subjects, are his historical plays: *Mäster Olof*, about the reformer Olaus Petri, and the problem of the revolutionary who allows himself to deny his beliefs; or *Gustav Vasa*, with its chilling scene where the Darlkarls are fetched out one by one to die. Technically, Strindberg was an excellent dramatist with his sense of horror mixed with normality.

Inside Sweden, Strindberg is at least as famous for his prose works. *The Red Room* is one of the few really good novels in Swedish literature;

it is a hilarious satire on the middle class and the civil service, but it also debunks the myth of the gay bohemian life. Sadly, the two sequels to *The Red Room* become progressively more misanthropic and hysterical. Strindberg was at his best in writing short stories. His two collections of tales from the Stockholm archipelago, *The people of Hemsö* and *Stories from the Skerries*, are idylls of the sea and the islands and those who live there, described with a vivid realism that prevents their being merely charming. Strindberg's humour is cruel, as when he describes the parson who gets so drunk at the wedding that he delivers his Christmas sermon. The writing of these stories began with homesickness in Switzerland at the worst stage of the Siri marriage. Strindberg's sense of history was superb, and he had a talent for giving reality to periods that were long gone by. *Swedish Destinies* is his best collection, and he always casts a fresh and original light on history, debunking the myth of Karl XII and the glorification of war. Strindberg's favourite king was Gustav III.

August Strindberg, by Anders Zorn

It was Heidenstam who introduced Strindberg to Nietzsche, in whom he found many of his beliefs confirmed. Strindberg was convinced of the uselessness of culture, and in his stories the educated and decadent are trampled on by the new and the brutal; he asks that almost inconceivable question for the nineteenth century, 'Is progress really going backwards?' In history, Strindberg maintained firmly that it was the people who counted not the heroes. At Uppsala, he had belonged to a political and literary group called the New Sweden, which included students like Branting, but the great socialist concluded reluctantly that Strindberg was useless for serious political work. So tautly strung a character was always on the verge of madness, and, indeed, Siri did once try to have him committed; for a while, he was convinced that his enemies were trying to destroy him with magnetic waves and slept in a bed surrounded with burning candles to keep the demons off. The product of that time is *Inferno*, a work of almost existentialist horror.

The late nineteenth century was also a time of several great Swedish painters. There was a little colony of Swedish artists in Paris, living the romantic bohemian life of the Third Republic, a group of friends who included Zorn, a barmaid's bastard, and Prince Eugene, one of Oscar II's sons. These were the years of the victory of Impressionism, and the young Swedes even had their own anti-exhibition to the Academy in Stockholm in 1885, which proved a wild success.

The leader of the young rebels was Ernst Josephson. At first his work is clearly impressionistic in the series of remarkable portraits for which he is best known; and his blacksmiths at work, painted on a journey to Spain with Zorn, have the brashness of Courbet. Perversely, however, Josephson seems to have become more romantic with the years and his later pictures are eerie northern landscapes. Essentially Nordic is 'The Watersprite' at Gothenburg Museum: a naked dark-haired boy who sits playing his fiddle in the middle of the rapids. Carl Larsson's career is similar. His early pictures, often watercolours, are delightful landscapes from Barbizon and Grez, but later Larsson turned to Art Nouveau, and his work, like the murals in the Gothenburg Museum, with their swirling lines and sculptural figures, had left Impressionism far behind.

Prince Eugene is, above all, a landscape painter. He was deeply sensitive to the beauty of the forests and mountains of Scandinavia, and to the exhilarating mood of the northern summer nights when the sun never really sets and, even at midnight, the light is shimmering on the lakes. He had various public commissions, including the murals in the new opera house at Stockholm, and the frescoes in the south gallery of Stockholm's town hall. At his home in Waldemarsudde, he assembled a unique collection of modern paintings, a patron as well as a colleague and friend to other artists.

The greatest of this group of painters is Anders Zorn, the only one to make a world-wide reputation, particularly in the United States. He was the illegitimate son of a poor girl from Mora in the heart of Dalecarlia fathered by a German brewer. His talent for drawing won him a patron in a fashionable architect, and his success was made with the picture of a widow in black at the Swedish Academy. He established himself as a portrait painter in London, but made several highly successful visits to the United States, where he painted American society from President Cleveland downwards. Zorn himself was a most likeable character, natural, extrovert and cosmopolitan, and it is easy to understand why he was lionized everywhere. He loved watercolours and has left some charming landscapes from Clovelly and St Ives, but, as he grew older, he used oils more and more. His financial success came as a portrait painter; but he was far more than a social photographer, for his portrait of Strindberg with staring eyes and unruly hair is a brilliant character study. Zorn's most well-known pictures are his female nudes, buxom girls from Mora bathing in the lake or walking through the summer forest – no anaemic studio models, but expressions of the joy in life. The folk-dances on Midsummer's Night, where the boys and girls are dressed in the colourful folk costumes, are a part of Swedish life that Zorn recorded with delight. The traveller remained deeply attached to his childhood home at Mora. He bought his old mother a cottage there that became the kernel of the Zorn Museum, which is a memorial both to the artist and to the province. On the hill in Mora stands Zorn's self-confident statue of Gustav Vasa.

Sweden owes a great debt to the historian Artur Hazelius, who in 1880 presented his private collection of archaeological and medieval treasures to the nation as the core of the Nordic Museum in Stockholm. Under his enthusiastic leadership, the museum grew into one of the finest national historical museums in the world. Not content with this, he went on eleven years later to found Skansen on open fields east of Stockholm. Skansen was unique, although it now has many imitators: the world's first open-air museum to which whole buildings were moved for the visitors to enjoy among trees and gardens. Precious relics from all Sweden's provinces are to be seen there in a setting that gives a unique sense of pleasure.

Another original Swedish institution that has had many imitators is the Nobel Prize. Alfred Nobel's father had been one of the many Swedish businessmen working in Russia, where he had been ruined by a political intrigue. His children grew up in real poverty, but all turned out to be true entrepreneurs, developing the oil fields of Baku and starting factories in St Petersburg. Alfred patented the use of nitro-glycerine in blasting and went on to invent the detonator. He became enormously wealthy, but never settled anywhere – the richest tramp in Europe – and never married. He was a lonely, melancholy man whose only strong belief was in science. Yet this pessimist who had made a fortune from dynamite was also an active pacifist. He once told a political meeting, 'My factories will end war sooner than your conferences!' He meant that they would do so by making the weapons of war too destructive, a theory which one hopes will be proved right in this nuclear age.

Darlkarl girls bathing, by Anders Zorn

When he died in 1896, his will came as a complete surprise. In his own terse, plain words, he left his entire fortune to finance five annual prizes to be awarded to those who, during the preceding year, had conferred the greatest benefits on mankind; the winners to be chosen in physics and in chemistry by the Swedish Academy of Sciences, in medicine by the Caroline Institute, in literature by the Swedish Academy, and in peace by the Norwegian Storting. The awards are made in the winter in Stockholm in a stately ceremony, and with an appropriate dignity. They are handed personally to the winners by the king (except for the Peace Prize) at the Nobel feast, and each recipient has to make a speech on his subject. There follows a dinner and a ball at the palace for the prize-winners and all their families. The choices have often been courageous, and in a century which has experienced two world wars, the Peace Prize has often justly been left unawarded, or has gone to institutions rather than men.

The same pragmatic idealism inspired the rise of the Swedish left wing. At Uppsala in the 1880s, the radical students' club Verdandi (the old norse for 'the Present') had no less than two prime ministers among its members, the liberal Karl Staaff and the socialist Hjalmar Branting, as well as intellectuals like Strindberg. Both politicians came from the *haute bourgeoisie*; Branting had been at school with the future Gustav V, and, in spite of his republican principles, remained on excellent terms with the king.

The philosophical battle of Swedish socialism was fought already in the last century between the revolutionary dictatorship sought by August Palm and the social democracy sought by Branting. To the lasting good fortune of the country, Branting won, and the concept of class warfare has not existed in Sweden until literally the last few years. In 1905, under Staaff, came the first of an almost unbroken series of liberal and social democratic ministries, which have given Sweden a uniquely just, humane and efficient government in this century. Unqualified universal suffrage was introduced in 1909. Staaff also began to build up the social services, schooling and old-age pensions, and to reform the spelling and script of the language.

At the same time the economy had taken a radical turn for the better. Protectionist trade policies allowed Swedish agriculture to recover, while the Industrial Revolution, which arrived late in a European context, provided the wealth to carry the costs of protection. The over-riding industrial problem of the time was the future of the *bruks*, those fully integrated, paternalistic economic units tucked away in the forests and based on an iron mine or a glass-works. One after another they were going bankrupt because they were too small, and with them died a traditional way of life in Sweden. Fortunately, many of them were bought up and rationalized as larger units by the banks. The most prestigious of Sweden's merchant banks is Stockholm's Enskilda Bank, founded by A. O. Wallenberg in 1856; Handelsbanken is an offshoot resulting from a policy split. Wallenberg was a pioneer in the capital markets. The early years saw the bank weather some very dangerous crises, as a result of borrowing short and lending long. However, it left the bank with important positions in several of Sweden's major companies, including the mining group Stora Kopparberg, L. M. Ericsson, and Asea. Another such conglomerate is the shipping empire of the Johnson family in Gothenburg. In a country that has been chronically short of capital, these interlocking empires have been the most efficient way of financing industry, and even left-wing governments have had the sense to let them stand. Other capital investments were simply beyond the scope of private enterprise. The government has had to build the railway network in what is one of the largest countries in Europe, and also to develop the enormous iron-ore fields at Kiruna, well to the north of the Arctic Circle.

Relations between capital and labour, although good, were by no means perfect. At the turn of the century, unions and employers formed central organizations, both able to negotiate from positions of strength, and the thoroughly professional style of the agreements between them has been a major factor in Swedish prosperity. There was one serious and unsuccessful attempt at a general strike in 1909, but otherwise Sweden has had an enviable record of industrial peace.

The major political crisis of these years was the collapse of the union with Norway. Sweden had always been the senior partner, but had never got anything out of the union except prestige. The union was only embodied in the person of the monarch, and the two countries had completely separate constitutions, the Norwegian one being in fact more liberal than the Swedish. The two countries were also different in their trade and foreign policy, Sweden looking to Germany and Norway to Britain.

By the end of the century there was a running crisis, with Norway demanding a separate diplomatic service and childish arguments about the flag of the union. In 1905, after a quarrel about the relationship between the royally appointed ministers and the *Storting*, the Norwegians declared that the union had ceased to exist. Oscar II was seriously ill and the regent, Crown Prince Gustav, was in favour of maintaining the union by force. Happily, calmer councils prevailed and the union was unwound at negotiations at Karlstad. Norway chose to remain a constitutional monarchy and invited a Danish prince to become king. For Scandinavia, the end of the union was sad, but it had never really been implemented.

Gustav V became king in 1907, and reigned until 1952. At his death he was aptly described as the world's oldest living diplomat, and one of its most successful. The fact that Sweden was able to maintain her neutrality in both world wars is, to a large degree, the personal achievement of Gustav V. His first queen was Victoria of Baden, a descendant of the exiled Gustav IV Adolf, and with her the Vasa blood returned to the Swedish royal house. By nature down-to-earth and realistic, he refused to be crowned or to indulge in the trappings of royalty.

There is one paramount fact about modern Swedish history, and that is that, through the dictatorships and horrors of the twentieth century, she has managed to avoid all wars. In the optimism of the early years, Swedish defence had been dangerously neglected. Staaff's government wished to spend all the available money on its social programme. When he refused to build another cruiser for the navy, the money was collected by subscription and the ship presented to the nation. Early in 1914, the farmers organized a vast procession in Stockholm to the king to demand an increase in defence spending, to which the workers held a counter-demonstration soon afterwards. As the clouds gathered, the king, who anyway disapproved of Staaff, dismissed him and appointed Hjalmar Hammarskjöld as prime minister.

When the war broke out in 1914, Sweden declared a policy of strict neutrality. Gustav V invited his fellow Scandinavian monarchs to a meeting at Malmö, where they agreed to form a Nordic neutral bloc. Swedish sympathies, however, were strongly pro-German. Germany had, after all, been the great power in whose zone Sweden lay, while German was their international language and the closest links from academics to businessmen existed with their southern neighbour.

The Swedish economy was very badly organized for the war. There was drastic inflation; and the profiteers were exporting everything edible they could lay their hands on to Germany. At last, in 1917, Hammerskjöld, by then nicknamed Hungerskjöld, resigned for a liberal government, but the just resentment was a boost for the socialists.

The Russian Revolution brought the war to Scandinavia, for the Finns seized the opportunity to regain their freedom at the cost of a bitter civil war against the Bolsheviks. A Swedish volunteer brigade fought under General Mannerheim, and Swedish support helped the white victory. Unhappily, peace brought an immediate bone of contention. The inhabitants of the Åland Islands, who are entirely Swedish-speaking, demanded to be reunited with their mother-country rather than to remain with Finland. The case was one of the first brought before the International Court of Justice at The Hague, and under pressure from the great powers, the decision went in Finland's favour. In spite of this evident injustice, Sweden accepted the verdict, and the only ones to suffer were the unfortunate Ålanders.

In 1920, Branting became the first socialist prime minister. For many years he had been a journalist, carrying left-wing papers out of his own pocket, until in 1897 he became the first socialist member of the *Riksdag*. He was an idealist and an internationalist, and at once applied for Swedish membership of the League of Nations. Here Branting became a member of the council, and made his mark as the defender of the small states against the great powers, which has become traditional Swedish policy. Unlike the victors of the war, he saw the League as a parliament not as a military alliance, and fought there for the implementation of many inconvenient ideals.

Sweden's cultural life has flourished in the prosperity of peace. The

Courtyard of the Milles Museum

Swedes were from the beginning fascinated by the new art of the film, and its foremost cult figure must remain the Swedish actress Greta Garbo. The visitor to Stockholm cannot but be struck by the City Hall built by Ragnar Östberg in a strange Nordic fairy-tale style which yet achieves beauty as its brick arches float above the water and the sun glints on the gilded three crowns at the top of the tower.

In a suburb of Stockholm is the remarkable memorial to one of the greatest sculptors of this century, Carl Milles. It is an open-air museum, housing his own collection and copies of many of his works. Milles was fascinated by the soaring figure, and is one of the first sculptors to use the full possibilities of modern technology in casting and materials. Much of his best work is in the United States, where he lived for many years:'The Fountain', 'The Meeting of the Waters' at St Louis and in Washington, 'The Fountain of Faith'. In Sweden he has left a magnificent, sensual Poseidon at the arts centre at Gothenburg, while the Folkunga Fountain at Linköping vividly tells the saga of that blood-stained family. The Sea-god in Stockholm turns this monster from the past into an abstract in granite.

For the inter-war years,Sweden followed the course of Europe. The temperance movement only just failed at a referendum to have prohibition introduced on the American model. At the depression, Sweden followed Britain off the Gold Standard. For her the most dramatic result of the economic crisis was the Kreuger collapse. Ivar Kreuger was a remarkable financier who had built up a world-wide empire based on Swedish Match, where he controlled one third of the world's matchstick production. The pyramid was, however, brought down by the slump, and in trying to save it, Kreuger used some very doubtful accounting. In 1932, he shot himself in Paris, and during the sorting out it was discovered that the prime minister, Ekman, had been accepting large bribes from Kreuger to give him Riksbank credits. The scandal led to an election which returned the first socialist majority government under Per Albin Hansson.

The Second World War found Sweden better prepared but more dangerously placed. Her armed forces supplied by the modern factories of Bofors and Saab were the strongest in the north, but the Soviet-German Non-aggression Pact had placed her in the same exposed position as had existed after Tilsit, and Gustav V wisely avoided any joint Nordic neutrality. Public opinion, however, wholeheartedly favoured the Western democracies and supported the coalition government of Hansson.

The war in Scandinavia began in November 1939 with the unprovoked Russian invasion of Finland. The Finns put up an epic defence of a heroism that ranks with the wars of Karl XII, and Mannerheim succeeded all through the winter in holding the Russian armies at bay. The Swedish reaction was as if their brother country had been overwhelmed by a natural catastrophe. Credit both in food and arms for Finland was limitless, tens of thousands of Finnish children were received as refugees, and the factories worked non-stop to supply the Finnish troops with weapons and munitions. Volunteers were already fighting with the Finnish army, but when Mannerheim appealed for regular Swedish forces to help, the government rejected this appeal. It was a humiliating order for a Swedish army, but it was unquestionably the right decision. A Swedish entry into the war would have been futile. It would only have destroyed the one asylum in Scandinavia. For the same reason, the heady request for the transit of Anglo-French forces to Finland was rejected. By March 1940, an armistice was signed leaving Russia in control of the most strategic points in Finland.

In April, Hitler invaded Denmark and Norway. Denmark was impossible to defend and Norway little better. It is still a mystery why Hitler did not also invade Sweden: there was, happily, no Quisling party there to welcome him, and Gustav V made a special personal visit to charm the dictator while reminding him that the Swedish iron-ore supplies on which Germany was so dependent would be cut off by a guerrilla war.

Concessions, however, were inevitable, for Sweden was entirely isolated from the West. German troops on leave from Norway were allowed transit through Sweden, and the export of iron ore continued. When Hitler invaded Russia, the Finns very naturally rose again to regain their lost territory, and the Germans demanded to be allowed to move the so-called Engelbrecht Division from Norway to Finland. This Gustav V forced through as a once-and-for-all concession.

As the tide of war turned, the Swedes cancelled their concessions one by one. An unexploded V2 that had landed in Skåne ended up in

London. In 1944, the Finns who had wisely halted their advance with the recapture of Viborg, were able with Allied and Swedish pressure to sign another armistice. Meanwhile, Sweden was receiving refugees from everywhere, Finland, Denmark, Norway, the Baltic States and finally even from Germany, where Goering, who was married to a Swede, allowed men like Count Folke Bernadotte and Raoul Wallenberg to take prisoners from the concentration camps. It was through Bernadotte that Himmler made his offer to surrender to the Western Allies. It is an irony that Bernadotte, as a United Nations representative, was later murdered by Jewish terrorists in Palestine, and Wallenberg, working for the Red Cross, was murdered by the Russians after the capture of Budapest.

When the peace came, Sweden and Switzerland were the only two houses standing in the ravaged city of Europe, and both have retained their neutrality, though there could be no return to pre-war pacifism, and Sweden continues to have one of the highest defence expenditures in the Free World. In foreign policy, Sweden joined the United Nations at the first possible moment, but in spite of some internal debate, has kept out of NATO. The reasons for this are partly the tradition of neutrality and partly the anomalous position of Finland. Finland is the only province of the Tzarist empire that the Soviets have not re-conquered, but, were they to occupy Finland, the Swedes would join NATO and bring the Americans to within a few hundred miles of Leningrad. Equally, joining NATO would probably bring about a Soviet invasion.

In the United Nations, the Swedes have played a major role, thanks to their non-alignment. Dag Hammarskjöld was the son of the prime minister, and when he was elected Secretary-General of the United Nations in 1953, he soon made it clear that, like Branting, he saw the organization as a world parliament to which he wanted to give a strong and useful executive. That this interpretation of his post brought him into conflict with the Great Powers is not surprising. It is too early to pass judgement on his policies, but what can be said with no contradiction is that without this very independent and brave man, the organization would today be very different and much less effective.

His most moving memorial is the old farmhouse he bought amid the meadows of Sandhammaren on the south-east corner of Skåne. Backåkra, as it is called, was restored by his friend the artist Beskow, who also designed the meditation room at the UN Headquarters in New York, and it is now a museum of Hammarskjöld's life. Tragically, he died in the Congo before he ever had time to enjoy this idyll of peace in his hectic life.

Sweden has also inevitably become a regular provider of troops for UN police missions, and has had volunteers serving in many of the world's trouble-spots. The commander-in-chief of the Congo operation was a Swedish general, Carl von Horn. The personal involvement of many young Swedes in UN work has made Hammarskjöld a national hero, and his funeral at Uppsala brought out an unexpected show of pomp among his countrymen.

Gustav V died in 1950, the oldest monarch in Europe; a survivor from the world from the First World War. His son, Gustav VI Adolf, was a distinguished archaeologist in his own right, and was succeeded by his grandson Carl XV Gustav, so that Sweden now has the youngest king in Europe.

Modern Sweden vies with Switzerland as the most prosperous country in the world, and is able to afford her citizens an unrivalled standard of welfare. Geography and an armed neutrality have enabled her to stand aloof from the conflicts of recent years. But it must not be forgotten that this is a prosperity which has been earned by centuries of bitter poverty and a neutrality which has been earned on the battlefields of Europe.

INDEX

Index

INDEX OF PLACES

Index

Index

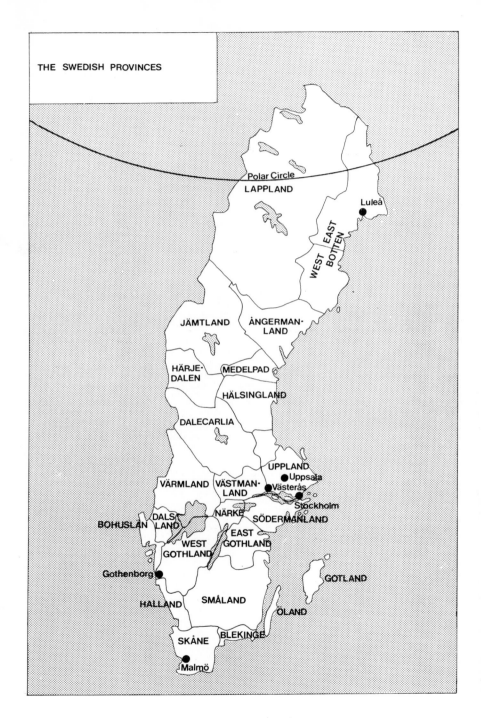

THE SWEDISH PROVINCES

Polar Circle
LAPPLAND

Luleå

WEST EAST BOTTEN

JÄMTLAND

ÅNGERMAN-
LAND

HÄRJE-
DALEN

MEDELPAD

HÄLSINGLAND

DALECARLIA

UPPLAND

Uppsala

VÄRMLAND

VÄSTMAN-
LAND

Västerås

Stockholm

NÄRKE

SÖDERMANLAND

DALS-
LAND

BOHUSLÄN

EAST
GOTHLAND

WEST
GOTHLAND

GOTLAND

Gothenborg

HALLAND

SMÅLAND

ÖLAND

SKÅNE

BLEKINGE

Malmö

The provinces of Sweden

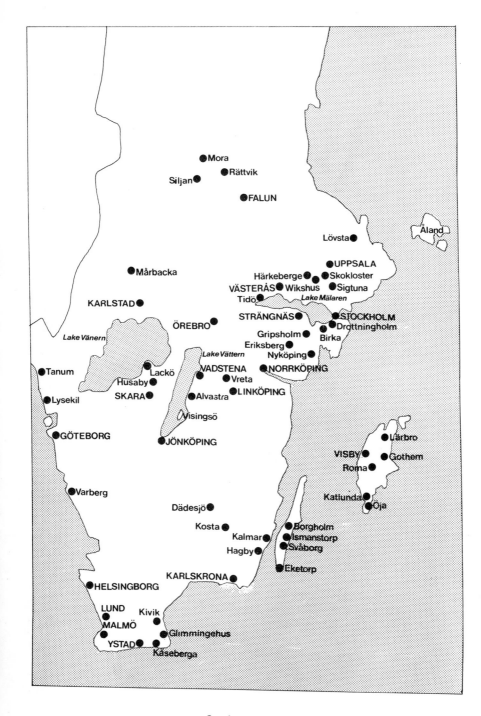

Mora
Rättvik
Siljan
FALUN

Lövsta

UPPSALA
Mårbacka
Härkeberge   Skokloster
VÄSTERÅS   Wikshus   Sigtuna
KARLSTAD
Tidö   Lake Mälaren
STRÄNGNÄS   STOCKHOLM
ÖREBRO   Drottningholm
Gripsholm   Birka
Lake Vänern
Eriksberg
Lake Vättern   Nyköping
Tanum   VADSTENA   NORRKÖPING
Lackö   Vreta
Husaby
SKARA   Alvastra   LINKÖPING
Lysekil

Åland

Visingsö

GÖTEBORG   JÖNKÖPING   Lärbro

VISBY   Gothem
Roma

Varberg   Katlunda
Dädesjö   Öja
Kosta   Borgholm
Kalmar   Ismanstorp
Hagby   Svåborg
KARLSKRONA   Eketorp
HELSINGBORG

LUND   Kivik
MALMÖ
YSTAD   Glimmingehus
Käseberga

Southern Sweden